Praise for *The Improv*

"The Improv was a cauldron of talent. Whetsell writes about it wonderfully and with respect for its importance to comedy."

—ROBERT KLEIN

"They used to say that if you made it in New York you could make it anywhere. Maybe so, but if you didn't make it at the Improv, it was time to pack your bags and move to 'anywhere.'"

—RICHARD LEWIS

"This book is a great walk down memory lane for me. All hail the Improv and all the laugh-filled times and wonderful nights that happened in front of those brick walls."

—BILL MAHER

"The Improv played a vital part in my early stand-up days as it did in the careers of the dazzling array of stars, eccentrics, and colorful characters whose stories adorn this bright and greatly entertaining book. Get at *least* two copies, in case you lose one."

—DICK CAVETT

"Here's a book I'll probably never finish, because for years to come I'll be picking it up again and again and rereading parts over and over, whenever I need perking up. It's the history of an art form, though that sounds way too stuffy, and of an institution—the great American comedy club, especially the Improvs of New York and LA."

—TOM SHALES, Pulitzer Prize–winning former television critic of the *Washington Post* and #1 bestselling co-author of *Live from New York* and *These Guys Have All the Fun*

"An entertaining ride through the glory years—the people, the stories, the feuds, the laughs—of the club that started the stand-up comedy boom in America."

—RICHARD ZOGLIN, author of *Hope: Entertainer of the Century* and *Comedy at the Edge: How Comedy in the 1970s Changed America*

"The Godfather of the comedy club is finally called to testify . . . and he sings like a canary."

—WILLAIM KNOEDELSEDER, author of *I'm Dying Up Here: Heartbreak and High-Times in Stand-Up Comedy's Golden Era*

THE
IMPROV

THE IMPROV

AN ORAL HISTORY OF THE COMEDY CLUB THAT REVOLUTIONIZED STAND-UP

BUDD FRIEDMAN

WITH TRIPP WHETSELL

FOREWORD BY JAY LENO

BenBella

BenBella Books, Inc.
Dallas, TX

BenBella

BenBella Books, Inc. | 10440 N. Central Expressway, Suite 800 | Dallas, TX 75231
www.benbellabooks.com | Send feedback to feedback@benbellabooks.com

Printed in the United States of America
10 9 8 7 6 5 4 3 2 1

Library of Congress Cataloging-in-Publication Data
Names: Friedman, Budd, 1932- author. | Whetsell, Tripp, author.
Title: The Improv : an oral history of the world-famous comedy club that
    revolutionized stand-up / Budd Friedman with Tripp Whetsell ; foreword by
    Jay Leno.
Description: Dallas, TX : BenBella Books, [2017] | Includes bibliographical
    references and index.
Identifiers: LCCN 2017012336 (print) | LCCN 2017028364 (ebook) | ISBN
    9781942952442 (electronic) | ISBN 9781942952435 (hardback)
Subjects: LCSH: Improvisation (Organization : New York, N.Y.)—History. |
    Stand-up comedy—New York (State)—New York—History. | Friedman, Budd,
    1932- | Theatrical producers—United States—Biography. |
    Businessmen—United States—Biography. | Comedians—United
    States—Anecdotes. | BISAC: BIOGRAPHY & AUTOBIOGRAPHY /
    Entertainment & Performing Arts. | PERFORMING ARTS / Comedy.
    Classification: LCC PN3166.N4 (ebook) | LCC PN3166.N4 I47 2017 (print) | DDC
    792.7/6097471—dc23
LC record available at https://lccn.loc.gov/2017012336

Editing by Vy Tran
Copyediting by Scott Calamar
Proofreading by James Fraleigh and Michael Fedison
Indexing by Amy Murphy Indexing & Editorial
Text design and composition by Silver Feather Design
Cover design by Jason Gabbert
Jacket design by Ivy Koval
Printed by Lake Book Manufacturing

Distributed by Perseus Distribution | www.perseusdistribution.com
To place orders through Perseus Distribution:
Tel: (800) 343-4499 | Fax: (800) 351-5073 | E-mail: orderentry@perseusbooks.com

Special discounts for bulk sales (minimum of 25 copies) are available.
Please contact Aida Herrera at aida@benbellabooks.com.

To my wife, Alix, for changing my life and
giving me everlasting love and happiness.
—Budd Friedman

To my mother, Anne Whetsell,
for always being the rock that grounds me and
the rudder that pushes me forward. Also, to my agent,
Peter Rubie, for never losing faith.
—Tripp Whetsell

Contents

Foreword

More than four decades have passed since I drove round-trip from Boston three nights in a row every week to go onstage at a dingy little club in New York's Hell's Kitchen called "the Improv." A lot has happened since then, but the Improv—then known as the Improvisation—was where I received my comedy education, and my long association with both the club and its founder, Budd Friedman, who was also my first manager, remains one of the most important of my career.

Though I had already been doing stand-up for several years at the time, the Improv was the first place where I truly felt like I had found a home, especially since I didn't know any other professional comedians in Boston, and when I told people this was what I wanted to do for a living, they didn't exactly take me seriously. Instead, they just assumed it was a phase I was going through, so I rarely mentioned it. Whenever I did, the response was almost always the same—they'd shrug their shoulders and roll their eyes, as if to say, "This guy's delusional."

This never happened to me at the Improv. All of the sudden, I fit in because I was finally surrounded by people who were like me, in a place where we could sit around until two in the morning, critiquing each other's sets and discussing who was good on *The Tonight Show*—conversations I never could have had in Boston. In fact, I've often compared my early days at the Improv to being in college. Budd was a wonderful professor, too, and I'll forever be grateful for the fact that he always put me on and gave me the freedom to experiment.

I didn't quite know what to expect that first time, and I'm not exactly sure how I heard about it, although the Improv already had a magical name by that point and hosted a mixture of comics and singers like

Bette Midler, whom Budd also managed, and Barry Manilow, who was the house piano player.

The one thing I did know for sure from the moment I walked in, however, was that this was where I was supposed to be, especially after meeting other young comics like Richard Lewis and Billy Crystal, who quickly became my friends. Then there were the more established performers like Robert Klein, Lily Tomlin, Stiller and Meara, and Dustin Hoffman, who used to occasionally drop in to play the piano, as well as a then-unknown Danny Aiello, who was the bouncer.

Being in their presence was the "brush with greatness thing," as my old friend David Letterman used to say. You didn't necessarily hang out with them, depending on how famous they were, but what amazed me the most was that you'd get to see all these people you had just seen on television, in person. The other truly amazing part was that we were all practically one and the same at the Improv, no matter how well known we were or weren't yet. It was as if all seniorities and superficialities were left at the door, and being at the Improv was like being at a big party every night where you never knew who might show up.

Then there was Budd with the monocle and goatee he wore then, who prided himself on being pretentious—and still does. At the time, my day job was delivering cars to New York for a place called Foreign Motors in Boston, which meant I showed up at the Improv in a different Rolls-Royce or Mercedes every night, and one of my favorite stories is how much this impressed Budd because he thought I was some rich kid, which, of course, I wasn't.

He could also be very gruff at times, but underneath that exterior is one of the most genuine and big-hearted people you will ever meet. Many a night he would even let me sleep on his couch when I had no place to stay. Budd is all of this and more; he's loyal to the people he loves and he's the first guy you can count on for a favor if you need it. Moreover, he was the first person to elevate stand-up to an art form by giving comedians a stage they could call their own in front of a willing audience.

In that sense, he's the father of the comedy club, and to this day, one of my greatest pleasures is going to the Hollywood Improv on Melrose

Avenue, even though the original New York club is long gone. It just feels like coming home.

I think that almost anyone else who has ever performed at the Improv for any length of time over the years and knows Budd feels the same way. After hearing him tell the Improv's story, complemented, and in some cases contradicted, straight from the mouths of the people who also lived it, perhaps you'll understand why our bond remains so strong.

—JAY LENO

Prologue

JERRY SEINFELD, comedian, actor, writer, and producer:
On a national level, I started out doing stand-up in New York, but you really had to go to LA to prove you could go onstage amidst those guys. They were the real killers, and the West Coast comics were honestly much stronger—especially in the mideighties. Back then, the Hollywood Improv on Melrose Avenue was *the* spot, and I can't tell you what being welcomed and finding a home there still means to me. It's where I was born.

JIMMY FALLON, comedian, writer, and current host
of *The Tonight Show*:
Budd Friedman is one of the greatest influences in comedy ever, bar none. He changed pop culture forever. For every person he's started, seen rise and fall, and then seen rise again, he's been through it all. He's like the Godfather. He's *the* guy. I'm so lucky I got to work with him and have him involved with my career.

BILL MAHER, talk-show host, commentator, writer,
comedian, and actor:
Of course he was—and still is—a true patron of the comedy arts, and Budd Friedman should be considered a giant because he is a giant. Before the Improv came along, comedy came out of the Catskills. That's where comics were coming from and their acts reflected it. By moving it into the city, he changed everything, and it just made comedy so much more hip and so different.

BETTE MIDLER, singer, songwriter, actor, producer,
and comedian:
The thing about the Improv was that if you were just starting out in show business, you were basically a student of professionals who were coming there to work in the way

they worked. They taught you how it was done, and your reward for being in the audience was that you got to get up there and try and do it. It was like a master class every night.

PAUL REISER, comedian, actor, and writer:
Everyone got these introductions back then that sounded so impressive to me. They'd say stuff like, "You've seen this comedian on such and such talk show." The fact that somebody could be in this club and then emerge the next week on national television was just staggering to me. I always said that if it wasn't for the pipeline that the Improv created, I never would have figured out how to be a comedian.

ROBERT KLEIN, comedian, singer, actor, and writer:
It had a wonderful aura that was steeped inside the old Greenwich Village tradition. Anything could happen and people like Lily Tomlin would drop in even though Budd had a hierarchy and you couldn't just walk in and go on. I had gone to the Yale School of Drama for three years, but they didn't teach stand-up comedy, so the Improv kind of became my training ground.

LILY TOMLIN, actor, comedian, writer, singer, and producer:
A singer could just get up there and sing, but a comedian had to have someone vouch for them. You didn't always know what Budd was thinking if you were new, but you knew he was the one who was going to say yes or no.

BILLY CRYSTAL, actor, writer, producer, comedian, and television host:
You really wanted to be ready to go on at the Improv because you really wanted to do well once you did. Then again, Budd's one of those guys that you'd say to yourself, "He really was there in the beginning of the rise of stand-up comedy." If the movie *Boys Town* was about comedians, then Budd would have been Father Flanagan because he gave you the chance to grow.

LESLIE MOONVES, president of CBS and former Hollywood Improv bartender:
What you always felt about Budd was that he was the best cheerleader for all these comedians. They were like his kids, or his kid brothers, and he was literally rooting for all of them.

ADAM SANDLER, comedian, actor, writer, producer, and musician:

The older I've gotten, the more I've come to appreciate what Budd has done. His whole life has been about making comedians feel comfortable, making us feel valued, and giving us a place to work. He always made you want to work, too, because whenever you were performing and he came into the club, you knew it wasn't an average night. To this day, there's not a time I don't stop in at the Improv whenever I'm on Melrose Avenue. I still feel like I'm missing out on something if I don't.

RICHARD LEWIS, comedian, actor, and writer:

I had a real love affair with Budd practically from day one. I was one of the few, perhaps, who got along with him, got what I wanted, and was supported. When things were happening and reviewers or producers would come in from the various shows, Budd would say to me, "Listen, the people from *The Tonight Show* are going to be here next Saturday night and you're on at ten o'clock." He was always there for me and he wanted me to succeed.

ALAN ZWEIBEL, writer, producer, Broadway playwright, and bestselling author:

Maybe it's a little severe to say that Budd scared the living shit out of me, but I understood his power, and I didn't want to be in his bad graces. I witnessed that on more than one occasion, and I can remember people who had been going on at ten o'clock being relegated to one in the morning because Budd was pissed at them for whatever reason. But I also wanted Budd's respect, and when he started calling me "Rookie of the Year," I knew I had been accepted. That being said, only a few people in my life have frightened me as much as Budd did.

JEFF FOXWORTHY, comedian, actor, writer, and voice-over artist:

Budd wasn't intimidating physically, but the power of what he could do for you was daunting, even though I always felt he was rooting for you to do well. But if you want his respect and approval, you have to work for it before he acknowledges you. And make no mistake about it, Budd's always watching—or at least he was when I was there. He knew who was there just trying to screw waitresses, who was really working at it, and who had arrived. As you were getting good, he'd kind of give you that arched eyebrow and smile. I used to call it the "Mr. Planters Peanuts" face because of the monocle he wore. Then he would actually speak to you and that's when you knew you'd arrived.

MARC PRICE, actor and comedian:
When I first became a regular at the Hollywood Improv around 1983, I was about fifteen years old. One of the things that stands out most was having access to guys like Jerry Seinfeld, Bill Maher, and Jay Leno, who were already well respected in the comedy world even though they hadn't become famous yet. What made this such an interesting dynamic was that they all wanted to do sitcoms, and I was already a regular on *Family Ties*, which was one of the biggest hits on television at the time. So there they were, wanting to be able to experience what I was experiencing. And here I was, wanting to be able to do stand-up as well as they did, which I couldn't do at that point and probably still can't.

JUDD APATOW, producer, director, actor, writer, comedian, and former Improv emcee:
For me and the other comics I came up with, what made our days at the Improv such carefree, magical times was that we basically had zero responsibilities—except trying to figure out how we were going to be funny that night.

JEFF DUNHAM, ventriloquist, comedian, and producer:
The Hollywood Improv to me was always a mystical place because I knew how many legendary names had gone across that stage. It was almost like the lyrics from Frank Sinatra's song "New York, New York"—if you could get onstage and kill there, you could probably do it anywhere. What I didn't understand was the Improv was a completely different room from the entire rest of the country. You either learned to play that crowd or you didn't, and even if you did, it didn't mean you could play Kansas City.

DAVID SPADE, actor, comedian, writer, and television personality:
I first heard about it when Johnny Carson was introducing comedians and he'd say they were appearing at the Improv. When I got into stand-up around 1984 or '85, the only two places that were really worthwhile in LA were the Improv and the Comedy Store. You had to get on at either one of

these clubs to get a foothold and both seemed so far out of my reach. I was around nineteen at that time, and I'd go to the Improv and just watch so I could catch a glimpse of these guys. It was more people watching and being starstruck. I remember looking at the chalkboard they had out front and seeing names like Bill Maher, Jerry Seinfeld, Richard Belzer, and Dennis Miller. They were all in one spot and it was like being at Disneyland. After that, Budd became my first Lorne Michaels, and he held the keys to the kingdom because he basically takes the best people in comedy and splays them out on the table for the rest of the world to see.

JOE PISCOPO, actor, singer, radio host, comedian, and former New York Improv doorman and emcee:
Once you did the Improv, you knew you could do anything in the entertainment business because it was live, flying by the seat of your pants with no safety net. Everything I ever learned at the Improv, I still take with me to this day.

HOWIE MANDEL, comedian, actor, TV host, and voice-over artist:
There wasn't a night that went by when somebody wasn't working on something huge or being discovered for something huge. Because somebody always got something or was getting something, you weren't only a part of the excitement that was going on at the moment, you were also a part of the landscape of what America was going to be watching and laughing at for decades to come.

LEWIS BLACK, comedian, actor, social critic, author, and playwright:
One of the things I'll always give Budd credit for is that he never tried to censor me onstage, although he did tell me once that I used the word "fuck" too much. I told him go fuck himself.

Introduction

Although the Improv certainly can't claim credit for inventing stand-up comedy, to say that comedians were seldom the main attraction prior to our opening on a frigid mid-February night on West 44th Street in New York City's Hell's Kitchen in 1963 isn't an exaggeration.

Up until then, only a handful of established comics, and even fewer headliners, performed regularly in America's nightclubs and predominantly Jewish resorts in the Catskill Mountains, many of which were already on the decline and where the emphasis was mostly on music. And practically all of them who did worked in between the singers when they weren't scrounging for stage time in strip joints.

Which isn't to say that putting comedians front and center—and, in the process, becoming what would be billed as America's first "showcase" comedy club—was ever my original intention either.

It's important to understand also that even though I'd enjoyed listening to comedians since my days as a teenager growing up in the Bronx, I didn't know the first thing about the comedy business, much less running a restaurant. Instead, my sole reason for opening the Improv to begin with—which began as an after-hours coffeehouse for Broadway performers—was because my goal after a brief and unsatisfying career in advertising was to become a theatrical producer, a career for which I was no more qualified.

The Improv was simply a means to an end, one that, if all went according to plan, I naively hoped would give me enough clout to help me find my first show to produce—and on Broadway no less. I certainly had no idea that the comedians would quickly come to dominate our stage or that helping to discover and develop them was to be my destiny, making it possible for me to go places, meet people, and experience things that I could have never imagined.

Of course, the how of how I did it might make for a lot more interesting reading if I could say that my decision to use comedians in favor of singers was part of an elaborate, years-in-the-making vision on my part to fulfill some unmet need in the marketplace (like Thomas Edison and the light bulb), or to modernize an existing product and make it more accessible to the masses (Bill Gates and the computer, McDonald's founder Ray Kroc and the hamburger, etc.). The truth is that it was all a complete fluke.

And yet, from these improbable beginnings came all this and more—all because I needed a way to support myself. And fortuitously when comedians started coming in to perform within weeks after the Improv first opened, New York in particular was riper than ever for smart satire. Though not yet the cultural phenomenon it would become in the decades that followed, the basic rules and subject matter were changing—thanks largely to the progressive, often controversial, routines of Lenny Bruce, Dick Gregory, David Frye, George Carlin, the Smothers Brothers, David Astor, and Richard Pryor—with Dave and Ritchie, in a symbolic twist of fate, being among our first comedians.

So while the basic art form of stand-up comedy was hardly new, the sensibilities were. And with the Improv's birth paralleling this revolution and providing a forum—presenting as many as twenty different comedians on the lineup on any given night with no headliners and no top billing—so were we.

The Improvisation, as it was originally called—and so named, because improvising in the sense of "anything can happen" is how it happened—was the first of its kind, not only streamlining the way stand-up is presented by featuring multiple comics on one stage in the same show, but also by osmosis, becoming the exact template for almost every other comedy club that followed.

Most importantly, we made people laugh, along with—I'm enormously proud to say—having had a hand, or at least a finger, in helping to launch the careers of most of the biggest names in comedy over the last fifty-plus years. There were also uncountable others who never made it, and though there was no way to predict when, if, or how somebody ever would, they were all there for the same reason: It was their calling.

When the Improv began, the number of professional stand-up comedians in the United States was fewer than 200. Today, the total number of full-time comedy clubs in practically every major and mid-sized American city far exceeds 500, while the number of professional comics worldwide is easily more than 100,000, with the vast majority performing in the US, and all of them fighting to appeal to the same youthful audience we helped delineate. This is on top of dozens of cable channels in addition to YouTube and Netflix, where many of these same comedians can be seen for free.

Yet despite this, and perhaps even because if it, the Improv remains one of the most dominant global brands in humor. Though the original New York club closed in 1992, our flagship club on Melrose Avenue in Los Angeles continues to thrive, while the Improv franchise now includes more than twenty-two locations nationwide. Even though the comedians may have changed, our mission has remained the same.

At the time I founded the Improv more than five decades ago, I obviously had no way of predicting what was to come. Needless to say, it's been a phenomenal journey, and this book chronicles the Improv story in the exact words of the people who've been along for the ride set against the backdrop of my own. As you can no doubt already tell, it's quite a lengthy list and each and every one of them holds a special place in my heart. Aside from asking for their participation, I had no input, nor did I place any restrictions whatsoever on what they had to say. I wouldn't have it any other way, even if it isn't always flattering.

My aim was to get a representative sampling of past and present performers—most of them comedians—but also singers, actors, writers, producers, managers, fellow club owners, friends, family, and current and former staff—thereby creating as comprehensive and chronological an oral history of the Improv from our inception to the present day as possible.

So here it is without further ado: the Improv story from the start. My own story begins less remarkably in Norwich, Connecticut.

PART ONE

Growing Up Fatherless and Struggling to Find My Way

Norwich, Connecticut, where I was born Gerson Friedman on June 6, 1932, could have easily passed for a scene straight out of a Norman Rockwell painting. It wasn't that small a town, but whoever first called it "The Rose of New England" had it right.

As the youngest child of three and the only male, I was doted on by my parents and two older sisters, Helene and Kala. My mother, Edith, and my father, Benjamin, nicknamed me Budd, and as a little boy I was often called Buddy, which in the English language means "friend." Since I've spent most of my life in the entertainment business nurturing comedians and singers, I would like to think this was prophetic, though I'm sure there are some who might disagree.

In 1925, my father's two older brothers, Irving and Joe, decided to leave New York and open an auto parts business in Norwich, and my dad joined them, which is how we wound up there, even though nobody knows for sure why they chose Norwich. Nevertheless, it was the height of the roaring twenties, and their new storefront enterprise on Thames Street flourished from practically day one.

We also felt extremely accepted, despite being one of the only Jewish families in a hotbed of anti-Semitism. Our house, situated on a hilly incline at 39 Wilmont Avenue, was small but comfortable. Some of my most vivid early childhood memories are of sledding with my two sisters during the frigid Connecticut winters and watching deer run across the yard from our living room window.

Helene, my eldest sister was an absolute knockout who became a World War II pinup model pictured in such prominent New York newspapers as the *Herald Tribune*, the *Journal-American*, and the *Daily News*. When she walked into a room, everybody took notice, and she had many male suitors. So did Kala, who always made up in personality what she may have lacked in beauty, although she also became quite attractive after our Aunt Gert paid for a nose job the year Kala turned eighteen.

Both are widowed and the three of us have remained extremely close. Sadly, Helene, now ninety, suffers from dementia and is in a nursing home in Hollywood, Florida. Kala, an amateur singer and mother of four who is eighty-eight, still has more energy than most people half her age. She also lives in Florida, and her selfless devotion as Helene's primary caregiver is truly remarkable.

At the beginning of my life, I'd describe the atmosphere of the Friedman household as traditional. Ever popular among the neighbors and with the help of a thriving business, my parents were frequent guests at dinner parties, where my dad often delighted in cracking jokes. My mother also had a great sense of humor, something that I indirectly credit for my own love of the spotlight and being a ham.

As much as I loved and knew I was loved by both parents, unfortunately nothing much in particular stands out about my father. For one thing, as the Great Depression dominated throughout the 1930s, he spent nearly all his time working in order to keep a roof over our heads. The only thing I really remember about him at all is the one nightly ritual I always looked forward to, which would ultimately cost him his life and leave me fatherless for the rest of mine.

Because his hands were always filthy from working on cars all day long, he had to use a special industrial-strength soap that came in a yellow tin can he kept in the bathroom. Every evening when he got home, my sisters and I would join him to wash up before dinner while he hoisted me up on the closed toilet seat so that I could reach the sink. But no matter how hard he tried, my father could never get his hands completely clean, which is what caused a small pimple on the inside of his nose to become so irritated when he scratched it that an infection developed and traveled all the way into his bloodstream. Penicillin was still in its infancy, and although the specific details are sketchy, he apparently spent the following year unable to walk and bedridden in a Newington, Connecticut, Veteran's Administration hospital. There he became so emaciated that he literally wasted away to nothing before finally succumbing in September 1936 at the age of thirty-six.

Though my father's sudden illness and horrific death must have seemed especially painful to my sisters, who had grown up with him, I was too young to understand what was happening. I also don't remember anything about my father's funeral or, for that matter, how I was even told he'd passed away. Nevertheless, I was always acutely aware of the void he left.

Aside from the emotional impact, my father's death raised a host of practical issues. The biggest one was how my mother was going to be able to take care of us, particularly since she was a high school dropout who'd been a housewife for her entire adult life, and my father didn't have an insurance policy. Instead of panicking, however, she decided that the best solution was to get creative and soon began selling plus-sized women's clothing out of our home. Though my grandparents and various aunts and uncles often pitched in, too, my mother took great pride in being able to support us, which was no small feat, especially considering that the country was still in the throes of the Great Depression.

To supplement her modest income from the clothing business, for two summers she also ran a sleepaway camp out of our home with the help of my Aunt Gert. Most of the kids came from New York City and slept on cots my mother managed to get from a local thrift store. The camp also gave me my first exposure to show business when my older cousin Leon decided to put on a talent show in the fall of 1936 and I sang "Little Sir Echo," the classic children's standard made famous by Bing Crosby. Though I was supposed to sing it as a duet with Will Sage, my best friend from across the street, at the last minute he got cold feet, so I ended up performing both parts, for which I was paid the princely sum of sixty-five cents. Through it all and no matter what she had to do or sacrifice, Mom continued to be our anchor, and while our lives were never completely the same after my father died, she stoically tried to make them as normal as possible until the Great New England Hurricane of 1938 sent us into another tailspin.

On the September afternoon it hit, they dismissed us early from school, and I returned home to an empty house where, at first, I tried to remain calm until the winds began picking up speed; then I went outside to hold up the trellis in our backyard. This is when Will Sage's mother realized I was all alone and immediately ordered me to come over to their house, which wasn't any safer. Just as I was going inside, a gust of wind came through, causing the swinging door in their kitchen to bang into my head, leaving a bump I still have. While none of us sustained any life-threatening injuries, the structural damage to my family's home was significant enough that my mother began having serious reservations about whether to remain in Norwich, although it would ultimately take another two years for her to decide.

To make the choice easier, in the summer of 1941, my Uncle Sid and Aunt Roz, who separately owned two competing ladies' undergarment stores, offered to pay a portion of the rent on an apartment in the Bronx, which we would then share with my maternal grandparents. Again, the transition was much harder for my two sisters, who were already teenagers in high school by this point and both had active social lives. But while being the youngest certainly had its advantages when it came to adapting more easily, I was also apprehensive about moving to the big city, even though practically my entire family on both sides had been born and raised there.

For the first seven years, we lived on the ground floor of a three-story apartment building at 1104 Grant Avenue in the Grand Concourse section of the Bronx, ten blocks from Yankee Stadium. Though I may have been initially apprehensive, these fears soon proved unfounded. Instead, mostly good memories come to mind when I think about my years here, many of them about sports.

I was always a decent athlete, which is probably the reason why the first thing I recall is watching a group of boys from our neighborhood play a game in which you bounce a rubber ball against the side of a building. I don't know what it was called or what the object was, but I remember one of the boys' fathers coming up to me afterwards and inviting me to join him and the other kids for a soda at the local candy store. It was a very touching moment because this was my first entrée into having friends in the Bronx.

Beyond these pivotal early friendships, the tide quickly began turning in the right direction for all of us after moving to the Bronx. While my mother eventually found steady employment as a hotel bookkeeper in Manhattan and my sisters completed high school, I attended PS 90. Though I continued to excel in sports, my lackluster grades would hardly qualify me for a place in the National Honor Society. It's not that I necessarily hated school, didn't do my homework, or resented authority figures. The simple truth was that even with my grandfather living with us, I really didn't have many male adult role models, especially since most of the guys I grew up with were fatherless also (or so it seemed).

In 1945, our family was dealt another difficult blow when my grandfather Jacob died of natural causes at the age of eighty-six, not long after my Bar Mitzvah. Despite his advanced age, he seemed immortal and his death came as a complete shock. Then, in 1946, we were forced to give up our apartment because the building had been sold and the new owner wanted it for himself—even though he was very lenient about it and gave us six months to find a new place. At that time, however, World War II had recently ended and there was a severe housing shortage in New York. There was also virtually no new construction, and so, with few alternatives, my mother decided to take a suite at the Le Marquis Hotel on 31st Street and Madison Avenue where she worked as a bookkeeper.

During my teenage years and into my early adulthood, we continued to hotel hop many more times, and although we felt like nomads, it wasn't all bad. I loved the excitement and diversity, something that sort of compared to being a poor real-life male version of Eloise, the fictional children's book character who lived at the Plaza.

As much as I enjoyed the adventure, however, I found myself faced with a bit of a dilemma when it came time to select a high school. Though we were living in Manhattan, the most logical place still seemed to be Taft in the Bronx, which Helene and Kala both attended, and which was coed. But this was never a viable option, because some girl had been felt up in the galoshes closet, and my sisters informed my mother that Taft would be a bad influence on me.

My choices were either Stuyvesant High School in Manhattan, which I didn't have the grades for, or Aviation High School in Long

Island City, which I had no interest in. Instead, it was decided that I would attend the all-boys DeWitt Clinton High School on Mosholu Parkway back up in the Bronx. In those days, DeWitt was considered one of the country's best public high schools, and it has boasted a raft of A-list alumni—including Ralph Lauren, Neil Simon, Stan Lee, Paddy Chayefsky, Garry Marshall, Richard Avedon, and comedians Jan Murray, Robert Klein, and Tracy Morgan.

The downside was the ninety-minute commute by subway twice a day. While occasionally I read, usually I found more dangerous ways to keep myself occupied, oftentimes by hanging my arm out the window of the moving train, running up and down the car, and having mock fistfights with my friends. Our shenanigans didn't end there, and while I hated schlepping to the Bronx every day, the good part was that after school I got to play different sports with guys from the old neighborhood. Usually, we played stickball, softball, or basketball, and I was always up for a game no matter what time of year it was.

During the summers, meanwhile, I escaped the sweltering city heat by returning to Connecticut, where my Uncle Joe owned a summer home on Oxoboxo Lake in Uncasville right outside of Norwich. Though being away may have cost me my first girlfriend, who burst into tears when she found out I was leaving and later wound up marrying one of my best friends, it turned out to be the best thing that could have happened to me. Aside from the change of scenery and exposing me to new things, it also kept me away from peer pressure because by the summer before my final year in high school, many of my friends in the city were already experimenting with drugs, including marijuana and even heroin.

I also spent one summer as a lifeguard at Tamiment resort in the Poconos when I was seventeen. It was there that I first saw comedians such as Imogene Coca from Sid Caesar's *Your Show of Shows* performing live onstage. Although it would be years before show business became my chosen profession, it made quite an impression on me. I also met and became very friendly with the brother of George Shapiro, the award-winning comedy manager who later went on to represent Jerry Seinfeld and Andy Kaufman.

Yet no matter how enamored I might have been with show business, I began to think about my future in more realistic terms as I approached high school graduation in 1950. Like most Jewish mothers, mine probably hoped that I would become a dentist or a lawyer or an accountant, although she never said anything, and I certainly didn't have the ability for any of these professions. I also wasn't about to subject myself to the City College of New York's entrance exam, much less four years of college, since I'd already suffered the disappointment of having my grade point average plummet because of DeWitt's foreign language requirement.

Initially, I decided to set my sights on simply trying to find gainful employment. My first job after graduation that summer was in the Catskills, the famed and predominantly Jewish Upstate New York resort region where almost any comedian and singer who was anybody in those years got their start.

We never had the financial means to vacation there, but I'd long been intrigued, especially after hearing about the stars that performed at places like Grossinger's, the Concord, and Kutsher's from our neighbor Arlene Strauss. Everyone called her "Crazy Arlene" and she was loaded by our standards. Her family was one of the few we knew in the Bronx who had a television when the medium was still in its infancy. Though there were only a handful of stations, and you had to turn on the set to let it warm up at least thirty minutes before your show came on in order to get a halfway decent reception, owning a TV then was considered the ultimate status symbol that few families could afford. Arlene and her mother used to let me and about five or six other kids come over and watch Milton Berle's comedy-variety extravaganza *Texaco Star Theater*, which was the show that forever made him one of America's biggest stars, along with earning him the nicknames "Uncle Miltie" and "Mr. Television." (Years later, after becoming a semi-regular at both the New York and Hollywood Improvs, Milton and I wound up as good friends right up until his death in 2002. Milton knew everybody and everybody knew him. Even though we were pals for nearly fifty years, I was always in awe whenever I was in his presence.)

During my second summer in the Catskills, I got a job at the Shawan-ga Lodge in High View, New York. I was hired as a boat boy, but while I was there, I also got more exposure to live comedians and singers. They were all "somebodies" and as it turned out, I got to be a "somebody," too. Not long after my arrival, I became the assistant stage manager, eventually playing the straight man to a burlesque comic named Sammy Smith.

My responsibilities also consisted of dancing with the mostly middle-aged female guests at the hotel, many of whom were married and had kids not much younger than me. When I say "middle-aged," I should add that any woman over the age of thirty qualified as middle-aged to me, and I found many of them to be quite attractive. Of course, I had the good sense not to pursue any of them romantically. I was also still a teenager, just barely out of high school.

Needless to say, I had an incredible summer and did very well there, but when it came time to return to New York that fall, I again realized I needed to find something steadier. I got a job as a hardware store stock boy in lower Manhattan, making a dollar an hour, which I hated, and where I only lasted about three months, even though it cemented my lifelong love affair with hardware stores. After that, I worked in the test kitchen of General Foods at 250 Park Avenue, around the corner from Grand Central Station. By 1952, however, it gradually occurred to me that I might want to reconsider college, and so I decided to study for the Brooklyn College entrance exam at the urging of a high school teammate of mine who was now on the Brooklyn College football team.

While I loved the camaraderie of it, picking up the pigskin again was also the worst thing that had ever happened to me up to that point—and the most painful. During our first practice, I intercepted the ball in the backfield, ran through the line, and was tackled from behind and thrown down, landing on the ground face forward. As I got back up on my feet, I realized my nose wasn't broken and I felt like a new person.

It wasn't long after when I decided it probably wasn't in my best interest to remain on the team. And similar to my lackluster academic performance all the way through grade school and high school, I wasn't any better when it came to college. Around the same time, I also began receiving draft notices and—voluntarily—decided to enlist in the army even though it was the height of the Korean War. After basic training in Pennsylvania, I was sent to biological warfare school just outside of Tokyo. Following three weeks there, I was posted to Korea, where all of the war was going on in the middle, with nothing happening in the south and north. Our unit literally went from Busan right up the peninsula to the main line of resistance in about a day and a half, as seemingly endless convoys shuttled men and equipment.

And then the next thing I knew, I was out on the front line in the middle of nowhere during the Battle of Pork Chop Hill on my first day in action. It was just like something out of a movie, and years later there was one called *Pork Chop Hill* starring Gregory Peck.

When we got to that battle, we were all dressed in freshly pressed uniforms and clean shaven. The rest of my guys were standing about fifteen yards behind me, throwing grenades up in the air. The sound was deafening and it worried me that I was at such close range, so I pleaded with them to throw the grenades to me with the pins in them, and to let me pull them.

At first, everything went fine, but then as I leaned forward and tried to duck for cover in one of the trenches, I was struck in the right leg and both arms by an enemy grenade. Minutes later, a piece of mortar also went through my helmet and scratched my earlobe as I was being hoisted up onto the mobile army surgical unit. By comparison, however, I got off easy, because the next thing I noticed, while being transported on the back of the tank, were five dead Chinese soldiers in the trench. One of them had his arm wrapped up in a bandage and he had lost a hand.

I was still recuperating in an Osaka military hospital, where I'd stay for four months, when a cease-fire went into effect and the war officially ended. After being discharged from the hospital and being awarded the Purple Heart and the Combat Infantryman Badge (CIB), I spent the next three weeks attending personnel management school. For the remainder of my twenty-one-month enlistment, I had a clerk's job just outside of Tokyo at Camp Zama. While I yearned to return to civilian life, my time in the military taught me survival skills that would later prove beneficial in many unexpected ways in the comedy world, and I'm grateful to have had the experience.

I came back to the United States in August 1954 and immediately reported to Camp Kilmer, New Jersey, although it would take nearly another month before my discharge became official. In between reuniting with my mother and sisters, I decided to return to Sha-wan-ga Lodge in the Catskills, where they put me in charge of security. I then moved back in with my mother, who was now living in Rego Park, Queens, and decided to give higher education one last try, first enrolling at the City College School of Commerce. Soon after, a letter arrived, informing me that I was eligible for more money from the GI Bill because of the injuries I had sustained in Korea, so I immediately transferred to New York University. Like I had during high school, I commuted every day to NYU's Greenwich Village campus by subway, this time from Rego Park. I also enthusiastically threw myself into my studies in a way I hadn't before. But it would take another two years after graduating with an advertising degree in 1957 before I finally landed my first "real" job in advertising.

My older cousin Leon, who was like a surrogate uncle to me, had already had a successful run producing television commercials, most notably with George Clooney's aunt, Rosemary Clooney, who was then a popular singer and recording artist best known for such hits as "Come On-a My House" and "Mambo Italiano." The problem was that Leon no longer worked in advertising. With no connections, I knew that getting a job in a New York agency would be next to impossible without starting off in the mail room, so I didn't even bother to apply.

Instead, in 1961, I decided to give Boston a try, where I quickly found work as a junior account executive at a small agency called Marvin & Leonard Advertising. Like me, they were two New York Jews who'd recently moved to Boston; they'd taken over the company after the previous owner retired. They had an office on Lincoln Street, and all of their clients were shoe manufacturers.

They were very nice men who paid me an extremely generous salary. I also had a great apartment in Beacon Hill and a very active social life, but as ideal as things were, working in advertising quickly grew boring even though I did it for nearly two years. And remaining in Boston as a single person also gradually lost its appeal.

The turning point was hitting thirty, plus my mother no longer needed my financial help because she was now collecting social security and had recently inherited $5,000 from my Uncle Sid. So when the question became, "What should I do next?" the answer seemed immediately obvious. That's when I made the decision to move back to New York in the summer of 1962 to finally try to do something in show business.

I knew I didn't want to be an actor, but I also knew nothing about becoming a Broadway producer. Still, I wanted to be one, and I decided to go for it. I also made up my mind that I was going to mount my first show within a year.

Broadway Bound and the Unexpected Detour

I returned to New York in June 1962. I still don't know how I ever thought I could make it as a Broadway producer, but failure was the furthest thing from my mind. The one thing I knew for sure is that I no longer wanted to work in advertising. I also knew that I needed to find a way to support myself before I could find my first show to produce.

Fortunately, my wonderful brother-in-law Gene, who owned a luncheonette on Madison Avenue, hired me as a waiter and let me work whenever I wanted. Another job I had for about three months was selling magazines over the phone, where one of my biggest sales was to the ex-wife of George "Bullets" Durgom, the legendary talent manager who represented such A-listers as Frank Sinatra, Jackie Gleason, and Sammy Davis Jr. She bought twelve subscriptions from me on the same day. After that, I did so well they eventually offered to promote me to manager, which I turned down, because I knew I wasn't going to stick around long. However, between this and working for my brother-in-law, I was able to share an apartment with a wealthy friend of mine from Boston named Burt Caldwell.

Burt moved back to New York around the same time I did to work for his family's tennis court installation company, and the Alphabet City apartment we shared was definitely a major step down from what I'd been accustomed to in Boston. It was a roach-infested hovel with exposed electrical wiring, a tub in the kitchen area, and no bathroom sink, which meant the kitchen is where we had to shave. The neighborhood was also riddled with drugs and crime in those days, and I couldn't believe that someone with all Burt's money was actually living there.

Even so, as two single guys, we had an amazing time in Manhattan. It was exciting and alive, especially at night, and I really liked Burt because he didn't take himself too seriously. It was also around this time that I began dating Silver Saundors, the woman who eventually became my first wife and indirectly helped plant the seeds for the Improv. We tied the knot nearly six months after the club opened, and although the marriage ultimately didn't work out, we had two wonderful daughters, Zoe and Beth. I also credit Silver for making me keep the menu prices down in the beginning.

We first met in the summer of 1961 at Logan Airport in Boston where she was on a layover from Nantucket, and we both happened to be on the same Eastern Airlines flight to New York, before I'd moved back there. She was five feet five with blonde hair and movie-star looks that I found very striking. Silver, then twenty-seven, was a chorus girl in the Broadway company of *Fiorello!*, which impressed me. I was intrigued, too, when she told me how she'd been named after Sime Silverman, the founder of the show-business bible, *Variety*, where her father was an editor.

SILVER SAUNDORS FRIEDMAN, Budd's ex-wife:

Budd kind of sidled over to me from out of nowhere. I was wearing a yellow car coat and a kelly-green hat. In all truthfulness, I was kind of dressed like a crazy person, but the ensemble went well together as far as I was concerned. This obviously must have made an impression on Budd, because the first thing he said to me was, "I bet you're from New York."

That was his opening line, and I was like, "Pardon me?"

And he goes, "I can tell from the way you're dressed that you must be from New York."

I'd missed the previous flight because I overslept that morning, and I was in no mood for small talk, so I said, "Yes, I guess I am if you say so." I was very aloof about it, although Budd was evidently unfazed because the next thing he did was ask me out for a drink if we couldn't get on the flight. I reminded him that it was one o'clock in the afternoon and told him I didn't drink at this hour, so he asked me out for a soda instead.

Then an announcement came over the loudspeaker that the flight had been delayed, so we ended up going to this little bar near the gate. I ordered a glass of tomato juice while Budd ordered wine and we sat for about a half hour. I then politely excused myself and went back over to the gate to stand in line. Meanwhile, Budd had somehow managed to get on the plane ahead of me because by the time I finally got on board he was waving me over to the seat next to him. It turned out Budd was going to New York to meet up with some friends and he asked if he could come see *Fiorello!*.

"Everybody can see the show," I said.

"Can you get me a comp ticket?" he asked. I told him no, but when I said that I could get him a discounted ticket, he was still undeterred and asked for my phone number.

"Can I call you and find out?" he said. I said yes, and then I gave him the number to the backstage phone at the theater we used in case of emergencies.

I don't remember Silver telling me the tickets weren't free or even asking. I guess I just naturally assumed they were because she was in the cast. So when I got to the box office the following afternoon and the clerk informed me they cost $6.50 a piece, I was shocked. Even though I could barely afford one ticket, I still wound up buying two with the idea that I could sell the extra and make some money. When it occurred to me that I would still be out six bucks, I couldn't believe what I'd just done.

Then, noticing there was a middle-aged woman standing in line behind me, and with the clerk now in the middle of another transaction, I offered to sell her one of my tickets. I'll never forget the exchange of words we had as long as I live. Embarrassed, but with nothing to lose, I said, "Would you like a ticket to see the show?"

"Yeah," she replied. "That's why I'm here. Is it a good seat?"

I was relieved someone would take the extra ticket, but what began innocently enough as an attempt on my part to inject some levity by delivering a clever comeback quickly deteriorated and put an end to any chance I might have had of closing the deal. I said, "Sure, it's a good seat. I'm going to be sitting next to you."

As soon as I said this, it became clear that she wasn't amused, as the look on her face turned to disgust and she snapped her purse shut. "I'll get my own ticket," she said.

I could hardly believe what was happening. I was also completely oblivious to the fact that what I was doing was illegal or that I could be arrested if a cop showed up, because I spotted another couple who immediately bought both of my tickets. As a result, I didn't see *Fiorello!* until right before it closed nearly a year later, although I still managed to get up enough courage to ask Silver out before I went back to Boston—only to have her say no. Her reason was that she was already seeing someone and didn't want to jeopardize it by being in a long-distance relationship.

But she also invited me to call her if I ever moved back to New York. By the time I did, some eight months after that, Silver was in the chorus of *How to Succeed in Business Without Really Trying*, which was the biggest hit on Broadway. Co-starring Robert Morse and Michele Lee, it also featured another young singer-dancer named Donna McKechnie, who in the mid-1970s would go on to achieve major fame playing aging dancer Cassie Ferguson as the lead character in choreographer Michael Bennett's critically acclaimed musical *A Chorus Line*.

DONNA MCKECHNIE, singer, dancer, choreographer, and actor:

Silver and I sat next to one another in the dressing room, and I liked her a lot. She had a great sense of humor and a great laugh, but there was also a tough exterior when you first met her.

She kind of became like a big-sister figure to me after a while. When it came to men, I was the girl who could never say no, so I'd have all these boyfriends, and Silver would try to educate me. I don't mean going all the way [sexually], but when somebody asked me out, I'd say, "Okay, sure." I also never kept an appointment book, which meant there'd often be two guys waiting for me outside the theater because I couldn't keep track of my schedule. It used to absolutely drive Silver nuts.

While we were doing the show, she and Budd were dating. I remember him being this funny guy who wanted you to think there was an aura about him. Silver didn't just want Budd to be an entrepreneur in his mind. After all, he had these great ideas.

Even during this period when I was at loose ends, and it was becoming increasingly evident that becoming a Broadway producer wasn't going to be in the cards—at least anytime soon—I would always come back to the fact that I didn't want to go back into advertising. Not only did

the idea of three-martini expense-account lunches and hawking prod-
ucts for some Madison Avenue agency hold little appeal to me, I knew
it would have meant working eighty-hour weeks and having to prove
myself all over again.

While I also had no particular interest in going into the nightclub
or restaurant business either, the early 1960s seemed ripe for the picking if you had the right concept. Back then, you could literally choose
from hundreds of clubs in New York that presented the top music acts
seven nights a week. You could also catch up-and-coming acts at a lot
of places down in Greenwich Village for practically nothing. At that
time, though, there really weren't any affordable bars or restaurants in
the theater district where young performers who weren't already stars
could go and unwind after their shows.

This dawned on me very early on in my relationship with Silver
when we'd go out with the cast of *How to Succeed* after the show, and I'd
hear them talk about this place or that place in Chicago and Philadelphia where the food was cheap and they could get up and sing. They also
lamented the fact that there was nowhere in New York where they could
do that, which I could relate to because I was on a very limited budget
myself. So the more I thought about it, the more I began kicking around
the idea of opening up something myself.

THREE
Building the House
That Built Hilarity

can't help but think that a part of me must have been insane when I look back now at why I decided to start the Improv. I also wasn't thinking in any specific terms about how it might evolve other than as a temporary, part-time venture to help me expand my contacts in the theater, which were nearly zilch at that point.

And that was basically it, although I, at least, had enough sense to realize I needed an existing restaurant so I wouldn't have to start from scratch. I also knew that it had to be between West 43rd and West 49th Streets and in between Eighth and Ninth Avenues. This was my target location, and my original plan was to open a coffeehouse that served food because I couldn't afford a liquor license. I also knew that even if I could serve liquor, I'd run the risk of the Mafia finding out, and I'd have to pay them off. At any rate, I must have started looking for places towards the end of the summer of '62, and I searched practically every day for almost five months.

In the meantime, I had a backup plan. My cousin Len, who's a year older than me and also wanted to go into show business, was running a pet store on Christopher Street down in the Village. He was very eager to sell it and I was all set to make a deal with him because by then I was feeling desperate.

And then, lo and behold—on the very same day I was supposed to sign the papers—I happened to pass a Vietnamese restaurant on West 44th Street near the southeast corner of Ninth Avenue that had just closed, and I saw the For Rent sign in the window literally two hours after it had gone up. This was in November, and the Improv opened a little over three and a half months later.

LOU ALEXANDER, former comedian and agent:

It wasn't a classy joint and the neighborhood was terrible, but Budd was able to make a deal and get a low rent. That's how it all started.

Even before I set foot inside, I was in love with it. Not only was it a block west of the famed Broadway watering hole Sardi's, it had once been the cafeteria for the Actors Studio, which was one block east. I also loved the fact that Marilyn Monroe reputedly used to eat lunch here.

However, there weren't any special deals. Not only did I have to borrow money from my mother, I eventually had to sell shares to be able to afford the $250 monthly rent. But the landlord, Emil Lublin, and his son were very nice to me. They owned the liquor store next door, which we later took over.

DONNA MCKECHNIE:

Budd was really excited about it and so was Silver, and they enlisted everybody's help because they had a deadline. I remember the brown paint, and lacquering some of the news-papers they used for wallpaper. Other things I remember are the tables coming in and the little upright piano they had over in the corner.

I still don't think I was really aware of what Budd was creat-ing at that point, but whatever it was, it seemed exciting. After it opened, the Improv became like a haven to me because I knew everybody and I could go alone.

Some of the people from *How to Succeed* and a few friends pitched in, which was a great help. But I was a pretty decent carpenter, so I did most of the renovations myself. I was also able to do them without a permit from the New York City Department of Buildings because I didn't make any structural changes, nor did I need a certificate of occupancy, which back then was only required if you had more than ninety-nine seats and we had seventy-four.

As an extra level of insurance to avoid prying eyes, I sealed off the windows with newspapers and did most of the work late at night. In terms of renovations, the first thing that had to be done was removing the huge counter in the middle, which the Vietnamese restaurant left behind and would have severely restricted our seating capacity. Then, although I knew nothing about plumbing, I started tearing out the pipes and nearly flooded the place because I used a hacksaw to cut the pipes without shutting off the water first. I also accidentally turned off the water supply to the entire building when there was a professional card game going on upstairs on the second floor. The next thing I knew, I was standing there completely drenched and up to my knees in water when this massive guy named Walter who was built like a football player suddenly appeared from out of nowhere. Staring me up and down for about a minute before he finally spoke, he said, "Hey, you shut off the water."

Although I replied, "I'm really sorry, but I don't know what the fuck I'm doing," I was suddenly really scared, too, because I thought he might try to beat me up.

But instead, he said, "Let me help you." Better still, it turned out that he was a fairly skilled carpenter-electrician-plumber, who then proceeded to help me out with everything for the next two months without pay. I'm not sure why, but he just did it, no questions asked, and I never found out his last name. I never saw him again after that either, except once when he came by the club about three years after we'd been open and reluctantly accepted a bottle of scotch.

Walter really saved me because once we got the plumbing done and then the floor, which was this beautiful terrazzo that only needed to be buffed, we were able to build our booths and cover them with fabric. We also put up curtains in the window.

Then I began tearing out the red lacquered paneling and mirrors, which is how I discovered the brick wall that has become a staple of stand-up comedy ever since. Like practically everything else I was doing then, this was pure happenstance. Once again, it was there just staring me in the face, and the reason why we didn't cover over the brick was because I couldn't afford drywall. So we simply cleaned the brick with muriatic acid and sealed it instead. Then my friend Aaron Heller, who was an artist, built a wooden fire escape on the wall, which looked real. But the brick wall didn't really become a focal point until years later when we expanded and I had to put in an emergency exit, which was behind the wall. In front of it, we had our stage and that's how the brick wall was used. It was a perfect buffer space.

Flying by the Seat of My Pants

T hat was how it pretty much all started. Exhilarating, exonerating, terrifying. From the moment I began making preparations to open the Improv towards the end of 1962, I never had any second thoughts about whether I'd made the right decision. And with the renovations coming along well enough by early January 1963, I started to believe I might actually make a go of things.

Slowly sprouting up almost like top seed, I would do this, and out of this came that, but I still didn't have any formal plans. In other words, it was all pretty much an improv. This was also how I came up with the name "the Improvisation," which we later shortened. Officially opening on a frigid, snowy night in mid-February, here's what transpired from day one.

DONNA MCKECHNIE:

Everybody from *How to Succeed* came over after the show and we all got up and sang. The way it worked was that you'd come in and they'd ask if you wanted to sing. You'd be like, "Let me eat something and see how I feel." But you never felt any pressure to do it, which was part of the appeal.

ROBERT MORSE, actor:

I don't know how close I was to Silver and Budd, but I adored them and they liked me. Silver was the first person who told me about the Improv the night it opened, and once in a while I'd get up onstage and do something terrible. I closed the place most of the time.

MICHELE LEE, actor and singer:

I didn't help them get ready, although I did come soon after the Improv opened and I was always comfortable there. It was the same kind of atmosphere that Elaine's, which also opened that same year, had. You knew you were protected from onlookers. Even though there *were* onlookers, there was a sense of security you got being at the Improv—and of course, you could eat, drink, and do whatever you wanted to. To me, it was the first of that kind of after-show hangout.

Unquestionably, having the entire cast of *How to Succeed in Business*, including Robert Morse, Rudy Vallee, and Bonnie Scott, show up that first night was a godsend. Another major triumph was that on the evenings that followed, many of them brought their friends, a boomerang effect that would replicate itself and pay huge dividends almost immediately, in large part because many of them were also on Broadway. At the same time, their presence unfortunately didn't make much difference when it came to our cash register, and to say that we were also living hand-to-mouth in the beginning is putting it mildly.

For one thing, we almost never had any customers until eleven-thirty, after the Broadway shows let out, plus we were only charging a fifty-cent minimum because I didn't know how to price anything. I also had no idea that there were wholesale restaurant distributors where you could pre-order the food to specification and have it delivered. So instead, I shopped for whatever we needed at the grocery store and invariably almost always paid full retail.

Ditto when it came to buying our meat from a butcher shop over on Ninth Avenue, which also meant that we never had enough. I constantly found myself running across the street to Smilers Delicatessen in the middle of the night to replenish our supplies.

SILVER SAUNDORS FRIEDMAN:

Because we didn't have a cover charge, we had to try to make whatever profit we had on the coffee and food, so Budd got creative. He'd put cinnamon sticks into the coffee and sometimes he'd just roast them right into the grounds. This became kind of a signature because there weren't coffeehouses on every block and Starbucks didn't exist then.

ROBERT MORSE:

I actually used to go there a lot with Rudy Vallee for the food in the beginning, because believe it or not, the Improv had a wonderful menu.

Though food was never the main reason why people came to the Improv—and it was frequently in short supply—we did manage to serve a fairly consistent menu. Besides coffee, some of our most popular items initially were black bread and cheese, matzo ball soup, hamburgers, and peppers and steak.

MICHAEL GOLDSTEIN, the New York Improv's first publicist:

In the old days, Budd would wander into the kitchen to get a sandwich for himself, but that was about it. I don't think he was ever that concerned about the food, even though he probably should have been.

SILVER SAUNDORS FRIEDMAN:

To Budd's credit, he knew enough about food to know if you jazzed it up, people would pay attention. The problem was that we often couldn't pay the meat bill for our burgers, so Budd got creative there, too. What he'd do is send out a check without signing it, which meant they couldn't cash it. Then he'd buy us some time by waiting a couple of days until we had the money and send them another one.

For all my constant worries about how I was going to pay for the food and whether we had enough, this was nothing compared to some of the eccentric, if not at times mentally unstable, kitchen staff we had preparing it in a chaotic hiring practice that went on for many years.

First, there was David, a 350-pound French expatriate who was also Jewish. David had been in a German concentration camp during World

War II and literally ate everything in sight. Later, we had a Puerto Rican
guy named Louie who once threatened Silver with a knife that comedian Robert Klein used to do a deadpan impersonation of: "Pick up or
I cut your balls off!"

By far, the most memorable staff member, though, was a chef from
India who wore an oversized trench coat, and often got picked on by a
group of teenagers from the neighborhood in a scene that resembled
something straight out of a Charlie Chaplin movie.

**CYNTHIA FROST, actor and former New York Improv
waitress:**

[The Indian chef] used to throw things at you whenever you
sent the orders back, so I used to beg the customers not to.
He was also very religious, and he'd sit down at a table facing
the wall, lay out a napkin, and pray. He was this nebbishy little
Hindu guy who couldn't stand women and wouldn't let them
touch him. So now get this: One day I'm walking along Broadway and I see the chef. He's coming towards me and he's got
a hooker on his arm that's about six two. It was surreal.

BOBBY KELTON, writer and comedian:

Once they started giving us food, it was like gold because we
were all broke and a lot of times it was the only meal we'd
have all day. Sometimes the comics would even wander into
the kitchen late at night to tell the waitresses what we wanted
to eat. But I'd also heard stories, particularly about the Puerto
Rican chef chasing people with a knife, so I made it a point to
steer clear of him whenever I did.

CYNTHIA FROST:

There was also a terrible mice problem, so Budd got the idea
to put cats down in the basement, hoping this would get rid
of them, which it didn't. One night, there was this huge mouse
that somehow scurried up in front of the drum set we had
onstage. Budd didn't even notice until someone from the
audience yelled out, "Hey, Budd, there's a rat." Then he picked
up a baseball bat from behind the bar, smashed the living day-
lights out of it and blood splattered everywhere. It was a huge
mess, but the people still came after that. God did they love

it—and they came in mobs every night because of the entertainers who would show up.

SHELLEY ACKERMAN, singer, actor, astrologer, and former New York Improv waitress:

During the week, the pace was a little slower, but it could still be very packed and you worked your ass off. If a table comfortably sat eight people, Budd would double that to sixteen. He'd squeeze as many people in as he possibly could, so there was very little room and you had to move through it and move fast to keep your eye on everything because Budd did.

For our bread, we used these round boards where we'd put half a loaf of pumpernickel and two pats of butter. If a customer wanted extra butter, Budd insisted we charge them five cents extra. I wouldn't call him cheap necessarily, but he was very frugal and watched every penny. This also meant that if a customer walked out without paying, it was our problem.

The Improv Gets Hot

SILVER SAUNDORS FRIEDMAN:

The crowds came based on the early press we got, which Budd was very good at because he'd been in advertising. Besides the singers we had from many of the Broadway shows and other celebrities performing and coming in nightly, another big crowd-pleaser in the beginning was this defective pay phone we had.

It was a leftover from the Vietnamese restaurant, and you could call anywhere in the world, often without putting money in. People were so fascinated by this that they'd line up just to use the phone. Somehow or another, Earl Wilson, who wrote a column for the *New York Post*, found out and he wrote an entire story about it.

The talent we had coming in almost nightly was in abundant supply from the get-go. This was already becoming increasingly evident by the spring of 1963, even though it was still anybody's guess where it would all lead. It was also during this early period when I suddenly began to realize that, if nothing else, we were prophetically living up to our name both onstage and off.

CYNTHIA FROST:

One night, there was a holiday of some sort and the place was packed when Budd came in with four or five strippers who must have been standing outside. The next thing I knew, they were all up on the table taking their clothes off. I don't know if they were professionals or not, but they were up on the tables dancing. We all just good-naturedly kind of took things in stride and the men went crazy. But God almighty, Silver was pissed off—and rightfully, I think—because she was afraid that if the cops came in they'd be out of business.

That same evening, my friend Jim Downey stopped in after his restaurant closed and when I told him what happened, he asked me to introduce him to the women, which I did. He said, "Ah, good evening, ladies. I'm Jim Downey. How are you tonight?" And then one of them reached into her blouse, took out her breast, and said, "Oh, hello, Jim. Have some."

CYNTHIA FROST:

Budd kept a mental list of who came in and who was more famous. He would always ask them to get up and there were some of them who didn't want to because they weren't getting paid, although there were others who were well known that wanted to and Budd wouldn't let them. He'd keep them waiting for hours.

Attracting an after-hours show-business crowd like we did, there were obviously a lot of drunks, although when I was there we didn't have a bar and we didn't serve liquor yet. Instead, Budd would sneak some booze to his favorite customers, like Rudy Vallee, and he wouldn't charge them. Rudy was very cheap. I would wait on him hand and foot, and when it came time to pay, Budd would say it was on the house. Rudy wouldn't even leave a tip.

To this day, I'm still obsessed with meeting and being around celebrities, which, aside from my desire to be a producer, could have well been another reason I started the Improv. This didn't occur to me until many years later, although when we first opened, I felt like a big kid in a candy store.

JAMIE DEROY, producer, singer, actor, and television host:

Budd was always very nice to me and I've got nothing but wonderful memories, although I'll also tell you an interesting story about him when it comes to having customers who were famous—even though mine probably echoes a lot of others.

I moved to New York from Pittsburgh in 1964 to study acting at the American Musical and Dramatic Academy, and become a singer and an actress. Like a lot of young performers, I had a lot of day jobs to support myself, although fortunately most of them were in show business. One of them was working for the Improv's publicist Michael Goldstein. He brought me there a lot and I worked for him off and on, which was great, but there was a time in between when I was collecting unemployment benefits.

As it still is, one of their requirements is that you have to be actively looking for work in your respective field in order to receive benefits. One day, I was down at the unemployment office and the clerk set me up for a job working for a British actor named Norman Wisdom who was very well known at the time. He needed help learning his lines for this upcoming television appearance he had, which proved to be impossible because he was impossible.

Anyway, one night after work we ended up having dinner at this hamburger place near the theater district. It was such a dump that there were literally flies in the food. It was just disgusting and I'm not sure if I even ate, but somehow afterwards I suggested we go over to the Improv. Needless to say, Budd, in his typical fashion, was absolutely ecstatic that I'd brought Norman into his club and we stayed for a couple of hours.

The next thing I knew, when the check came at the end of the evening, Budd picked up the tab for both of us, which he never did when I was alone.

ROSS BENNETT, comedian:

Budd loves talent, but he loves being around celebrities and power even more. I'm not sure if it's him or just the nature of show business, but that's what he gets his charge from.

BUDDY MANTIA, comedian, actor, and singer:

I think Budd's bark was always much worse than his bite, although you could always feel his wrath when he'd yell at you to get out of the aisle—especially if you weren't famous yet, because it made you fearful that you wouldn't get spots. But the thing was that it could be just about anybody and he'd say the same thing: "Get the hell out of the aisle." Back then, it was his mantra.

SILVER SAUNDORS FRIEDMAN:

In the beginning, Christopher Plummer would come in a lot, and sometimes Jason Robards would meet him because they were friends. I loved Jason as an actor and I certainly respected his talent, but he was a drunk and he was almost always plowed. As a matter of fact, he came in one night not long after we opened and then proceeded to relieve himself on our brick wall.

I remember saying to Budd, "If you don't reprimand him, I will." However, he refused to do anything. He said, "We can't do that. He's drunk. Number one, he'll never remember that we reprimanded him, and number two, we have to be careful who we reprimand."

Well, that was that. This was where Budd and I had our biggest differences, even though I didn't fight with him over this particular instance. I also understood the importance of "marketing" as much as I hate that word, although Jason never came back with a decent party and he was almost always drunk.

Not long after that, I'm guessing sometime around late 1963 or early 1964, I remember hearing this commotion coming from outside the men's room. Naturally, because we only had one toilet and there were three guys in there, I immediately became suspicious, and I started pounding on the door with my fists. It was one of those things where impulse just sort of takes over.

When nobody responded, I kicked the door in and busted the latch. The next thing I knew, I saw Jason, Christopher, and this other guy named Al Lewis, who was an aspiring actor that ran his father's parking garage. All three were just standing there, passing around a bottle of vodka like a bunch of teenagers and getting completely shitfaced. They didn't even have cups, but I didn't want to seem like the bad guy either, so I finally just said, "Don't stay too long," and turned around and left.

I guess you could say I was something of an enabler, although nobody knew about those things then. There was a police precinct about two blocks away, and there were these six detectives who used to come in after they got off duty to have a drink and blow off steam.

What they'd do is get a bottle of whatever from another bar, then come in and have a drink, and leave the rest for me to give to some of our more famous customers like Christopher and Jason. So many stories involving them and alcohol come to mind, but probably my all-time favorite was the night that Christopher was there singing some sort of a duet with Jason at the little sixty-six-key upright piano we had.

And then—God knows why—Albert Finney and Tuesday Weld decided to join in. Both were already famous actors, and Tuesday, who had won a Golden Globe Award for the Most Promising Female New-comer in 1960 and was dating her future husband Dudley Moore, was one of the biggest sex symbols in Hollywood at the time. Teenagers and grown men alike were absolutely besotted by her, myself included. You can only imagine what a thrill for me it was to have her in my club. Only this night, she became the main attraction, because just as Christopher and Jason were singing, a very sexily clad Tuesday stretched out diago-nally on the piano top while Albert Finney began beating on the back of a chair like a pair of bongo drums.

The audience just went ape shit and I remember bolting from the back of the room where I was tallying up checks to the front so I could get a closer view. My mouth was literally hanging wide open like some teenager. I can still see Tuesday stretched out, sultry and sensual, and every other male in the room ogling her. I'm sure that any man who was there that night and is still around shares this memory.

On this very same evening, and whenever Jason and Chris were performing together at the piano after that, they'd often have a third person with them named Mort Shuman, a songwriter who'd written for Elvis Presley, Bobby Darin, and the Drifters. Mort worked in the nearby Brill Building and he always brought his guitar with him. This happened frequently and he was a very pleasant, easygoing guy, although I was hesitant about putting him on despite his pedigree because rock 'n' roll wasn't in keeping with the Improv's musical-theater theme. Usually he was just fine with that, so it was never a problem.

However, on this particular night, Mort insisted on joining in. I can't remember if it was before or after Tuesday and Albert, but I do remem-ber saying yes and letting him go on anytime he wanted—all because he sent his friend out to get champagne from his home and we wound up staying until the sun came up. It was the perfect example of countless other evenings that followed.

Over time, I also became very friendly with Mort's writing part-ner Doc Pomus, who spent most of his life in a wheelchair following a childhood bout with polio. He was married to the female lead in

Fiorello!, which Silver had been in. Doc was a great guy, and he's the one who taught Bette Midler how to sing rock 'n' roll. He saw her at the club one night and said, "I'll tutor her." And he did.

BETTE MIDLER:

Oh my God, Doc was a blues singer—a white blues singer—and he'd been in a wheelchair for a long, long time, but that didn't stop him from having wonderful relationships with a wonderful family who adored and looked after him. He lived on 72nd Street on the West Side somewhere, and the Improv is where I first met him. He was also a terrific songwriter who wrote mostly blues and blues-inflected songs. I think he thought he could help me, but I wasn't sure he liked my voice. I never really got that feeling, and I don't think I spent enough time trying to get a firm grasp on what he was offering. He gave me some songs he thought were appropriate for me that I either butchered or didn't come up to snuff with. But Doc was truly one of the giants and he knew a lot of the same people I wound up knowing.

DANNY AIELLO, actor, singer, and former New York Improv bouncer:

Doc Pomus was my boy. He was working somewhat with Bette and he used to come to the club a lot even when she wasn't on. His car would pull up to the entrance and then I'd carry him inside and put him near the stage. There was a waiter named Jerry Green who worked at this restaurant called the Colony on the Upper East Side where Doc also went a lot, and he knew we were friendly. One time, I was having dinner there and Jerry came up to me out of the blue and asked me if I knew why Doc wrote the song "Save the Last Dance for Me," which I later recorded on one of my albums.

It was a very touching story because Doc's wife had been a professional dancer and he used to enjoy watching her dance with other people even though he couldn't accompany her because he was confined to a wheelchair. That was the inspiration for this song where the last line was, "As long as you're going home with me." Doc was dynamite.

A Future Film Legend Wanders into West 44th Street and I Nearly Produce My First Show

In April 1963, I decided to hire a piano player. Given our precarious finances, it was another expense I could barely afford. But from what very little I still knew about show business at this point, I also knew enough to realize that singers sang that much better if they had a regular accompanist who was familiar with their material and could play in their key.

The first person we had was Bob Murdoch, whom I paid fifty dollars a week and who was in the chorus of *How to Succeed* with Silver. Bob came in almost every night after the show and was an immediate hit. When he got another gig and left several months later, I was devastated. Luckily, however, I wasn't left completely high and dry because not long after that another classically trained pianist from California who had recently moved to New York to become an actor wandered into the club and sat down at the piano.

When I say "wandered into," which was how a lot of people found their way to the Improv in those days, I'm not exaggerating. I also didn't try to stop him after I discovered he could play, although I couldn't tell you the song he did or what our first conversation was if my life depended on it. The whole thing sounds strange, yes, but he was always welcome during the six months he came in after that.

Whenever he did, it was mostly without fanfare, mainly because it was usually during our early evening lull. But I liked him a lot, even though the melodies he played typically fell somewhere in between slow and serene to sullen and moody. Nevertheless, it worked because of his tendency to scrumptiously blend into the background. And yet despite his enigmatic playing style, there was also something about his personality that made you want to like him.

The young man's name was Dustin Hoffman. Many years later he would say that the only reason he was never a flop is because I never formally introduced him. I don't say any of this for vindication, but his claim is also only true because he never asked me to.

In any event, when he first began coming into the Improv in either the late spring or early summer of 1963, Dustin was living in an Upper West Side hotel with a young male opera singer who also came in fairly often. One night around this same period, the roommate told him that he was bringing a girl with him to the club and Dustin said, "I'll meet you there." As fate would have it, the girl was Anne Byrne, a young ballet dancer and actress who eventually became his first wife.

PHOEBE DORIN, actor and the New York Improv's first waitress:

I went home with Dustin one night. Dusty is a tiny little guy and I'm a tiny girl, and he liked me because I waited on him. At the time, he was several years away from *The Graduate* and light-years away from instant recognition. He was living on the West Side not far from me, and he asked if he could take me home on his motorcycle. I'd never ridden one so I was like, "What do I do? Do I sit on the back?" And he said, "Yeah." He was very charming and adorable, but I didn't invite him up because I didn't know where it was going to go. Instead, we ended up going out for pancakes and just talking until four in the morning. Even though he told me he was struggling, I could already tell he was going to be a humongous star.

I can't say that Dustin and I were ever close friends, and I haven't spoken to him in many years, but we were always friendly. I remember one night in particular when he came into the club in late 1975. It was right before I moved to Los Angeles and Dustin was in town filming *Marathon Man*.

He was already a major star by this point and I hadn't seen him in several years, but as we were about to close, Dustin informed me that he was due on the set in a few hours, which meant he didn't have enough time to go back to his hotel and sleep. Then he asked me if I still went to Brasserie, a popular all-night French restaurant in the Seagram Building that has since closed. I told him I did, although I was also tired and I wasn't too thrilled about going at first. Then again, I also didn't want to seem like a bad sport, nor did I want to pass up an opportunity to be seen in public with Dustin Hoffman in one of New York's hottest restaurants.

So we went and, needless to say, had a great time, although when I went to see the film after it came out I remember noticing that Dustin appeared to be exhausted in one of the scenes. That was when it suddenly occurred to me that our night out on the town months earlier might have been the reason why.

Along with Dustin and Louis Gossett Jr., who occasionally sang and played the guitar, we had many other talented piano players at the Improv over the years. Early on, most notably, they included Charlie Small, who went on to write the original Broadway score for the *The Wiz*, and John Meyer, who wrote a musical about the Vietnam War called *The Draft Dodger* that I wanted to produce in 1965.

JOHN MEYER, composer, lyricist, and former New York Improv piano player:

I got to the Improv around 1964, about a year after it opened. It was still called the Improvisation, and it was already quickly gaining a reputation as a place where singers and comics could drop in and try things out. Around this same time, I met another singer named Betty Rhodes who later became my girlfriend and lived right around the corner from the Improv. One night, she suggested we stop in to meet Budd and see if we could get on. I'm not sure if he'd heard of either of us yet, but he was instantly enamored of Betty even though he was married to Silver, and he immediately put Betty on.

Betty was one of the sexiest women you could ever meet on top of having an incredible voice. She was just the complete package, and we were all gaga over her, particularly Budd, who practically fell over himself that first time we came in. But he also liked the way I played, so not long after that he hired me to become his piano player for seventy-five dollars a night. This was a fortune back then, but he knew I was his secret weapon for keeping Betty around, so he somehow managed to come up with the bucks and paid me weekly in cash.

In any case, I had a blast and in the coming months and over the next year or so, I was there almost every night. The comics loved me and used to call me "Knuckles" because I had a theatrical instinct for punctuating their routines musically with things like car chases or love scenes to accompany the setup of their bits, plus I could hold my own doing shtick and throwing them lines.

I had also recently co-written a musical satire called *The Draft Dodger* about a rich kid who evades the army during the Vietnam War, which was already five years old at the time and very controversial. When I told Budd about it, he loved the idea. He had this friend named Eddie Blum, who arranged for us to audition the show with the legendary Richard Rodgers, who wrote the music for *Carousel*, *The King and I*, *South Pacific*, and *Oklahoma*.

We were all ecstatic, and Budd even held a backer's audition at the Improv. There was subsequent interest in a film version and we sold the rights to a small company called Commonwealth United. There was also interest from Warner Brothers, although the lawyer we had at the time loused up the negotiations and the whole thing just completely fell apart.

When John first told me about his idea, I was instantly intrigued. Unfortunately, I think the reason why it probably never got off the ground was because ultimately everybody thought the Vietnam War would soon be over and they got cold feet. Needless to say, it wasn't, and giving up on the show so easily probably wasn't the greatest decision on my part.

Nor was it the last time I made a choice that I'd later regret.

SEVEN
The Singing Waitresses

I n the good decisions column, one of the best I made in the beginning was to hire singing waitresses. Similar to my decision to hire a piano player so that the singers would have an accompanist, the idea was that we would always have entertainment on hand even if no one else showed up, and it was a practice that continued long after I opened my second club in Los Angeles in 1975. Elayne Boosler and actor Karen Black were probably our most famous ones, but there were many others like Phoebe Dorin, who started with me very early on.

PHOEBE DORIN:

Like Budd, I came from an advertising background, first at CBS, and then in the art department of Dell Publications, where I was miserable. I'm not sure how I first found out about it, but everyone in the acting community already knew about the Improv, and I think I just went over there when I found out Budd was looking for waitresses, and he hired me. He wasn't particularly personable back then, and sometimes he could berate you and you'd think, "My God, I'm just a waitress. This isn't rocket science."

But since I'm one of the ones who made the transition to becoming a performer, I also think he had great respect for me. I was twenty-three or twenty-four at the time. Unlike being an aspiring actress at other places, if this is what you wanted to do and you were waiting tables at the Improv, everyone else knew it—especially if you were also singing there. The interesting thing about it was that the people who came in and the people who waited on them were practically one in the same. It was like a network. Our roles could switch at any time, because we were all in the same boat. Nobody knew where anybody was going to wind up.

JUDY ORBACH, talent manager and former New York Improv assistant manager:

I come from a show-business family. My dad's cousin was Jerry Orbach from *Law & Order*, and my father, who was originally from Germany, sang at the Berlin Academy of Music and later Carnegie Hall. My mother was a Juilliard graduate and my brother Ron was in the original Broadway cast of Neil Simon's play *Laughter on the 23rd Floor*.

Show business was always in my blood. I started singing when I was three years old, and by the time I got to the Improv, I'd been doing it almost my entire life. I was already writing songs, and I was ready to move to New York. The first time I went there, I was sitting in the audience with my mom listening to these waitresses and I was like, "Shit, I can do that." And with a completely straight face, she looked up at me and said, "Go talk to somebody."

So I got up from our table to ask one of the waitresses who was in charge, and she pointed Budd out to me. I went right up to him and said, "Are you Mr. Friedman?"

He said, "Yes." And after telling him I could sing, he looked me up and down and told me I was up next. Then he hired me to be a hostess and a singer even though I lived in New Jersey. It didn't scare me, because I was already a performer. My mom played for me that night. I did a couple of songs from *Funny Girl* and then I did some of my own stuff.

SHELLEY ACKERMAN:

I knew I belonged at the Improv from the moment I first heard about it. Back in early 1971, I was home watching television one night and there was a documentary about the Improv on PBS. Actually, it was more like a special where they featured comedians and singers, sort of like *An Evening at the Improv* was years later. Each one of them was fantastic, and I was absolutely mesmerized both by the talent and the magical feeling in the arrangement.

I had already been singing at several showcase clubs and this little place on Second Avenue called The Apartment where Jimmie Walker, who was an Improv regular, also performed. Jimmie had been in the documentary I watched and a couple of months later I saw him at The Apartment. We started talking after the show and I told him I wanted to sing at the Improv.

"All right, there are auditions. I'll bring you there," he said. I auditioned for Budd not long after. I brought my own accompanist, Robin Field, who used to play only in the keys of C and F. I was doing a lot of Stephen Sondheim material back then, and I did one of his songs and Budd loved it. I wound up working there from July 1971 until 1980, first as a singer and soon after as waitress also, even though I was only seventeen at the time.

I still had a shitty day job collecting rents at an apartment building, which I hated, and I figured it would be much more convenient to work where I sang. But when I told Budd I wanted to be a waitress, he told me there weren't any openings. Two months later, I was singing at the Improv and miserable in my day job when one Friday afternoon I got a call from Budd and Silver asking me to babysit for their two young daughters.

While in his house that night, he called and told me I would start as a waitress the following evening—at which point he added, "I've never hired anybody who was fat before." I was probably thirty pounds lighter than I am now and I was adorable, and he hurt my feelings. My theory at the time was that he must have thought he was Hugh Hefner, but he hired me anyway. That was the dichotomy about Budd. On the one hand, he could be downright nasty and just explode at the drop of a hat—especially if you left something on the table or there was a napkin out of place—but then there was also a very tender and generous side to him.

In my case, I think it spoke volumes about his recognition towards me not only as a singer and a waitress, but also as somebody that he could count on to help him run the club. After I'd been there for about a year, he came up to me one night and told me I needed singing lessons. I was flabbergasted and I didn't quite know what to say, so I said, "I do?"

He said, "Yeah, your voice brings me joy, but you don't always hit the high note right." When I told him I couldn't afford them, he offered to pay for half, which he did. I've never forgotten that. When Budd decided you were talented, he would help any way he could—and his help was invaluable because he always seemed to be connected and he always tried to facilitate. I remember one time early on before I was ready, he took me to an audition at Radio City Music Hall. They were looking for a Judy Garland type. Although I could sing like her, I didn't really look like her, and I don't think I was more than eighteen at the time. He also took me to the Playboy Club and brought me to this Sunday night showcase they used to have at this hotel up in the Catskills.

He was always doing things like that. So for all the crap some people might say about him and how penny-pinching and cheap he was, I saw another side to him. Even though he could be ruthless and mean, he always had a heart, and when it came to helping me become a better singer, he put his money where his mouth was. There's really no one like him. He was part P. T. Barnum, part ringmaster, and part British music hall impresario.

EIGHT

Liza Minnelli and Judy Garland . . . Onstage at the Improv

I n keeping with our name, there have been many unplanned moments that have happened at the Improv over the years, but one of the first that stands out—probably *because* it was one of the first—was the night I put Liza Minnelli on. At the time, she was fifteen or sixteen and a student of actor Charles Nelson Reilly, who taught a musical-comedy class in Greenwich Village and was also in *How to Succeed in Business Without Really Trying* on Broadway with Silver.

We'd only been open for a couple of months. On this evening, Liza came in and asked me to let her sing because her father, the famed director Vincent Minnelli, was in the audience and had never heard her perform before. It's still like a picture in my mind. I already knew who she was, but I was busy making coffee, and when she tapped me on the shoulder and asked if she could sing, I just sort of brushed her off. And then because it hadn't yet sunk in that Vincent Minnelli was actually in my club, I continued to ignore her. By this point, she was practically in tears.

"Oh, please, Budd," she begged. This is when I finally caved in and said, "Oh, okay," as if I were doing her a favor. And then when she went on and I heard her sing, neither of us could have been happier. While she had a young voice that wasn't fully developed yet, she was still Judy Garland's daughter and when she opened her mouth, it was absolutely mesmerizing.

SILVER SAUNDORS FRIEDMAN:

A few months later, Liza brought her mother and her future husband, Peter Allen, to hear her sing, and we had to form a reception line in the doorway. As Judy Garland made her entrance, it was as if we had crossed swords over her head like she was the Queen of England, and then we all shook her hand and she sat down.

Finally, Liza got up and sang, and then Judy did a number, but she couldn't remember all the lyrics, so she tried to inject some levity. From the stage, she pointed to Liza who was sitting at a table in front and said, "Come up here and save the family name." It was perfect.

JOHN MEYER:

I'm the one who first brought Judy Garland to the Improv. By this point, I was no longer the piano player and I had a gig at this other club called Three. One of the regulars was this very flamboyant gay sound archivist named Richard Stryker, who came up to me one night and told me he was putting together an act for Judy, who was very down on her luck at the time. Richard was a big fan of mine, and he asked if I had any material that would be suitable for Judy.

Well, as it turned out I did. And then the following afternoon, I came over to his apartment in the Carnegie Hall studios and did a song, which Judy later did on *The Merv Griffin Show*, called "I'd Like to Hate Myself in the Morning." I did the song for him and he loved it. Then he asked me if I'd had dinner, and when I told him I hadn't, he proceeded to ask me if I wanted to have an orgy—at which point he pulled out this amyl nitrate capsule (a popular sex drug at the time) and shoved it under my nose.

Now, I'm completely straight, so of course I said no and immediately left. But a couple of nights later, Richard invited me over again. At first, I was like, "You're not going to try and fuck me again, are you?" As it turned out, Judy was living with Richard at the time, which was really amazing considering the fact that she was a major star and he was basically nobody. But Judy was also practically destitute and depending on the kindness of anybody who would take care of her, which Richard happily did.

So here comes the kicker. I arrived at Richard's apartment and there was Judy with her secretary. She was really depressed, but then when I sat down at the piano and started playing, she came to. She even anticipated the lyrics and we finished the song. Immediately afterwards, Richard got up and left the room. That's when Judy looked at me and said, "Let's get the fuck out of here."

I remember being in awe, but also feeling panicky, too, because it suddenly hit me that Judy Garland and her secretary were expecting me to entertain them for the evening, and when I reached into my pocket, I discovered that I only had forty-five cents. This was before the days of ATM machines, but even if they existed I was flat broke, so when we got downstairs and into my car, my mind began racing about what the hell to do next.

That's when it occurred to me to drive over to the Hudson River and West 56th Street, which was the municipal pound where they took cars that had been towed and loaded them up on barges. I was desperate for something to do until I could figure out what to do next and so we drove over. I figured that it might amuse Judy, but after parking near the pier for about twenty minutes, the guard finally told us to leave and that's when we headed over to the Improv where at least I knew I could get a free meal.

As soon as he saw us, Budd nearly fainted, as did Rodney Dangerfield, who was also there. Rodney was practically catatonic as he tried to speak. He said, "Miss Garland, I do'wanna sound like a schmuck, but really, sincerely, there is no one, and I mean no one—"

Eventually, Judy got up to sing and I sat down at the piano, but neither one of us could remember our keys, although we ended up staying at the Improv until four in the morning. But when it came time to leave, Budd wasn't about to let us go until he could capture the moment for posterity. So, he called a friend of his, who was a newspaper photographer for the *New York Herald Tribune* and asked him to come over and take a picture. Then Budd followed us out to my car, which was parked on the street in front of the club, and rested his elbows on the passenger side making small talk with Judy as I started the motor. This went on for like six or seven minutes, but the photographer never showed up. Finally, I said, "Budd, we're going home." And then we drove off.

The night Judy Garland came in with John was just incredible. And then several months before she died in 1969, we had Judy, Liza, and Liza's boyfriend Peter Allen unexpectedly drop in. There were only about ten people in the audience, and an actor friend of mine named Jack Knight was also there. Judy, Liza, and Peter were performing, and all of a sudden I decided to join them—with me seated in a chair, Jack pushing me around, and all of us singing "Under the Boardwalk." At the time, of course, we were just in the very beginning, and I still had barely the slightest inkling of who and what was to come. Perhaps that's why those memories of having Liza Minnelli and Judy Garland continue to linger so strong after all these years.

NINE

Not So Blown Away by
Bette Midler . . . at First

As extraordinary as Liza Minnelli's debut appearance turned out to be, not everyone's first time on our stage turned out so well, reminding me also that while first impressions are often the most lasting, you can't always judge a book by its cover.

One of the best examples of this is Bette Midler, who was never a waitress at the Improv, contrary to popular belief. Instead, she was already playing Tzeitel in *Fiddler on the Roof* on Broadway when she first came into the club around 1967. My friend Helen Verbit, who was also in the show, is the one who brought her in.

BETTE MIDLER:

I moved to New York from Hawaii in 1965 and got *Fiddler on the Roof* in 1966. I started going to all of these little clubs around town about two years after I got there, particularly during my last year in *Fiddler*. Like a lot of kids on Broadway in those days, I did it because you were always looking for places to put together your twenty or forty minutes of new material so that you could do something besides just stay in the show you were in.

Like it still is now, the jobs were few and far between. The musical theater itself was also in transition from a kind of legitimate, traditional grown-up American musical to the rock 'n' roll musical, most of which I always thought were pretty awful. So most people were looking around to see what else was going on, and Budd's club was a great training ground. I must have heard about it from somebody in the show, and if Budd says it was Helen Verbit then I'll take his word for it. Helen was a wonderful woman who lived on the West Side and gave me matzo brei for the first time. I'd never had it and I'd never heard of it. I just remember thinking it was so interesting that people would even eat it because it was so strange.

Helen was this very social woman who loved to go out. She was in the chorus of *Fiddler* and I believe she understudied Yente, the matchmaker, who at that time was Florence Stanley.

Bette was already in *Fiddler*, so when Helen brought her in and told me about her, I put Bette on without thinking twice. I forget what she was wearing that night or what she said to me, but she was very sexy and playful, almost flirtatious, and I got a big kick out of her. She was also funny, and I thought she was going to be a slam dunk. But then the material she sang just didn't deliver the way that I expected it would. Mostly they were dirges, which were heavy and awkward. The audiences just didn't like it—or her, for that matter.

BETTE MIDLER:

I'm sure I sang something from *The Threepenny Opera*, because when I came to town I had my three little piano arrangements that I had paid for. Those were my audition pieces and I sang them whenever I was required to. They were extremely complicated because I was in the torch-song singing business, which was also torture, but I was very proud of them. They were dirges, there's no question, and then somewhere along the line my boyfriend at the time introduced me to Mae West. Not literally, but introduced me to who she was and what she had done. I had never seen or heard of her before because I came from Hawaii, so I didn't know anything about her.

But when I first saw her movies at this theater down in Greenwich Village where they used to play old revivals, I fell in love with her. She was so funny and so big and blonde and so sexy and so different from the sort of square-type talent that you saw everywhere you looked. I just adored her, but I didn't know if she was alive or dead. I assumed she wasn't with us anymore because these were movies that were made in the 1930s and she didn't look like a spring chicken in those days.

So I thought that she had passed on to her reward and that it was fair game to sing a couple of her songs. I think that's sort of where the comedy started because the songs were "Come Up and See Me Sometime" or "I Wonder Where My

Easy Rider's Gone" or "Frankie and Johnny." Songs like that had a little bit of an edge to them. That was the first time I started to do songs that were a little bit funnier than my usual dirges. It was a slow transition, but I made it really fun at Budd's place and at the various open mic nights around town.

JOHN MEYER:

If I can say something about that—and I don't even think I was there that particular night she auditioned—but Bette was always smart and she was funny. The only reservation I had about her in the beginning was that like many girls who aren't too attractive (which Bette has since become), they want to present themselves as a sex symbol. Bette had tits, and she insisted on showing them and flashing them around. It clashed with her image early on, and that's why I think she adapted the Mae West persona initially.

Nevertheless, Bette seemed to be taking it all in stride. If she was upset after her first time at the Improv, you sure couldn't tell it. She was cool as a cucumber and she never lost her composure. I was also very nice about it, though, and not wanting to offend my friend or hurt Bette's feelings, I made some offhanded compliment and quickly introduced the next act. But then about three weeks later, I went to see a waitress of mine named Rosalind Harris, who later appeared in Bette's role in the film version of *Fiddler on the Roof*, perform at another club not far from the Improv called The African Room and was absolutely blown away when I discovered that Bette was there and I saw her perform again.

BETTE MIDLER:

The African Room was very dark. It was like a themed room, so they had a lot of highly combustible décor—jungle stuff, conga drums, and banana trees. I really didn't get it, plus the acoustics were terrible and the piano wasn't great. There was hardly anybody there and it seemed like it wasn't going to be a very exciting booking. Actually, to tell you the truth, I don't remember whether I was ever formally booked there or if I was doing an open mic night the second time Budd saw me.

The African Room had this big stuffed ape when you walked in, and as I was sitting there nursing a glass of wine waiting for Rosalind to go on, Bette got up and sang "Am I Blue?" This time, it was absolutely jaw-dropping. What struck me the most was that she could sing that loud, yet she also sang soft and delicate without ever missing a single note.

From the moment I heard Bette perform for the second time at The African Room, I immediately knew that she had superstar quality. When you believe that about someone and they live up to your expectations, it's one of the most satisfying feelings in the world. Of course, the opposite is also true when things don't pan out, and the pain and disappointment can be excruciating. But in Bette's case, my instincts obviously proved correct. She was just delicious, and not long after she became a regular at the Improv, I became her manager even though I didn't know the first thing about being one and still had ambitions about someday becoming a producer. I also figured that if I became a manager, it would get me that much closer to Broadway.

So I did, but it didn't.

BETTE MIDLER:

Budd came up to me right after I sang that night and asked if he could manage me. I thought, "Why not." And that was it. He was very nonchalant and casual about it, and I wasn't exactly sure what was going to happen, but it seemed to make sense and so we signed a one-year agreement.

BUDDY MANTIA:

Whenever Bette came in to the Improv, she always got great spots because Budd was managing her. But she also had this great concept of what she was doing, especially when she started doing songs like "Boogie Woogie Bugle Boy," and it all kind of just evolved from there.

DANNY AIELLO:

The first person who really made me realize Bette was going to be a star was my sister Rosebud who came into the club one night and proclaimed, "She's good." Most people who weren't there at the time don't know this, but I used to sing backup behind Bette—me, Buddy Hughes, Bobby Alto, and Buddy Mantia, who was also in a doo-wop group called the Untouchables with me.

The other thing about Bette was that even back then she was a wonderful actress. One night—I don't remember the specific year—Bette was onstage singing when this guy from the audience threw a glass of wine at her. She walked offstage in a huff, but then a couple of minutes later she came back on and started crying. Of course, it was all just a put-on, but the audience was absolutely captivated. And then she launched into this amazing love song.

JAMIE DEROY:

In the beginning, I remember that Bette was always very hard on herself no matter how well she'd done. When she came offstage, she'd say, "I did terribly." And I'd be like, "Terribly? What do you mean? You were great."

LENNY SCHULTZ, comedian:

Bette was also very civic-minded. Hell's Kitchen in those days wasn't exactly what you'd call the garden spot of America, and Bette had this thing about cleanliness and litter. Whenever she saw somebody throwing something on the ground, she'd scream at them at the top of her lungs. She'd say, "Hey, what the hell are you doing?" Sometimes she'd even chase cars down the block. Littering drove her crazy.

JOE PISCOPO:

By the time I got to the Improv in the midseventies, Bette was already a major star and she wasn't a regular anymore, but she'd still come into the club from time to time and we'd perform for her. She was very quiet and she'd sit way in the back, and we'd all get up onstage. I played the piano and we were all basically just goofing around—which she probably doesn't even remember—but Bette really seemed to enjoy that.

ROBERT KLEIN:

I keep thinking Bette came in about six months after me, which was the first time I saw her. She was in *Fiddler on the Roof*, and she looked like she wore the costume home. That's what I remember. She had on a vintage outfit and she wasn't very pretty, although she had a beautiful body. I've said this a million times—you could tell who had it and who didn't at the

Improv—and Budd was obviously astute enough to see that in
Bette's case for sure.

Bette became a regular at the Improv as I learned the ropes of what
being a good manager entails. However, our audiences didn't always
warm up to her in the beginning because of some of the offbeat songs
she sang. There were instances when they'd be talking and I'd have to
exert my club owner side and tell them to be quiet, although the further
she got into a number the more mesmerized they would be.

Not long after I began managing her, I remember taking Bette to a
Friars Club showcase where she entered from the back of the room. At
first, people were laughing at her and I was heartbroken. But within the
first two minutes after she got onstage, they were laughing with her and
she had them wrapped around her finger.

It also wasn't long before I began having some success managing
her even though we'd never really mapped out any sort of formal game
plan. The first television show I booked her on was with local New York
personality Joe Franklin, who had a daily talk show on WOR. My goal
at this point was simply to get her any kind of exposure I could, and
my persistence paid off. Soon she caught the attention of David Frost's
talent coordinator after I invited her to the Improv to see Bette. It was
also one of the first times that Bette's famously powerful voice would
prove to be an enormous advantage because the talent coordinator, who
was hard of hearing, immediately offered us five shows in a row. The
only problem was that they were syndicated, which meant they didn't
air consecutively.

So the David Frost shows didn't have the impact they should have,
and while we were both disappointed, this quickly led to five appearances
on *The Merv Griffin Show*, all within a year's time. Not long after that, I
got Bette her first appearance on *The Tonight Show*. The story leading up
to this, which she told on Johnny Carson's final show in 1992, is that she
knew a woman who liked her singing and made two satin gowns for her.

She wore one of them to the audition, and as we were driving over in
a taxi, the gown split down the middle—whereupon Bette leaned over
to me and said, "I can't go in like this. Give me your jacket and I'll wrap
it around."

However, instead of giving it to her, all I could think to say was, "I can't give you my jacket. What about my dignity?"

And that's when Bette shot back with one of the cleverest, off-the-cuff comebacks I've ever heard. She just looked up at me and said, "What about my ass?"

Of course, we were both laughing but also panicking, as we got out of the cab and got some safety pins from a drugstore before making our way over to this little theater on West 49th Street near NBC where they were holding the auditions. Needless to say, we were nervous. But then at the appointed moment, after hearing her sing "Am I Blue?"—the same song that won me over back at The African Room—the producers flipped, and we were immediately told that Bette was going to be on the show.

CRAIG TENNIS, former talent coordinator of *The Tonight Show*:

I wasn't involved in the Bette-Budd drama that day, but here's how I remember the events leading up to it and afterwards. For a while—and it was only slightly successful—we decided to have open auditions at the Johnny Victor Theatre in Rocke-feller Center, which was owned by RCA and sat about sixty people. Johnny Carson came to about three of them before deciding it wasn't worth his time, and the way it worked was we'd see about fifteen acts and maybe one would get a shot.

Anyway, Budd was managing Bette and he called me up to see if he could bring her in. Of course, I said yes, but then they got there and Budd said, "Bette's wearing an antique dress and it tore. She doesn't want to go on." I think I said something like, "Budd, this is a once-in-a-lifetime thing. Get some safety pins, put the dress together, and have her sing."

Obviously, she did, and everybody thought she was won-derful because the following day in our production meeting, the associate producer John Gilroy said, "She's not pretty good. She's unusual." So we booked her and Johnny adored her immediately. What I remember specifically about her first audition for us, though, is that I really pushed Budd to push her.

BETTE MIDLER:

It was one of the most humiliating and terrifying moments of my entire life. I had auditioned for *The Tonight Show* several times before and I never made the cut. So I was understandably very nervous about it and then my dress ripped right as we were getting out of the cab. I certainly wasn't laughing about it. I said, "Budd, my panties are showing. Give me your jacket."

It was just awful. But instead of trying to help me out, he was really being mean about it. He just looked at me and said, "I can't go into *The Tonight Show* in my shirtsleeves."

Making matters worse, we got upstairs and nobody had a safety pin. I wound up undoing a paper clip somebody gave me and going into the ladies' room to try and sew my dress back together. I remember the distress—and the anger—I felt over the fact this happened and no one helped. In the end, though, I gave what turned out to be a fantastic audition, because I got the gig even though I was so outraged. And then I went on and that was that. But I'll never forget it. I mean, those kinds of things are indelible.

Looking back, not giving Bette my jacket in the cab is something I shouldn't have done and I regret it, although at the time—and in my defense—I also wasn't doing it to be mean or insensitive. If anything, I think I did it because I was nervous, too, and simply caught up in the moment, plus I didn't want *The Tonight Show* people to think I was a slob because I wasn't dressed properly.

In any case, things turned out fine because Bette got *The Tonight Show*, which was ninety minutes in those days, meaning that guests sometimes got to do an encore if time allowed for it. Fortunately, we decided to come prepared just in case. The number Bette chose was "Sh-Boom," a big, soaring doo-wop tune that afforded her the opportunity to show off her range beyond the downbeat, melancholy ballad "Am I Blue?"

Bette's audition turned out to be phenomenal and she went on Carson about a week or two later in a different gown. When it came time to taping the show that afternoon, Bette launched into "Sh-Boom." However, this time the gown she wore was so flimsy that everything underneath started to jiggle because she wasn't wearing a bra. Suffice to say that when the startled crew looked out from the control booth, Johnny Carson was literally writhing in his chair with his mouth wide open. It's not that he was necessarily trying to look, but he just couldn't help himself. None of us could, and Bette was one of his favorite guests from then on.

BETTE MIDLER:

This friend of mine named Annie Flanders had made a dress for me and I wasn't wearing a bra. It was the height of the bra-burning years, and I wasn't wearing one because I thought it was the feminist thing to do. In my case, it wasn't a good thing to do and I was bouncing around a little bit, but there wasn't anything ripped.

I think I sang one of Mae West's numbers, and not long after that, I received a letter from her lawyer telling me to cease and desist. I just thought it was hilarious, first of all, because I didn't know she was alive. That was for starters. The second thing was, apparently her estate had somebody monitoring this who turned out to be a Mae West impersonator. The whole thing was really an education.

I really enjoyed my time with Budd, even though I decided to part company with him after the incident of tearing my dress. I'm sure he had his reasons, but I really felt betrayed. So we went our separate ways, although I never disliked him. I always adored him and I always thought he was smart, strategic, and shrewd. He was all those things you would hope to find in a manager, although what I didn't have was him not putting himself before me. But I always loved him. I think anybody who's ever come in contact with him in any significant way will for the most part tell you that they're grateful.

I can't remember the exact date we decided to stop working together, but it wasn't right after her first appearance on *The Tonight Show*. I can say this with absolutely no hesitation, because I was still representing Bette when she got her next five appearances on *The Tonight Show*, which I was directly responsible for. I was also with her for a period after that in the early seventies when she began performing at the Continental Baths, an openly gay Turkish bathhouse in the Ansonia Hotel.

In any case, when we did part company it was very painful, even though the decision was mutual. But deep down, I resented it, especially as she grew more famous. At the same time, however, both the Improv and my life were already slowly veering off into a direction that was about to take a comedic turn I never expected.

Comedians Start
Coming to the Improv

L ike I've said from the very beginning, it was never my plan for comedians to become a part of the Improv, much less eventually take over. I should also add here that ending my yearlong management arrangement with Bette wasn't the catalyst, although it wasn't long after we parted when I began to realize that I enjoyed listening to comedians more than singers. If I had to place a name and time on it, however, a big reason for this was David Astor, a popular comedian from Brooklyn who became our first comic when he came in one night and asked to go on the year after we opened in 1964.

At the time, Dave was appearing at the Blue Angel, a hip nightclub on Manhattan's Upper East Side where Mike Nichols and Elaine May got their start. With material ranging from beat poetry and the nuclear arms race to a popular routine about the First Family ("Caroline Kennedy, an absolutely brilliant child . . . of course, her father's never, ever gonna let her plan another nuclear invasion"), Dave was what we call a comic's comic and he struck a chord with me immediately.

SILVER SAUNDORS FRIEDMAN:

By about the sixth or eighth month, there were already a lot of people getting up who weren't in theater or even necessarily singers for that matter. Mainly they were doing improv sketches where they'd take suggestions from the audience.

There was a class of about five or six of them like Ron Carey, Martin Friedberg, and J.J. Barry. They were all amazing, but the guy who stood out most was Dave Astor. He was just incredibly fast and sardonic and he seemed to know a lot more about language than the others did.

HOWARD STORM, director and former comedian:

David Astor and I were very good friends back then and that's how I first heard about the Improv. In fact, when my first wife and I split up, I moved in with Dave. He had a two-bedroom apartment on the Upper East Side. And then, as fate would have it, Dave moved in with me after his wife left him. I loved Dave, and he was brilliant, but living under the same roof with him was absolute madness because he was also nuts. He was kind of our ringleader at the Improv.

Years later, he bought a farm in Ventura, California, and turned it into a pot farm where he sold marijuana. He made a ton of money doing it, but the sad part was that he didn't need to because he was a very talented guy. No matter how well things were going, he'd always find a way to fuck them up.

LOU ALEXANDER:

Dave was a very troubled and self-destructive person, but you can't take away the fact that he still deserves a lion's share of credit for what the Improv became. Basically, he came in one night to break in new material and that was it.

Once again, fate intervened and we were living up to our name. Yet as much as Dave opened my eyes and gave me a newfound appreciation for comedians I'd never had before, I certainly wasn't going to throw the baby out with the bathwater by no longer presenting singers—at least initially. Not only had they been our backbone from day one, they were also still enormous crowd-pleasers and I'm convinced that the Improv wouldn't have survived if I'd done away with them completely.

Coincidentally, one of the most popular acts in between the period when I first heard Dave and began managing Bette was her future musical director Barry Manilow. Barry would, of course, go on to become one of the most successful male recording artists in popular music history, with a monumental string of hits in the 1970s like

"Mandy," "Copacabana," "Can't Smile Without You," and "Weekend in New England."

By the time I hired him to become the Improv's house piano player in 1969, he was already making a name for himself, as an accompanist, arranger, producer, and soon-to-be jingle writer for Kentucky Fried Chicken, Alka-Seltzer, State Farm Insurance, Band-Aid, and McDonald's, some of which are still on the air today. We met the previous year when he was the lyricist and musical director for the off-Broadway musical *The Drunkard*, which I'd wanted to invest in.

Although it never came to pass because I couldn't come up with the money, I continued to be on the lookout for other shows. In one sense, however, the fact that I wasn't able to be involved in *The Drunkard* would prove prophetic. With comedians now coming into the club with more frequency towards the late 1960s, not only did my preference for stand-up intensify, it also convinced me I should run with it.

Or at least jog.

One reason was that the more comedians I heard, the more I began to realize that I had a much more receptive ear when it came to hearing the same jokes repeated and improved upon with nuances versus listening to the same songs over and over again, which quickly grew tiresome. What I enjoyed most, though, was the setup and then the build leading up to the punch line when everybody in the room was feeding off of one another. You got a vibe that was completely different from only having singers. And then, all of a sudden, without fanfare, even more comedians started dropping in.

Besides Dave Astor, who was our Pied Piper, there was also David Frye, a masterful impressionist, who was already well known for his spot-on political impersonations of Lyndon Johnson, Bobby Kennedy, Richard Nixon, and Spiro Agnew, as well as film stars like James Cagney, Henry Fonda, Kirk Douglas, and George C. Scott.

BILL SALUGA, comedian:

David Frye was an oddball and he wasn't very outgoing. He also couldn't do an impression unless he was looking at a picture of the person he was imitating. Whenever he'd turn around onstage, he was looking at their photograph.

MARTY NADLER, screenwriter and comedian:

Frye was fine except that he just didn't have any personality because he was imitating all these people, so you never knew who he really was. One night, a bunch of us were standing at the bar with Rodney Dangerfield when somebody came up to us and said, "David Frye is here."

And Rodney goes, "Good, who's he here as? You know what I think of David Frye? He's a mimic. They're three places below a juggler." Rodney was always commenting on everybody and if he didn't like them, he'd let you know it.

Without missing a beat, David would usually come into the club with a drink in his hand and do about five minutes onstage, then leave. He used to also practice his impressions in the men's room, so if you hadn't seen him when he first arrived and you walked by the men's room and heard voices, you knew it was him.

FRED WILLARD, comedian, actor, and writer:

You'd always hear stories about people going into the bathroom and hearing voices from the adjacent stall. This was David going over his bits before he went on, and when he wasn't performing, he ran hot and cold. There was always some anger and some slight he sensed somewhere. He could be your best friend one minute and then he wouldn't talk to you the next. As a comic, though, he was one of the ones who made me laugh harder than anybody else.

BETTE MIDLER:

What a horrible, inconsiderate man David Frye was. One time when Budd was managing me, he had me booked at this nightclub outside of Boston called Paul's Mall. Jay Leno used to perform there a lot. Anyway, the time I was performing there they didn't have a dressing room for me. I wound up changing in this little area behind the kitchen where they kept the tomato sauce. It was kind of a big pantry where there were no mirrors and about an inch of water on the floor, so I poked my head into David Frye's dressing room to see if my makeup was okay while he was onstage.

Somehow, he got wind of it because afterwards David came up to me and started screaming: "If you ever put your face in my dressing room again, I'll have you fired." I think I may have played there a couple of times after that, but that night with him was horrible.

SILVER SAUNDORS FRIEDMAN:

David was very talented—and crazy—which was fine with us, because the two usually went hand in hand, and we'd be crazy right along with him. But he was also an alcoholic and a serial womanizer who'd supposedly had a number of kids out of wedlock, and he became increasingly paranoid that one of these women was going to shoot him.

As a result, he wound up having a vasectomy that backfired. Occasionally, he'd have to excuse himself during the middle of his act, and then he'd go backstage and pee in a bucket. I think that probably ruined his sense of self and his career.

DANNY AIELLO:

When I was working at the Improv, some of the performers occasionally hired me to do side jobs and one of them was David. He paid me $500 a week to be his road manager on a West Coast tour he was doing. That was a lot of money back then, and Budd was always very cool about it, although I was basically a glorified gofer.

But as masterful as David was when it came to doing impressions, he was also a heavy drinker on top of having a weak bladder, which didn't make for the best combination—especially since he had to go often, and even though he incorporated it into his routine by sneaking behind a partition in back of the stage to pee in an ice bucket at regular intervals. The audience had no idea why he was doing this, and they found it funny. I didn't, particularly when he told me that part of my job was to empty the piss-filled bucket.

Needless to say, I refused, and everything was fine until one night we were at the upscale Fairmont Hotel in San Francisco and he walked right off the end of the stage like Wile E. Coyote during the middle of his James Cagney impression and without missing a beat went outside. He never came back after that.

Then there was Jackie Vernon, a former trumpet player turned comic, who often carried a cornet as a prop even though he seldom played. Dubbed the "King of Deadpan," he was a veteran performer who supplied the voice of Frosty the Snowman in the animated Christmas special of the same name and was an occasional opening act for Judy Garland. At the Improv, he used to sit in the back with his writers until I could coax him to get up onstage. But once I finally did, there was no stopping him. Jackie's signature opening line was, "To look at me now, it's hard to believe I was once considered a dull guy," and with material on topics like prisons, trying to turn a watermelon into a house pet, and traveling to the Grand Canyon only to find it closed, his routines often veered from the darkly surreal to the absurd.

I also had a great deal of affection for him personally because when I was managing Bette Midler, he hired her to be his opening act at Mister Kelly's in Chicago, which was a huge break for her. He also performed at the Hollywood Improv after I first opened on the West Coast, and then a number of times after that when we had a club in Las Vegas.

Not only was Jackie talented and extremely loyal, it was electrifying when he and other comics went on. Their performances, both good and bad, brought the entire meaning of stand-up as an art form home to me. Yet, while the residual impact of seeing them so closely, along with hearing the laughter, was exhilarating, I still had no idea that I had stumbled on a viable new business model for showcasing talent.

SILVER SAUNDORS FRIEDMAN:

They were blessings. No doubt about it, the addition of comedians was a blessing for us, and they all pretty much came up from Greenwich Village and did whatever they were doing down there. If they had talent, they knew Budd would eventually give them stage time. He was very good when it came to validating acts and he didn't mistreat them. I like to think I had something to do with this in terms of creating an environment where they got appreciation and respect because the audiences were good.

In the beginning, I was often the emcee, which I loved. Besides being onstage itself, one of my favorite parts was bringing up newcomers because there was always an element of surprise. This was perhaps first evident in 1964 when future talk-show legend Dick Cavett came in—and fell completely flat with the material he did, even though he already had a formidable reputation as a comedy writer. He was also nearly two years into his second tenure working for *The Tonight Show*, where he'd served as both the talent coordinator and then-host Jack Paar's monologue writer.

I first met Dick through his manager, Jack Rollins, who along with his partner, Charles Joffe, were two of the biggest power brokers in comedy long before there was such a term. Jack got his start in show business as a Broadway producer in World War II, then founded a one-man talent agency that represented writers, dramatic actors, and singers, including Harry Belafonte. Charlie worked briefly as an agent for MCA before joining forces with Jack in 1953 and eventually handling comedians almost exclusively from the early 1960s through the late '80s—among them Dick Cavett, Woody Allen, Robert Klein, Joan Rivers, Nichols and May, Robin Williams, Billy Crystal, and David Letterman. If Jack and Charlie represented you, you'd made it.

MARTY NADLER:

Part of the magic of the New York Improv was that once they got to know you, you'd have all these mentors who would help you. When I say that Jack Rollins was incredible to me, I'm not exaggerating. Besides doing stand-up, I was also writing material for a lot of other comics, so Jack would always ask me if I had a script because he knew I wanted to break into television. As a matter of fact, I wrote one spec script for *All in the Family* and Jack offered to pass it along to Norman Lear.

The premise was that Rob Reiner's character, "Meathead," was involved in a Vietnam War protest, and sure enough, Jack showed it to Norman. About a week or two later, he called me into his office up on West 57th Street near the Russian Tea Room and handed me a letter. It was from Norman and it was a rejection, telling me he liked my script but that they didn't have any room on the writing staff—meaning that it really wasn't that good.

Jack was still very encouraging, but the even more amazing part was that he opened up his desk and pulled out this huge stack of rejection letters held together by a rubber band. At first, the only thing I could think of was that they were all for me. But then Jack looked at me and said, "No, these are all Woody's."

Jack was great. And you know what? I eventually showed that *All in the Family* spec script to Garry Marshall, which is how I got my first job as an apprentice writer on *The Odd Couple*.

Not only was Jack the model for the title character in Woody Allen's 1984 film, *Broadway Danny Rose*, he was the one who had initially convinced Allen he should try stand-up. And it was Dick Cavett who was put in charge of grooming Allen for his first appearance on *The Tonight Show*.

DICK CAVETT, author, former talk-show host, and comedian:

Not long after I got there, *The Tonight Show* sent me to the Blue Angel in New York to see this new, young comic named Woody Allen. By the way, at this point Jack Paar was saying to me, "I'm not sure if trying to make Woody Allen a stand-up comic is one of our genius ideas." As it turned out, it wasn't, because Woody hated it and he'd throw up before he went on. Then, once he finally made it up onto the stage, he stood with his face right behind the bulky microphone and the audience kept talking.

I was stunned. It was like being at a convention where there's a boring speaker and the whole audience is talking. But suddenly, the genius jokes firing from Woody to me at the back of the room were better than the best line any comedian had in their act that night. Some of the funniest were the ones about Woody's first wife, Harlene Rosen, who later sued him for doing jokes about her. Anyway, I put him on the show and Jack Paar didn't like him. Then he later claimed that he started Woody's career.

Woody Allen came to the Improv a few times, but he was never a regular. His manager, Jack Rollins, of course, was. Though I was also very friendly with his partner, Charlie, and their wives, Jane and Carol, I was especially close to Jack in New York. We were both Upper West Siders and played poker together. And when it came to his management skills, there was and still is nobody else like him, so when he made the case for Dick, I gave him the go-ahead without hesitation.

DICK CAVETT:

I had never been to the Improv before, and when I got there I just remember it being this kind of a joint with some tables and chairs that had a stage and nothing else. The thing about it was, you knew when you walked in that the Improv was where you *wanted* to be allowed to go.

The routine he did about attending the wedding of a wealthy classmate from Yale, unfortunately, faltered during the second joke. The problem was that the setup, which began with a bit about his friend being so rich they had caviar flown all the way in from Beluga, was so highbrow it went over everybody's head as it had when he'd done it the previous evening at The Bitter End in Greenwich Village. Still, I liked it and I thought he had something special, so I invited him back. And after eliminating the caviar joke, which I still found amusing even though I also didn't understand it initially, Dick did much better the following week and the half-dozen times he went on after that.

DICK CAVETT:

My lifelong friendship with Woody Allen began when I was grooming him to do *The Tonight Show*, and he's the one who introduced me to Jack Rollins, who encouraged me to try stand-up after I told him I'd been a magician as a kid and that I liked performing. He said, "Why don't you try it, lad. You know how you've been watching Woody and seeing how we've been trying to turn him into a performer."

I thought why not, although when I told Woody, he attempted to warn me how difficult it was. He said, "You might be able to churn material out at lightning speed for another performer, but when it comes to writing for yourself it could take hours just to get one good joke."

What Woody said to me was right on the money, but I wanted to give stand-up a shot anyway. One of the first places I appeared was down at The Bitter End on Bleecker Street in Greenwich Village. In those days, comics like Bill Cosby, Lenny Bruce, Mort Sahl, and Joan Rivers were there. George Carlin would also show up occasionally and there was a ferrety-looking guy with a guitar on his back who I thought was never going to get anywhere.

This turned out to be Bob Dylan, and there were a lot of others you could never be completely sure about, but anyway I went to The Bitter End and did this routine about Beluga caviar at a wedding. It failed so spectacularly that I literally had sweat damming up over my eyebrows, so I tried to stay still because I knew the sweat would run down my face if I moved. Before I was even halfway through, I remember looking into the audience and noticing that Jack Rollins and the owner Fred Weintraub had discreetly stepped outside because they couldn't bear to watch the murder that was taking place onstage.

Bombing at The Bitter End was the bitter beginning for me in terms of stand-up. The Improv kind of became my redemption, because right after that, Jack came up to me and said, "Well, lad. You fouled out tonight, but you'll be back in the saddle tomorrow night at a place called the Improv." When I said I didn't want to, he told me I had to, and I did. As soon as I got there, Budd was extremely friendly and encouraging. The first thing he said to me was, "Jack Rollins thinks you're going to be great." And then he put me right on. It was a real watershed moment for me in terms of confidence.

ELEVEN

The Anointment
of King Richard

ichard Pryor also started coming into the Improv around 1964, and I became a fan immediately. Though I don't remember exactly what he did the first time, I do recall receiving complaints on several occasions about his constant use of the word "fuck" onstage, which wasn't nearly as commonplace with comedians as it is now. He was also doing drugs, although I'm not sure which ones.

Speaking of drugs, I should also say here that I was completely oblivious to anyone's drug use back then. Yes, we were a New York club that catered to a late-night, largely show-business crowd, and it was the 1960s, but all I drank was red wine. Plus, I detested cigarettes, which I begrudgingly had to tolerate, even though my clothes used to reek of secondhand smoke every night. So if people were doing drugs—and of course, they were—they did them behind my back and it came as a complete surprise when I found out.

I know this makes me sound incredibly square, but once we had a comedian you've never heard of auditioning who took out a cigarette and removed some of the tobacco to make it look like a joint. Then he proceeded to light it onstage and began doing some sort of routine about pot. Naturally, that's what I thought he was smoking, even though there was no odor to suggest he was.

Even so, I immediately became suspicious. My first impulse was to grab the Louisville Slugger I kept for protection behind the bar. Slamming it down on the table as hard as I could, I screamed, "That'd better be a real cigarette!" I'm still not sure if it was or it wasn't, but I do know that I scared the living shit out of this guy. As soon as I yelled at him, he bolted like a scared rabbit through the fire exit door onto West 44th Street and I never saw him again after that.

But getting back to Richard Pryor, he was a good friend of David Astor's, which I didn't discover until many years later. Like George Carlin and Joan Rivers, who only came in a handful of times, Richard was already a regular at places like the Village Gate and the Cafe Wha? on MacDougal Street, where the owner, Manny Roth, had become his first manager shortly after Richard moved to New York in 1963.

Somewhere in between, Richard met David, and along with Ron Carey—who later appeared in a series of Mel Brooks films and as New York City police officer Carl Levitt on TV's *Barney Miller*—they did an improvisational act for us on Friday and Saturday nights. Ron, too, was an extraordinarily gifted comedian, particularly when it came to physical comedy and characterization, and together the three of them were brilliant. We had this one little microphone that was barely audible and Dave would sit in the corner and tell a story, which Ron and Richard would act out.

All three of them were terrific together and alone. However, Richard, without a doubt, was the most magnetic, and we all knew he was special from the beginning. He was also already a force to be reckoned with as well as a solo performer, even though his material initially was still far less controversial than what was to come. And one-on-one he could be absolutely charming. Still, his well-known volatility could also surface at any moment without warning.

One night, he stormed into the club high as a kite and accused me of taking advantage of him and not paying him because he was black. When he said it, I was stunned. After I told Silver about this later that evening, her reaction was that I should have told him I took advantage of all performers, regardless of race, color, or creed—meaning that *none* of them were getting paid.

About six months later, he came back very contritely to apologize and nothing more was ever said. We even exchanged manly hugs, and on this particular evening he was with a very attractive-looking black woman. It was the first time I had ever seen him with a female companion who wasn't white, although he was also there to pick up one of my white wait-resses, a woman named Paula Best, whose father, Larry, was a well-known Catskills comedian.

As I look back at my relationship with Richard, I think that it was the confluence of both of those temperaments—not to mention the fact that he remains to this day the funniest comedian of all time—that always endeared him to me. For those who knew him both at the Improv and outside of the Improv, I truly believe this is how most of them feel as well.

DAVID STEINBERG, comedian, director, actor, writer, and talk-show host:

By the time he got to the Improv, Richard had pretty much mastered his political radicalism. He was always dangerous after that.

ROBERT KLEIN:

Not long after I got to the club, we did a lot of improvs there a la Second City, and Pryor could be very sweet. He also paid me the greatest compliment once when he said we got our material the same way. I'm paraphrasing here, but one night at the club he took me aside and said, "You know, we're alike in a way, because it all comes off our head. We make faces." And you know what? He was absolutely right. I mean, my comedy isn't like Richard Pryor's, but the process of how we got from point A to point B was essentially equal.

JACK KNIGHT, actor, longtime friend of Budd's, and Improv stockholder:

At the time he was performing at the Improv in New York, Richard was just like the rest of us. He wasn't a star, although he was beginning to get known because of his outspokenness. It was like whatever came into his head came out of his mouth and there was absolutely no filter.

PHOEBE DORIN:

Richard Pryor was a doll. I thought he was absolutely ador-able even though he was also a huge dichotomy who hated everything and everybody but still wanted to be loved. The first time I met him was when he came over to my table to talk to me. It wouldn't get busy until after midnight because that's when people started coming in, but the waitresses had to be there early to set everything up. Once you were done, though, you could sit and schmooze before it got busy, and I remember Richie coming in and just riffing before he went onstage.

He would talk to us about his childhood growing up in a brothel in Peoria, Illinois, and honest to God, I don't know how he survived. He saw an awful lot of shit. What might have shocked me as a little Jewish girl that grew up in a sheltered environment, Richard embraced his background out of necessity and turned it into comedy gold.

BUDDY MANTIA:

Richard was one of the very first comedians I ever saw at the Improv. His comedic mind was so sharp and so brilliant that he could have you doubled over laughing one minute and in tears the next. I also think he could have been as funny without the booze and drugs. The ideas were all there. They came from the way he grew up, not a drug state.

CARL REINER, writer, actor, director, and producer:

Absolutely, unequivocally, there was no one like Pryor. He was maybe the most brilliant comedy mind ever. Not only was he an incredible performer, his ideas were just off the charts and he was his own writer. Even though he had writers, I don't think he ever necessarily needed them.

JERRY STILLER, comedian and actor:

Richie Pryor came on with a bang. Let's put it that way. Before he became famous, we all looked at it with a little bit of shock. What rescued him, of course, was the fact that he could pull it off because he was funny.

MARTY NADLER:

We did a lot of improvs at the Improv, and on one such occasion in the early seventies, I was onstage with Richard and Steve Landesberg, who later went on to fame on the sitcom *Barney Miller*. I can't exactly recall what the setup was, but right in the middle of it, Richard pulled out a switchblade and held it against Steve's throat. There's not much to tell other than we were speechless—and scared shitless—but we kept going and nothing happened. It was just Richard being Richard.

DANNY AIELLO:

Here's the weird thing about Richard—and how or when we became close, I don't know. I mean, I was always bowled over by his talent as a comedian and I always respected his honesty onstage, although I don't ever recall a time when we sat down and discussed our friendship. To the best of my knowledge, I don't think we ever once hung out together outside of the Improv. But somehow, not too long after my daughter Stacey was born, Richard found out she was about to be baptized and he offered to be the godfather. He was completely serious about it even though it never happened because he was working. However, the fact that he offered was interesting. It was an incredibly kind gesture and the last thing in the world I ever expected.

JOHN DEBELLIS, screenwriter, director, actor, comedian, and author of *Standup Guys: A Generation of Laughs*:

Pryor's years at the Improv predate mine, but I remember him coming into the New York club one night in the late seventies when he was the biggest star in comedy and sitting down at a table. Then he got up and left after about ten or fifteen minutes but not before leaving two crisp one-hundred-dollar bills for a tip. I'm not sure why he did it, but we were all in awe and I just remember being amazed by his generosity. Richard was like a god to all of us.

HOWIE MANDEL:

Pryor was the first guy I saw that showed us that the Improv and these other comedy clubs were great gymnasiums. He was the first one that made this really clear because whenever he came in, it wasn't just to perform. He was also there to write and experiment, which meant that even at his worst, he was better than most because he was willing to take chances.

BYRON ALLEN, television executive and former comedian:

Seeing Richard perform live was the first time I saw a comedy rock star in the flesh. Picture it. I'm a kid, Richard Pryor comes through, and he's got these comedy albums. Then he shows up and people are going bananas. They're screaming for him like he's Elvis. They're like hanging off the side of the building.

Then he goes onstage, they announce him, and they go even crazier. He probably gets a five-minute standing ovation going to the stage. But then he gets up there and he won't repeat any material that he has on the album—Mudbone and the monkey fucked me in the ear, all that kind of stuff. He just didn't do any of that and he bombed night after night. And then all of a sudden, ninety minutes of absolute brilliance and that's the ninety minutes of *Richard Pryor: Live in Concert*. He overcame the pressure of people screaming his name like he was one of the Beatles. He literally bombed, but he kept doing it until he worked out that new material, which was amazing to watch.

BOB SAGET, comedian, actor, and television host:

Watching Richard live was like seeing Obi-Wan Kenobi. It was him being honest about what he was going through and that was always the most astonishing thing to watch.

LIZ TORRES, comedian, actor, singer, and former New York Improv waitress:

Once he became famous, nobody wanted to go on after Richard because he would get up there and just absolutely destroy the crowd. He also liked to come in late when hardly anyone was there, which is when I preferred going on also, despite the fact that by this point in the evening most everyone would be squirming in their seats and asking for their checks so they could leave. The reason why I liked performing then was because I sang and did comedy, and I had this trick where I could turn the room around and get their attention back by mixing things up and doing both.

Richard absolutely loved that and he wouldn't go on if I wasn't there. What he'd do is finish his set, then leave the club, circle around the block, and come back in just as I was going onstage so I could see him. He said he liked seeing me turn the room around, which I thought was the biggest compliment in the world coming from him.

One night, he was at the club when there was practically no one else in the audience, and Budd came over to me and said, "Get up and do something." So I did, and I was right in the middle of my set when I looked over towards the VIP section and saw Richard sitting by himself drinking a Courvoisier. But instead of watching me, he was hunched over the table scribbling something into a notebook. A few minutes later, Budd asked Richard to go on, which he did, even though he was drunk and stoned. When he got up onstage, he said, "Tonight, I'm going to recite some poetry."

The next thing I knew, he opened up the notebook and started reciting the most incredible romantic poetry I had ever heard in my life. I swear, what Richard did that night was on a level with Byron or Keats. He didn't pause or hesitate for a second, and it was literally coming out of his pores like music. As soon as he started reading it, the room got completely quiet and all I could think of was the fact that there was hardly anybody there to appreciate it. This went on for like fifteen or twenty minutes. He had the entire room in the palm of his hand, and I'd never seen anything like it. Then he got offstage, put the notebook back on the table, and went over to the bar to order another drink—at which point I made a beeline for the notebook only to discover there was nothing in it. I will never forget that night. Never. Richard Pryor absolutely blew me away.

MICHELE LEE:

I had a childhood friend named Suzie visiting me in New York from Los Angeles, and one night we went to the Improv when Richard was on. Afterwards he came and sat at our table, and after suddenly realizing or noticing that Suzie was new in town, he looked at us and said, "Come on. I'm going to take you girls for a ride. You're going to see New York." He was a complete gentleman about it, and the next thing we knew we were in Central Park sitting in a horse-driven carriage—and where, for the next hour or so, we rode around the park with Richard acting as our tour guide and pointing out all these buildings.

Of course, half of what he told us was made up, but it was a very special night. We were great friends at the Improv, although we didn't remain that close after he became a superstar. At the time I knew him, I wasn't particularly aware of his drug use or any of his other vices. But in my head I always knew he was a little crazy, and I was attracted to that.

TOM DREESEN, comedian, actor, writer, and producer:

Pryor and I connected right away because we basically grew up in the same kind of neighborhood even though I'm from the South Side of Chicago and he was from Peoria. So we had that in common right off the bat and we became good friends even though I wasn't his Ace Boon Coon. When I was going to record my album *That White Boy's Crazy* in front of an all-black audience, Richard wanted me to call it *That Honky's Crazy* because he'd done *That Nigger's Crazy*. The only reason I didn't—and I told him this—I said, "Richard, no black guy has ever called me honky in my life." They called me white boy by affection, and to this day they still do.

PART TWO

 TWELVE
Revelry and Rivalry

BILL WEEDEN, actor:

I'm not sure what the ratio was, but by the time I got there in the early 1970s with my performing partner David Finkle, there was still a fairly even mix of singers and comics. David and I had been collaborating ever since we were prep-school classmates at Andover, which we continued to do at Yale and then at various clubs in New York after we graduated.

Budd had seen us at a place called The Duplex after reading a review in the *New York Times,* and he invited us to come to the Improv immediately after that. Since David and I sang comedy songs, we were in a really good position because he could put us in between the comedians and keep the laughs coming but still have music. It was the best of both worlds and it guaranteed us a lot of prime-time action.

While sporadic, Richard Pryor's appearances continued into the 1970s as his star rose and more comedians came in. At the time, *The Tonight Show* and *The Ed Sullivan Show* were the two most important vehicles for launching comics. Both originated from New York, and by extension, the number of both new and established performers we had showing up to try and get seen by the people who booked these shows also increased nightly, forcing the singers to share the stage—and sometimes breeding resentments.

To say that it was a near-constant power struggle in which attempts to upstage one another weren't uncommon is putting it mildly. In fact, one of the earliest and most notorious incidents involved Richard Pryor himself.

LIZ TORRES:

Perhaps hate is a strong word, but let's just say there was no love lost between the comedians and singers, especially after the comics started to dominate. There was this one time that we had a female singer onstage when Richie was there. Right in the middle of her set as I was serving drinks, he waved me over and said, "Watch this."

I said, "Okay." Well, right about then he went into the men's room, which was right behind me, and I returned to the table I was serving. When Richard came back out about five minutes later, he was completely nude—although not totally naked because he still had his tie and shoes on. But other than that, you could see the whole enchilada. Anyway, he walked past me and up onto the stage—where he then proceeded to stand right in front of her for about a minute before going back into the men's room, getting dressed, and returning to the bar to finish his drink. Now here's the amazing part: As Richard was parading around in front of her, the singer continued her song as if nothing happened. She didn't blink.

SILVER SAUNDORS FRIEDMAN:

The streaking incident with Pryor happened a year after we'd been open. At that point, he was still doing a lot of clean material so this was before he really became Richard Pryor. We were having a party to celebrate our first anniversary, and the name of the singer that night was Betty Rhodes. Richard was also on the roster and around one in the morning, he decided to go parading around the club in his birthday suit. He made a loop around the entire room, which wasn't that big then, and made his way towards the stage. Although I tried not to stare, I couldn't help myself and after looking at his exposed genitalia, I turned towards Budd. I said, "There goes another myth."

JOHN MEYER:

Actually, Betty Rhodes, who was my girlfriend at the time, originated that line and Silver appropriated it, unless they said it at the same time. What happened was, we were there that night and Betty was singing, with me accompanying her on the piano. Her big number back then was "I Happen to Like New York" by Cole Porter. I know that it was a great night because we were celebrating the club's first anniversary and everyone was in a wonderful mood.

Anyway, Betty was in the middle of her act about halfway through, and Richard Pryor was sitting at the bar, when all of the sudden he took his clothes off and began streaking diagonally across the floor. I don't know what he thought he was accomplishing except to draw attention to himself, which he did. So Betty just said, "Well, he just made a liar out of a legend," and then she went right back to her song.

Though I still liked and would continue to use singers for many years to come, even as my growing fondness for comedians morphed into a love affair, I never wanted to earn the reputation of "playing favorites." But while the way I structured things pretty much remained the same, looking back now I realize that this still created some degree of unintended antipathy—especially since nobody was getting paid.

ANN ANELLO, singer and songwriter:

Let's put it this way. If you were a singer, you just knew you had to be damned good if you were going up against these comics, even if the material you were doing wasn't necessarily tried and true. The bar was always higher and there was a much smaller margin for error if you were a singer, especially if you weren't one of Budd's favorites.

JAMIE DEROY:

Even if a singer was funny, they couldn't be funnier than a comic. Case closed—and if they were, there might be trouble.

STEWIE STONE, comedian:

There's no question that Budd created an ingenious system. However, for somebody like me who was already accustomed to getting paid in places like the Playboy Club and the Living Room, I also kind of resented the fact that the Improv and a lot of these other clubs only gave you a free sandwich and a soda for performing. Budd didn't even do that at first.

I never wanted the Improv to have the reputation of being a "pickup joint," so I didn't encourage it, particularly among the performers. But like drugs, of course, it still happened right under my nose.

RICHARD LEWIS, comedian, actor, and writer:

Sadly, I was a womanizer back then—even though it was always consensual. Also, I was a budding alcoholic. What happened was, I was just focusing on my set and then leaving, hanging out and trying to meet women. And I did. I did it as long as I was doing these clubs. That was my reason for living. My father was dead and I didn't get along with my mother. I didn't really see much of her, and my sister was living in Pennsylvania with four children. So it was just the microphone, women, and booze—not unlike a lot of comedians, to be honest.

BETTE MIDLER:

I have to say that I was on the outside, because there was no way you could deal with some of these guys. There was no point in trying. First of all, they were mainly men. And mostly they weren't interested in women as anything other than what they could fuck. If you didn't want to fuck them, then there was no way in. They weren't going to ask you, "How did I do?"

SHELLEY ACKERMAN:

No question about it, there was a lot of extracurricular activity going on—and when I say that the waitresses were kept quite busy servicing the comedians, obviously I'm not just talking about bringing them food. But there were also some liaisons that became real relationships and even marriages. Richard Belzer and I lived together in my walk-up studio apartment on East 52nd Street. We were a joined-at-the-hip couple for over a year and almost married. A year was a long time back then.

Once the comedians began to dominate the lineup, Silver used to complain that the singers were landfill for comics, although I used to do both so I could hold my own. I was a strong singer, but because I was there and I was funny anyway, I started to develop a lot of comedic patter.

If a comic had a car, they'd often end up driving me home after closing. When I lived on the Upper East Side, Andy Kaufman would drive me home regularly. David Brenner would often drop me off in a cab, and Robert Klein did that also when we both lived on the Upper West Side. Naturally, I would have these long 5 AM conversations with these guys, and believe me, there's a lot of bonding that goes on at that hour.

More often than not, though, the conversations weren't sexual at all. Instead, they would be about life, careers, show business, the Improv, who was trustworthy, why this person was going to make it. There was just so much drama with each move everybody made that you'd eventually end up talking about everything. At times, some of these conversations escalated into heated emotional exchanges that weren't conducive to a good night's—or morning's—sleep afterwards. But all in all there was a camaraderie that couldn't be denied and experiences that couldn't have happened anywhere else.

THIRTEEN
Stiller and Meara

While the collective popularity of comedy teams would ebb and flow, they were always a major draw on West 44th Street. Chief among them early on were husband-and-wife duo Jerry Stiller and Anne Meara, whose act focused on domestic material with a twist: Jerry was Jewish and Anne was Catholic. Though far more common today, back then this was considered a rarity and so were Stiller and Meara.

As the story goes, they'd met during an audition in 1953 when Jerry heard a woman screaming and saw Anne running out of an agent's office in tears. When he asked what happened, Anne said that the agent had literally chased her around the room, whereupon Jerry immediately went in and confronted him, and the agent began chasing him also. Afterwards, Jerry and Anne went out for coffee to commiserate about the hard-luck lives of struggling New York actors and soon began dating. Their relationship quickly blossomed and they were married a year later, although it would be some time before they started working together as a comedy team—in large part because Anne not only didn't think of herself as a comedian, she loathed them.

JERRY STILLER:

Anne didn't like slapstick at all and she couldn't stand things like The Three Stooges, but ironically she was as funny as anybody who was considered a giant in comedy back then. This was unusual because there were very few women, and the ones who were funny like Totie Fields, Phyllis Diller, and Joan

Rivers mostly made fun of themselves and their looks or the fact that they didn't get dates. We filled a gap in some ways because we dealt with two people in terms of relationships and what was going on in our minds.

When they first arrived at the Improv in 1966, Stiller and Meara were hot as a pistol. They were already regulars on *The Ed Sullivan Show*, where they eventually made thirty-five appearances—most notably as an interreligious couple named Hershey Horowitz and Mary Elizabeth Doyle. Jack Rollins, who was Stiller and Meara's manager, introduced us and we became very fast friends.

JERRY STILLER:

Aside from being this little dive where you could go in, get a cheap hamburger, and then get up onstage if you were a comedian or a singer, the thing I loved most about the Improv was that almost anything you did was acceptable as long as it was funny. It was that simple. This is the best-case scenario in an environment like that. With Budd, you always pretty much knew you had a free hand.

Jerry and Anne often brought their kids, Amy and Ben, in with them, several years before we added a children's variety show on Sunday afternoons. They were both also always a joy to be around.

AMY STILLER, actor, and Jerry Stiller and Anne Meara's daughter:

I remember Budd had this big collage on the wall where you'd go in and see all the performers, and my parents were on that. I also met my first boyfriend at the Improv. At the time, he was still in high school and he'd do his homework in between sets. I was kind of living through him because I loved watching stand-up, plus I was very shy and so it was always exciting to be there.

JUDY ORBACH:

Anne Meara taught me how to put blush on my face. Anne and Jerry used to come in and work out their sets for *The*

Tonight Show and they would bring the kids. Amy was twelve and Ben was about ten. Everybody just adored the Stillers. I'm still really good friends with Amy.

SILVER SAUNDORS FRIEDMAN:

Anne and Jerry were luscious. That's the word. You would watch them and listen to their wonderful culturally mixed ideas and you would just think you were eating apple pie and cheese— which was one of the things on our menu. You never had to worry about them hurting a customer or causing a scene. They were very down-to-earth people.

FREDDIE ROMAN, comedian and Dean Emeritus of the New York Friars Club:

And smart, too. They weren't your typical comedy team.

SHELLEY ACKERMAN:

When Stiller and Meara came into the Improv, it was a big event, plus they were funny and they were always very supportive of anyone who they liked and deemed talented and worthy. Whenever I sang anywhere, if they didn't show up they'd send flowers. If they didn't send flowers, they would send a telegram. If they didn't send a telegram, they would send balloons. They did this their entire lives. At the Improv, Anne always ordered a Vodka Gibson and I can still remember the putrid smell of those onions. I also remember Jerry giving advice to this young comedian once, and Anne saying, "Who is he, the Albert Schweitzer of comedy?" It was priceless.

DANNY AIELLO:

Besides my own family, there wasn't a man closer in life to me than Jerry Stiller. When we were doing *Hurlyburly* together on Broadway, we loved each other so much that half the shit we did was unscripted. It was unprofessional and we weren't supposed to do it, but we'd wrestle onstage—especially if he broke me up and I started laughing. People didn't know what the fuck we were doing and we'd be completely out of character, but if something funny happened, we'd go behind the couch and wrestle each other to the floor because we couldn't control ourselves. We'd just be screaming like hell.

One night during intermission, we were backstage with our co-star Christine Baranski and her husband who was also an actor. They'd just had a newborn daughter, who he was holding, and as I came out of my dressing room to do the second act, I looked at her and said, "Hey, Christine, how would you like your daughter to make her Broadway debut?"

She just grinned at me without saying a word, which I took to mean yes, and I lifted the baby in my arms and went back onstage. And she was totally fine with that even though the character I played was a drug addict and I had a big monologue coming up. Well, as soon as I came out from the wings and the lights went up, the baby started screaming at the top of her lungs. The audience went nuts, and trying to get back into character, I handed the baby to Jerry, who then handed her to Frank Langella. We were literally passing this poor kid around like a football.

But Jerry and I used to do crazy shit like that together all the time. Anne was also an absolute sweetheart, even though she had a bawdy sense of humor and could curse like a drunken sailor. At the Improv, they did spoofs on the wine commercials together. They were both wonderful and so were their two kids.

AL FRANKEN, US Senator from Minnesota and former comedian, writer, and actor:

Me and my writing partner, Tom Davis—who I first met when we were in high school in Minnesota and later collaborated with on *Saturday Night Live*—were also a comedy team. And, of course, so were Stiller and Meara. Back when we were performing at the Improv and I was still a student at Harvard, we had this thing where we'd drive down to New York from Boston on the weekends and hang out at the bar before our sets and talk to the other comics. One of the biggest thrills for us was getting to spend time with Stiller and Meara, who were always very encouraging. Tom and I were both still in our teens—and a team who'd followed them for a long time—so getting Stiller and Meara's approval was a very big deal. We got nothing but encouragement from them.

JOE PISCOPO:

They always had a great story, and they gave me the best piece of advice that anyone in show business ever has. Back when I was doing stand-up at the Improv, I was using the stage as a means to an end to get where I wanted to go, which was doing movies and television. Commercials weren't part of that equation. In fact, I hadn't even thought about doing them until an agent saw me one night at the club and told me he wanted to represent me for commercials.

I didn't know what to do—especially since I didn't want to do them—and so I consulted Anne and Jerry, who had a popular series of ads for Windex and Blue Nun wine that were running at the time. You know what they said? They were like, "Joe, you should always do commercials—always." When I asked them why, they both looked at me with a completely straight face and said, "Because it's fuck-you money." I immediately understood what they were talking about. I never lost sight of it either.

FOURTEEN

More Momentum, My Monocle—and Lily Tomlin's Grand Entrance

MARTY NADLER:

One of the craziest nights bar none was the New Year's Eve show. There'd always be a packed house and about ten minutes or so before midnight, Budd would get up onstage and say, "All right, we're getting ready for the countdown." Every year, he'd choose one of the male comics to be the New Year's baby and Father Time, which meant that underneath your Father Time outfit you'd have to dress up in a makeshift diaper and a sash with the year across your chest. On top of that, you'd put a cloak on with a hood.

The setup was that while Budd was up onstage, you'd have to go outside and stand next to the window freezing your ass off in subzero temperatures until he called you up. Finally, he'd open up the door and go, "Oh look, here's Father Time. He's going to ring in the new year." Then the lights would go off, you'd throw off the cloak, and you'd be standing there next to Budd in the diaper and sash.

One year—I guess because I was still a newcomer—I was the guinea pig and I was in this little room upstairs pinning on the sash and a bedsheet to look like a diaper when a couple of other comics who had already performed walked in. One of them turned to me and said, "Maybe we should go over to Times Square." Perhaps it's the cynical New Yorker in me—although the particular comedian who said it was also from New York, and from the Bronx no less, where we'd grown up and both attended the same high school as Budd—but I just looked at him and said, "Are you crazy? Are you out of your fucking mind? You're going to go to Times Square and stand in the middle of seventy million people scrunched together?"

But he was completely serious about it. And with a totally straight face, he just looked at me and said, "You're standing there in a diaper about to go outside in eight-degree weather and you're calling me crazy!" It was priceless and not atypical of some of the things that went down at the Improv.

JACK KNIGHT:

We used to have a Saturday night talent show where there'd be three performers and someone from the audience. The prize was a free bottle of champagne, and when I was on, I would sing. Budd had it rigged so that whoever participated from the audience always won and he would come up to the front table, which had an oil tablecloth, salt and pepper shakers, sugar packets, and an ashtray.

While I was singing, what he'd do is grab the tablecloth like a magician and everything would inevitably come crashing down on the floor, which was part of the act. Well, one night he did it and nothing fell, so none of us knew what to do. In addition to pulling the tablecloth off, part of the bit would be that the person who'd won would come up onstage after- wards—at which point we'd get up there also and Budd would be handing him the champagne and purposely drop it on the floor, where it would smash into a million pieces and splash everywhere. The tension in the room was so thick that you could practically cut it with a knife. But then, Budd would pro- fusely apologize and say, "Gee, I'm so sorry. Why don't you come back next week and see if you can win again?" Even though the regular customers knew what was going to hap- pen, it was a fun thing we did and it was always a big crowd- pleaser. Only once did he pull the tablecloth out when nothing broke.

As the attention about the Improv continued to increase, it was largely by word of mouth—and also because we had Damon Runyon Jr. who was then an editor at the *New York Herald Tribune* and often came in and took non-flash black-and-white pictures of the performers, some of which now make up a collage on the wall of the guest bathroom in my Los Angeles home.

Damon was a wonderful guy, although like his legendary father, he had a terrible drinking problem. Still, he was always welcome at the

Improv and it was in part because of some of the pictures he took that I also decided to hire a press agent.

MICHAEL GOLDSTEIN:

I'd been a Broadway publicist, and I first found out about the Improv through somebody I knew who was performing there. By this point, I'd already started my own agency where I represented clients like Janis Joplin and Jimi Hendrix and films such as *The Graduate*, so I was already making a lot of money when I agreed to do the Improv's publicity for free, thinking that I might be able to pick up a client or two.

The first thing I remember about Budd was that he wore a monocle, which I thought was so silly it was just perfect, although he said it was necessary. It was like there was this Jewish-English gentleman holding court at the Improv.

Even when I'm interviewed today, one of the questions that always comes up is: "What's with the monocle?" Not only do they want to know why I wear one, they also ask why I decided to wear it in the first place, so let me explain how it all started.

Like most clubs, the New York Improv was darkly lit and very often during the early days, when one of the waitresses would ask me to approve a check, I couldn't see it. I've often compared it to being like the sheriff in the old western town going blind, although because I was too vain, I'd never admit it. Plus, I only needed glasses to read, which I no longer do since having cataract surgery about ten years ago. Anyway, that's how I came up with the idea to wear a monocle because I could hang it around my neck.

Incidentally, I don't need the monocle anymore either, but I still wear it. It was very effective then, and it's become a great affectation that has made a distinct impression on practically everyone I've met since.

And while we're on the subject of distinct impressions and some of the other young performers we had who helped us get press in those days, Lily Tomlin was serendipitously soon one of them. We met through Louis St. Louis, another piano player I had during this period who later became famous for writing the song "Sandy" in the 1978 film version of *Grease*. Louis was a friend of Lily's from Detroit, where they'd both grown up, and when he recommended her to me in the fall of 1966, I immediately told him to have her come in for an audition.

Aside from Louis's endorsement, which always helps when it comes to getting me to take a look at a performer I've never seen before, part of what sparked my interest was that she had recently made her first national television appearance on *The Gary Moore Show*, which was then one of the most popular weekly variety programs in the country. But little could I have imagined that my initial encounter was to include a limousine.

LILY TOMLIN:

I'd already been living in New York for several years. In the summer of 1966, Madeline Kahn got me a job at the Upstairs at the Downstairs. Then that fall I got a job on *The Gary Moore Show*, but I was dropped after about three episodes because I argued with them all the time about material. I didn't hold out, but I was friendly with a couple of young guys from the show who had been working with Ron Carey, who was already a regular at the Improv.

Louis St. Louis might have recommended me to Budd, but it was through Ron that I heard about it and I may have even gone there once or twice just to check it out before my audition. In the old days, the club had a glass window in the front, and I had a lot of vintage clothes, which is what I decided to wear that evening. I remember I had on a blue velvet halter dress and a white fox fur that was pretty beat-up, but it looked pretty good at night. So I put it on, and took the subway from where I was living on 5th Street between Second and Third Avenues all the way uptown to Times Square. When I came out of the subway, I walked over to the St. James Theatre a few blocks away from the Improv and spotted a limousine parked out front.

Obviously, I wanted to impress Budd, and so I gave the driver like ten dollars or something to have him take me over to the club and wait for me. I went in and did a very solid monologue with several characters in it that Budd loved, even though it didn't have a particularly great ending. Perhaps it was heightened by the fact that I showed up in a limousine, but Budd immediately began giving me spots.

I happened to be standing out in front of the club when this limousine pulled up and it immediately got my attention. Lily was wearing this very chic avant-garde outfit and she was putting on these little white gloves when the driver opened the door. I'm not sure if I said it out loud and she heard me, but I definitely said to myself: "What the fuck is this?"

Then she said, "Are you Mr. Friedman?"

I said, "Yes."

And she said, "I'm Lily Tomlin. I'm supposed to audition for you."

So I invited her inside and she did this monologue with about six different characters, each one better than the next. I think I told her she could perform anytime she wanted, although it wasn't until about three weeks later when she finally started coming in on a regular basis that she confessed to me how she'd paid a limo driver to bring her to the Improv so that she could make her grand entrance.

LILY TOMLIN:

I came in and I didn't know much about Budd, even though I'd wanted to impress him—and I'm not even sure if I thought about it being an audition. After that, I came back and just started working on stuff.

JOHN MEYER:

I was one of Lily's voice coaches. She didn't have a musical act back then, but what she did do at the Improv was a precursor for all of her later characters like Edith Ann and Ernestine the telephone operator. Even then, she had an incredible range, and she was always wonderfully funny and imaginative.

FIFTEEN

The One and Only Rodney Dangerfield

n mid-1966, the Improv scored what was to be one of our biggest home runs hurled out of left field in the form of a fidgety, hard-drinking curveball. By the time he came to my attention—after having adopted the name Rodney Dangerfield, which I later discovered he'd chosen from the phonebook—Rodney was already well into what would be a long road towards the second phase of his stand-up career, even though he was still at least another five years away from becoming a major star.

One afternoon in the midsummer, I stopped off at the newsstand around the corner from the club and picked up the *New York Post*. As I sat with my coffee and began reading the paper, the first thing I noticed when I turned to the features section was a small one-column review of Rodney, who was appearing at the Living Room on Manhattan's Upper East Side. And then, in a "truth is stranger than fiction" twist of fate, he showed up on our doorstep unannounced that same evening.

I was completely taken aback, although much less due to the fact that I had read a review of him only hours earlier. It was because when Rodney walked in, there was no resemblance whatsoever to the urbane Ivy League type the newspaper had described. Instead—and to put it absolutely bluntly—he was shitfaced. Dressed in a wrinkled suit and wearing a stained tie that dangled loosely around his neck, I could immediately smell the booze on his breath as he staggered in, even though I was standing in the opposite direction. When he spoke, his words were slurred. I forget what was said, but with the review still fresh in my mind—and in spite of his inebriated condition against what ultimately proved to be my better judgment—I put him on anyway and he absolutely bombed. And so badly, I should add, that you could literally feel the chorus of boos ricocheting off the walls as customers began asking for their checks and clamoring to leave.

But then, he came back in again the next night stone sober and asked to go on again. It's like somebody had put him up to it on a dare. And you know what? After I reluctantly relented, this time he killed it, as if to say, "I'll show these people." And in as much as his first set was one of the biggest flops I've ever witnessed, the second one was also one of the most spectacular comebacks I have ever seen.

So giving Rodney another chance turned out to be one of the best things I ever did and he immediately became a regular after that. And for the next two and a half years, he was my unofficial emcee, a practice that he occasionally continued long after becoming famous and even when he'd opened his own club, Dangerfield's, on First Avenue in 1969. Rodney was always a crowd-pleaser among customers and comedians alike. One of the most unforgettable evenings at the Improv was the night he emceed with Bill Cosby in the audience.

Cosby was already an established comedian by this point, having also broken the race barrier to become the first African American prime-time television star on the NBC action-adventure series *I Spy*. I'm not sure what the occasion was or who was with him that night, but Bill Cosby was one of those people you didn't ask to perform, so I didn't even bother trying.

But Rodney never had any inhibitions as far as that was concerned. He just kept goading and goading him, until finally Cosby got up and went on for thirty minutes. It was amazing.

Another time, I remember being with Rodney at Jerry Stiller and Anne Meara's apartment for Passover. They lived in a gorgeous building on the Upper West Side not far from me, and every year they had a seder. It was wonderful, and they'd invite thirty or forty people, some of whom weren't even Jewish. One year, Rodney was there drinking martinis, and by the time dinner was served, he'd had about six of them. Then the next thing we knew, he'd passed out facedown at the Stillers' dining room table. He was completely obliterated, but none of us did anything as we continued eating for about another hour.

At that point, we all went into the living room while the caterers, one of whom was a former acting school classmate of Anne's, began clearing off the table. About twenty minutes later, he came running in from the kitchen and said, "Mrs. Stiller, Mrs. Stiller. The man's an animal."

Annie was like, "What are you talking about, Bruce?"

And he said, "That guy Rodney. He's in the kitchen ripping apart the turkey and he's just destroying everything." He kept going on and on, growing more and more agitated, until finally Anne looked at him and said, "I never promised you a rose garden."

It was so funny at the time, especially because of the way Anne said it, and we were all in stitches. Years later, Rodney's daughter Melanie became a TV producer and my daughter Zoe was working at Comedy Central as a producer and they became reacquainted through a mutual project they were working on. Though they were familiar with each other, they didn't realize they had been to many functions together as children.

As for Rodney and me, as time passed we never really became friends, despite the fact that he continued to perform at the New York Improv well into the 1970s and also at the LA club in the eighties and early nineties. Though we were both Jewish and obviously shared similar professional and cultural backgrounds, I think the main reason was that I found him very unapproachable and difficult to talk to. He could also be moody and argumentative, especially when he'd been drinking or smoking grass, which led to more than one verbal altercation that nearly became physical, so I tended to keep my distance. For all of Rodney's shortcomings, however, I will always be grateful for what he did for me and the Improv. In one way or another, like Richard Pryor, he touched the lives of practically everyone he met both inside and outside of the club—and even some he hadn't.

JIMMY FALLON:

I was probably ten or twelve when I first realized I wanted to be a comedian. My parents were funny and my grandparents were funny, so there was always a lot of joking around, and my sister was funny, too. Irish-Catholic family, always joking, always making people laugh, so no matter what I did, I was always making people laugh.

After a while, I was like, "This is something I'm good at." Then I started listening to comedy albums like The Smothers Brothers and Rodney Dangerfield. My dad would actually take a key and scratch out the dirty words in Rodney's albums, so it would skip over the curses and I would never hear the F word.

It was so Irish-Catholic, and it also screwed up the punch line. I didn't understand half the bits, but the setup was great. I would just listen to them over and over again and then I found that I could kind of impersonate people. As I got older, my parents would give me a dollar. They'd be like, "Go do Rodney for everybody."

JERRY STILLER:

We all respected Rodney for his ability to get up without any material, talk, and include everybody in the audience in his act to the point where they all felt very connected to him, like he was their father. Other comics didn't necessarily look at him as a comedian. Instead, they just saw him as a person who happened to have the ability to get up in front of an audience and make them laugh.

FREDDIE ROMAN:

Rodney was the character of the Western world. The man was high every night of his life. Budd opened the Improv before Rodney opened Dangerfield's, and the strangest thing about his club was that he hardly ever worked there. If he had to do a *Tonight Show*, he would also go to the Improv to break in new material instead of his own club, which made no sense.

RICK NEWMAN, producer and founder of Catch A Rising Star:

Rodney always used to kid around at the end of his act. He'd go, "I know you're wondering why I'm up here. But why would I want to be bad at my place? I'm trying out new material."

It was very funny that he would work out at the Improv and Catch A Rising Star when he had his own place ten blocks away. But he always used to say, "I don't want to be bad at my place."

ALAN ZWEIBEL:

He was the first guy I wrote for who had a defined character. When you'd write for those Catskills guys, you were just writing for a guy in a tuxedo. If this tuxedo guy didn't like the joke, he'd give it to the next tuxedo guy. Rodney already had, "I don't get no respect." It was really easy for me to build on that and have him say, "Even as an infant, I didn't get no respect. My mother wouldn't breastfeed me. She said she liked me as a friend."

I used to hang out with him. Even when I was doing *Saturday Night Live* and he hosted, I hung out with him that week. I learned a lot from him because here was a guy who totally reinvented himself from being Jack Roy and all of that. There was a hipness to him because he had been friends with Joe Ancis and Lenny Bruce. As commercial as he was, there was an underground Bitter End kind of quality to him, plus he did coke.

BILL SALUGA:

I don't think I ever saw Rodney do a bad set, even though he was half in the bag all the time. One night not long after I got to the Improv, there were these two Irish women who got up to sing. They were these pure, lovely looking girls and they sang some sort of virginal song. Well, that was all it took to get Rodney going because afterwards he said, "Hey, weren't they great? You know what I'd like to see, ladies and gentlemen? I'd like to see them cum together." You could literally see their faces turning bright red as they got offstage. You could also hear the collective gasps of shock from the audience when he said it. But that was Rodney. As crude and insensitive as he could be sometimes, he almost always managed to pull it off because he was so funny.

BOB "UNCLE DIRTY" ALTMAN, comedian:

I knew Rodney from the Improv, of course, but then when he opened his own club, Dangerfield's on First Avenue in New York, we all used to go over there and get high down in the basement. People would do lines of coke like you wouldn't believe—we're talking like an eighth of an inch and three inches long like vacuum cleaners.

BILL GULINO, author, pianist, composer, and arranger:

I was at the Improv in New York with Rodney one night sometime in the late seventies or early eighties when he spotted this woman who was a total stranger and said to her, "Hey, honey, can I bum a cigarette from you? Mine are in the machine." It was just such a Rodney joke.

JOHN DEBELLIS:

Rodney was one of a kind, and it's not a stretch to say they broke the mold when they made him. One evening after some road gig, we went back to the Improv to have a nightcap and we were standing at the bar. By this point, he had about three or four drinks in him, and all of the sudden he looked at me and said, "Hey, John, let me get you a prostitute. We'll go back to my place and we'll have hookers."

Well, suffice it to say, the thought of seeing Rodney naked in a room with a bunch of hookers was beyond repulsive to me. I must have used every excuse I could come up with to try to get out of it. I think I may have even told him I had a girlfriend who I'd been going steady with for a couple of years. I mean, there was just no way I was going to do this. Rodney didn't persist, but I remember he always used to say to me, "You know, John, in life you think you've gotten the perfect blow job and then a week later you think you can get a better one." Honest to God, that was his philosophy.

MARTY NADLER:

One night he was in the middle of his act at the Improv and an interracial couple came into the club. He was black, she was white, and as soon as Rodney spotted them from the stage, he interrupted the bit he was doing and said, "If there's anything I hate, it's a white woman going out with a Jew." Of course, everyone just started laughing hysterically and then he goes, "What do you think, I'm going to get killed here?" He was absolutely brilliant at that kind of stuff—and fearless, too.

The other thing about Rodney was that he was even funnier offstage. I remember another night several years later at the Hollywood Improv when I and a few other comics went over to Canter's Deli on Fairfax Avenue to get something to eat afterwards. We walked in and before we sat down at a table, the first thing Rodney noticed was another comic named Joe E. Ross, who wasn't part of our group but happened to be there also.

Joe was a mediocre comedian at best, but he'd had a fairly successful television career back in the fifties and sixties playing a second banana on sitcoms like *The Phil Silvers Show* and *Car 54, Where Are You?*, where his signature line was, "Ooh! Ooh!" Before that, he and Rodney used to perform in strip clubs together and Rodney hated his guts.

So finally we got seated, and just as the waitress was about to bring out our food, Joe comes up to us without even saying hello or apologizing for interrupting our meal and says, "Rodney, it's not fair. I mean, you're funny, but I'm funny, too. You do Carson every month and I can't even get on once."

By this point, Rodney was really starting to get annoyed and he looked over at Joe and said, "Joey, if life was fair you'd have been dead twenty years ago."

Not too long after that, Richard Lewis and I went to see Rodney at his club back in New York. Either before or after the show, we were downstairs in his dressing room and the first thing we noticed was a framed copy of Joe's comedy album that was prominently displayed. Because we knew how much Rodney loathed him, we naturally wanted to find out why. So we asked him and his response was this: "So that I can look at it and know that I'm not the ugliest fucking man in the world!"

FRED WILLARD:

The funniest night was when a bunch of us comics were all together at the New York Improv. Rodney was the emcee. Dave Frye did his act. Then another comic named Jimmy Martinez, who never went too far but was one of my favorites, went on. He made me laugh so hard. Anyway, Rodney came on and there were no boundaries to what he did that night. He got extremely, inappropriately blue. Some guy was heckling him and he turns around and goes, "Oh, you're going to judge me now." Two young girls who were twins were there, and he made some inappropriate sexual remark. I can't remember what it was, but it was just hilariously funny.

As much as I loved Rodney, the thing about him was that he kind of put up a fence around himself. There were a couple of times after I got to know him when he would come over and say, "Hey, Fred, listen to this joke. Do you think this is funny?" He'd start telling me jokes and then suddenly he'd stop. He'd go, "What the hell am I trying it out on you for?" So one night, I came up and I told him I had an idea for a joke for him. The premise was that he was in a Las Vegas casino disturbing the peace. He looked up at me and said, "Fred, you can do a joke like that, but when I get onstage I gotta do heavy damage."

That really stuck with me. Every time I see somebody who did a great job, I think, "You did heavy damage."

DANNY AIELLO:

Rodney used to quote me all the time and he made my career. He'd go on all the talk shows like Johnny Carson, Mike Douglas, Merv Griffin, and Dick Cavett and talk about me. He'd say stuff like, "Danny took me to Randall Avenue in the East Bronx. Looking over the water where his family lived, the most attractive thing about it was a toothless tire floating." Then he'd say, "Danny said make a straight right and a straight left." Of course, at the time I was a nobody, but he'd go on national television and mention my name as if everyone knew who I was. He'd do that on every show.

JIMMIE WALKER, comedian and actor:

Rodney was on another level. He was the guy who was like twenty or thirty years older, coming back for his second comeback. He was just a party cat. You wouldn't think a guy who was twenty years older than everybody and had been through what he'd been through would be that kind of guy. He was just one of the cats, man.

BOB SAGET:

Once he told me I had a "Jew head"—that I was never going to be able to rest at night because I couldn't stop thinking—but he'd seen me on *The Merv Griffin Show* and thought I was really funny. It was a pretty special thing and my friendship with Rodney was a big influence.

JUDD APATOW:

In LA, Rodney used to come in late at night, but I don't think I ever saw him do his act. He'd just go onstage and talk to the audience. A lot of the time he would just seem depressed and he would be insanely funny, but it wasn't the same Rodney Dangerfield. He would look at a woman in the crowd and say, "Oh, you'd love me for who I am. You'd be different." It was really funny—and really, really dark.

I think he did this because he enjoyed going on when he didn't have the pressure to be the Rodney Dangerfield character. It's like he enjoyed the tension of not doing *those* jokes for the crowd.

EDDIE BERKE, actor and longtime Hollywood Improv bartender:

My personal history with Rodney Dangerfield goes all the way back to when I was a kid. My dad, Irving, was the social director at this place called the Hotel Gibber in Kiamesha Lake, New York, in the Catskills. Part of his job was to hire the entertainment, and he was one of the first people that gave Rodney work as a stand-up comic way back when.

So we had that link and Rodney had known my father very well. Unfortunately, by the time I was at the Hollywood Improv in the late seventies and Rodney started coming in, he was heavily into drugs, booze, and all this other stuff. He actually came into the club one night dressed in his pajamas wanting to go on. Needless to say, whoever was emceeing at the time wouldn't let him because on top of how he was dressed, Rodney was also shitfaced or doped up—I don't know which.

That aside, though, Rodney was basically a very nice man who had issues. The other thing about Rodney—and this isn't unlike most entertainers—was that he had this big thing about age. My father was also one of these people with good genes who always looked a good ten or twenty years younger than he actually was. Even though they'd known each other forever, Rodney never believed my dad was really his real age.

Sure enough, every time I would see him at the Improv, the first words out of his mouth after I'd told them that my father had said to say hello to him was, "How old is Irving?" Whenever I'd tell him what my father's age was, he'd say, "I don't believe that!"

JOE PISCOPO:

I remember one night when I was emceeing in New York, Rodney came into the Improv unannounced, and I said, "Come on up here." He did, but then afterwards he came up to me in the bar and said, "You gotta introduce me. You can't just say come on up here." I listened intently to that, and to this day I've followed his advice. It's like if I'm doing a charity gig, I'll say, "Ladies and gentlemen. We're very privileged to have this person with us. Please give a nice round of applause for so and so."

Rodney taught me that. He was a scientist when it came to comedy and he was probably the purest comic I know. We would watch him formulate his *Tonight Show* set six weeks ahead of when he was supposed to go on. He would come in and just start to formulate the jokes. What he'd do is pull up in front of the club in this old Buick Electra. It was like a Cheech and Chong movie with all of the weed smoke coming out, and then he'd come in and come on.

I also remember once when I was just starting out, I was about to go on. When you're at that stage of your career, your heart's in your throat and you're dying because you've got to go on up in front of all these people. Then I remember Chris Albrecht, who was managing the club at the time, putting his hand on my chest and saying, "Rodney's here."

You knew that meant you were bumped for Rodney, and that he'd destroy a room like nobody else could. I mean, when I tell you that you never heard a laugh that big, it's true.

RITCH SHYDNER, comedian, writer, and actor:

There were some comics who'd try and stick it out to the end of their set, but I usually cut things off as soon as I saw Rodney even if I was in the middle of a joke. I'd say something like, "So this guy . . ." Then I'd say, "Hey, folks, I've got a big treat for you." Rodney always appreciated that and he'd say to me afterwards, "Hey, kid, you know how to move. I like that."

One night—and I'm not sure if Rodney had been at the Improv or not—I walked over to Times Square after my set and I lit up a cigarette as I stood there soaking up the scene. About a minute or two later, I felt somebody brushing up against me, and before I could get scared that I was about to be mugged, I looked up and it was Rodney. He goes, "Hey, kid, it's all happening out here." Then he spotted a hooker and said, "There's my girlfriend." Basically, he blew me off after that so he could go over and talk to her.

JACK KNIGHT:

I was seated in the audience in New York once with David Frye the impressionist, and Rodney—who couldn't stand David—

was up onstage. Back then, the light fixtures were in this kind of art-deco leaded-glass motif, and while Rodney was in the middle of his set, he spotted these two women who had just walked in. He stopped whatever joke he was doing and said, "Hey, look who just walked in!"

When he said it, I stood up in my chair so I could see the women and I hit my head on one of the lights and it disintegrated to smithereens. Broken glass fell onto the table and onto the floor—all of which got a big laugh and Rodney went on with his act. Meanwhile, one of the busboys came out with a broom and a dustpan and began quietly sweeping up all of the glass.

Then he carried it to the back of the club and dumped it into an empty metal garbage can. You can only imagine the noise it made when he did, but Rodney's timing was perfect because he came up with the fastest, funniest ad-lib I had ever heard in my life. He said, "Hey, it sounds like a robot throwing up!"

The interesting thing about Rodney is that he would come offstage after trying out a new bit and ask some stranger what they thought. Obviously, you couldn't get an honest opinion out of that, but I don't think he was very secure about a lot of stuff. I was actually the entertainment at Rodney's son Brian's ninth birthday party at the Improv. I forget what I did, but there were some songs and some carry-ons and we all had a great time. Come to think of it, I probably had a second piece of cake.

DREW CAREY, actor, comedian, sports executive, and host of *The Price Is Right*:

This is a really good Rodney/Improv story, and I'm extremely proud of this night. I hadn't become famous yet, but I had recently passed my *Tonight Show* audition and having just come off doing eighteen consecutive months on the road, my chops were really strong. I was also getting great spots at the Improv.

Normally, this was during prime time, which was generally any time between 9 PM and midnight. But no matter how good you were, one of the unwritten rules they had—and this is pretty much standard at any comedy club—is that if somebody else more famous than you shows up, you automatically get bumped. It has nothing to do with how funny you are. It's just the natural pecking order of things. Any comedian will tell you this and you just accept it, hoping there'll still be an audience left by the time you finally go on.

One night in 1991, I was at the Hollywood Improv hanging out in the bar with a buddy of mine. I was waiting to go on and going over my material in my head when either the emcee or the manager came up to me and said, "We're going to have to push you back from your normal time because we have someone coming in to do a guest spot."

Of course I was disappointed, but the only choice I had was to wait, and so I said, "All right." Well, the next thing I knew, the guy going on wasn't just any guest—it was Jerry Seinfeld, who had the hottest sitcom in America at the time. He absolutely murdered the place.

After that, in comes Jerry's best friend, George Wallace. George is still great and he works mostly in Las Vegas these days, but at the time, euphemistically speaking, he was a murderer onstage. Back then he could destroy any club, which he did that night as another guest who wasn't scheduled. By the time he finished his set, people were just pounding the tables.

I was like, "Fuck! I can't believe this is happening to me." What happened next was even more unbelievable, because just then the emcee tapped me on the shoulder and said, "We've got one more guy coming up—Rodney Dangerfield." So it was Jerry Seinfeld, George Wallace, and Rodney Dangerfield, all on the same bill, right in a row. But the emcee was great. I can't remember who it was, but he did me a really nice favor because after Rodney was done, he got up onstage and said, "Hey, folks. Not many people can follow Rodney Dangerfield, but this guy can. Please welcome Drew Carey." While the crowd was still laughing at Rodney, I went on and hit them with a joke just to get the ball rolling. After that, I did a good solid fifteen-minute set and killed.

ROBERT WUHL, actor, writer, and comedian:

Of all the places I performed, the Improv was the best of the bunch. First off, I was still living at home with my parents in New Jersey and I was coming from the Holland Tunnel, so it was closer. Also, I liked the intimacy of the room because there wasn't a high stage, which I preferred, because I never liked talking down to people.

And I was treated well because I was writing for Rodney Dangerfield. At the time, I idolized Rodney and I knew his club on First Avenue, so I wrote a couple of jokes for him and walked in one night off the street. I'd never performed there and they didn't know me from Adam, but when I went in I went right up to the maître d' and told him I had some jokes for Rodney. He never questioned me or tried to turn me away. He just said, "Rodney's downstairs. Go down there."

So I did. I walked down this flight of stairs next to the show room and knocked on the door. The next thing I heard was Rodney's unmistakable voice. He said, "Come on in," and I turned the knob. Now picture this: It's less than a second later and I'm in Rodney Dangerfield's dressing room. He's standing there in front of the sink and he's wearing a bathrobe that's wide open and he's taking a leak. His dick is on full display and he's doing his business because there's no toilet.

But somehow I still managed to say to him, "Hi, Rodney, I've got some jokes for you." I'm not sure if I even introduced myself, but without looking up he said, "Okay, kid. Let me hear them." So I told him my jokes and he said to me, "The jokes are good, kid, but don't imitate me." Then he said, "I pay fifty dollars a joke." Before I knew it, I gave him a few more and started writing regularly for him.

Being the huge partier that Rodney was, we used to smoke pot together. He also spent a lot of time running jokes by me, which I considered the supreme compliment. He'd say, "You're a good comic editor." One of my favorite rituals with Rodney was when he would leave jokes on my answering machine and then pause for the laugh. He'd call me up and say stuff like, "Boy, I worked some rough places. I worked at Vinney's Boom Boom Room and on the menu they had broken leg of lamb. Okay, so what do you think?"

Rodney also used my jokes on *The Tonight Show*, so that gave me gravitas at the same time I was developing my act. At the Improv, what he'd do is drop in to work out bits and take his cuts in the batting cage. Especially for the younger comics, he was a great role model, because he was fast and he'd be there just banging jokes out one after the other.

Rodney would also hang out there afterwards and sit in the back getting high. The thing about him was, he was the greatest supporter of comics who had something to say. If you didn't, though, he had absolutely no patience. You'd hear it especially when there was some greenhorn up there trying to do observational humor. Like for instance, there'd be a guy going, "You know, it's interesting when you're waiting for a bus and the sign says this."

Rodney would go ballistic. All of a sudden in the middle of their act you'd hear: "Come on, man, tell me a joke. I don't want to hear about your bus. Next you're going to tell me about where I buy shoes. Tell me a fucking joke. Make me laugh." So yeah, Rodney could be tough, but if he liked you and you took chances, you could do no wrong.

BOBBY KELTON:

By the time I met him, he was already a huge star, but he still came to the Improv a lot to work out. I can't remember how I first got to know him, but like a lot of the other comics, I was one of the ones he bought jokes from. One of his favorites, which he did on *The Tonight Show*, was about the Surgeon General offering him a cigarette. Another one was where he said, "I offered to donate my body to science and they gave me a doggy bag."

To this day, I have a stack of his handwritten letters on stationery from various Las Vegas hotels thanking me for my jokes. I was also out in Vegas once when he was performing at the MGM Grand, and Rodney got me and my brother tickets. During the middle of the show, he even said, "That joke was written by a very funny young man named Bobby Kelton who's here tonight." Then he invited me to get up and they shined the spotlight on me. I was blown away, but Rodney was like that. For all his shortcomings, he always had a good heart.

ROBERT KLEIN:

Rodney was by the book—even though there was no book—and he was of that old style. The rhythms of his jokes were so superior that he took you to another level. For example, some of his early material was every bit as good as Art Buchwald or William Safire. The point is that first and foremost, Rodney was a stand-up comedian. And street smart with only a high school education, talking about stuff like, "I'll tell you, our streets aren't safe, our schools aren't safe, our parks aren't safe, but under our arms we have complete protection."

This was social commentary and it was absolutely brilliant. My whole thing with him personally was a whole other story, and it became very intense after years of hanging out with him. But I always knew he loved me, and more than that, he respected my education and my intelligence even though we were exactly twenty years apart. On his very first comedy album, *No Respect*, when he autographed it for me he wrote: "To the next dimension." He called me the next dimension. He loved my sort of intellectual, slightly arrogant intelligence. It's not what he was used to where he came from, but he knew funny from funny.

Rodney was the indisputable king of the Improv, just starting to have his first commercial success on the night I began performing there. Though I'd never seen or heard of him before, he made quite an impression on me because all during my set I kept noticing this odd-looking guy dressed in a black suit and red necktie, nervously tugging at his collar. He looked miserable and I didn't quite know what to make of him, but just as I finished, he came up to me and said: "I'll tell you, you were fucking brilliant, man. I'm a tough cocksucker, but you have to come in here every night for three years to get it right."

I followed his advice, and from then on I went there every night for like the next three or four years. It was wonderful because I was single at the time and I met so many girls there, plus I learned so much from Rodney both from seeing him at the Improv and spending time with him at many of his gigs outside the club. Beyond the fundamental basics of understanding the construction and nuances of a joke, I also learned many of the crucial technical aspects, like how to hold a microphone and when to remove it from the stand.

Most important of all, though, he taught me how to size up an audience, how to take command of a room, and how to deal with hecklers. In short, he was my Yale School of Drama for comedy, whom I came to consider both my mentor, as well as a surrogate father figure rolled into one. In fact, I even used to kiddingly call him "pop" until he told me to knock it off. But while we had our fair share of disagreements over the years, I always loved Rodney. There will never be another one like him.

Robert Klein Elevates Stand-Up—and the Improv—to a New Level

The next major shot fired in the direction of the Improv's comedy arm was Robert Klein, the brilliantly acerbic Bronx-born comedian who arrived not long after Rodney in 1966 and immediately became his protégé, even though their styles couldn't have been more different.

In terms of topical, trendsetting, cutting-edge material, Robert was the perfect fit. On the most fundamental level, he was hysterical. Not only was watching him perform live like seeing a one-man band who could play every instrument pitch-perfectly, more broadly and indirectly, he would go on to influence multiple generations of comedians, from Jerry Seinfeld, Jay Leno, Richard Lewis, and Bill Maher to Jimmy Fallon, Stephen Colbert, and Jon Stewart.

JAY LENO, comedian and former host of *The Tonight Show*:

Robert Klein was *my* comedian. I say this because before Robert came along, most of the comics were older Jewish men like Rodney Dangerfield or Alan King. Or there was Pryor who was black and he was talking about that experience. There was no middle-class white kid out there and Klein was. He was talking about things I could relate to, like how bad television was back then. I was like, "Here's somebody who's talking about the exact same things I am." To a certain extent, George

Carlin was, too. But I wasn't a hippie and I didn't smoke dope, so Robert was my guy and to this day he still is.

RICHARD LEWIS:

I didn't get to the Improv until 1971, which was a few years after Robert, and he had already gotten hot by then. I had begun dabbling in comedy writing while I was still a student at Ohio State University, even though I got a degree in marketing and became an ad copywriter, which I had to supplement with a lot of horrible day jobs once I decided to become a comic. The turning point that got me back to the East Coast was when I heard that Robert Klein was hosting a summer replacement show on network TV in 1970, and a friend of mine somehow connected me with his manager Buddy Morra. I immediately set out to write some material for Robert, which I then mailed to Buddy, who liked it enough that he passed it along to Robert. When I followed up about a week later, Buddy told me to call him the next time I was in New York.

I couldn't get there fast enough and the meeting was life changing. Even though Robert turned me down, telling me that he didn't buy other people's material, he also said he liked what I'd written. Then Buddy promised to hook me up with some other comedians, which he did, even though he never managed me. The biggest one was Morty Gunty, who was a big star in the Catskills at the time and began buying jokes from me. There were also others I wrote for, and I made a decent living, but then I ultimately pushed forward on the same path as Robert and started performing the material myself. I owe a lot of that to Robert because of the encouragement he gave the first time we met.

Without a doubt, the Improv would have also been a much different place without him—both less funny and certainly not as intelligently funny. That's because Robert, whom I have always considered to be comedy's first "modern comedian," made you laugh and think at the same time. This is no easy feat, of course, and so in that sense he truly became our tipping point.

Steeped in recognizable human behavior that was always socially and politically relevant, Robert's razor-sharp observational style was an instant hit from the moment he got on our stage. Over the next five decades, he enjoyed a legendary career that included such milestones as releasing his seminal debut comedy album, *Child of the 50's* (1973), followed by starring in HBO's first comedy special (1975), eventually ranking him in the supreme pantheon of the greatest comedians of all time, an acknowledgment he deservedly received from Comedy Central in 2005. Needless to say, I am enormously proud that we were one of the first places where Robert did stand-up and I will always remember our times together with great fondness.

Aside from what he added to the club in talent and creativity, my respect and affection for Robert also had a brotherly kinship from day one. First of all, he talked about subjects I knew very well, like being a middle-class Jew from the Bronx, which we both are. On top of that, we'd both attended DeWitt Clinton High School. In addition to his observational bits that were often accompanied by songs and the harmonica, one of my earliest favorites was a routine he did on his old teachers in public school, which I could obviously relate to well. He'd say: "They had these older women who had gone to normal school in 1899, graduated in two years, took religion and first aid. They gave them each a bun in the back—a chignon—a large black dress, and Boy Scout shoes, and sent them into schools to say, 'No talking.'"

It was incredible and so was Robert. His father, Benjamin, was a textiles salesman and an impressionist who told funny stories and was a friend of the Yiddish-dialect comedian Myron Cohen. His mother, Frieda, was a medical secretary who later became the assistant to Leo Davidoff, the world-renowned neurosurgeon who had once operated on Albert Einstein and was immortalized in journalist John Gunther's 1949 memoir, *Death Be Not Proud*. Robert's mother also played the piano by ear and she would often accompany herself while singing Broadway show tunes. Even though he had initially planned to become a doctor, Robert, too, became interested in show business at a very young age when his abilities gravitated equally towards music and comedy—even forming a doo-wop group in high school, which years later he reprised into a trio with Buddy Mantia, Marvin Braverman, and later Danny Aiello at the Improv called the Untouchables.

In 1964, Robert left the Yale School of Drama after one year to pursue acting roles and supported himself by working as a substitute teacher. He then decided to try stand-up on the Greenwich Village amateur circuit in local folk clubs. He joined Second City in Chicago in 1965, spending a year there before returning to New York with the road company in the spring of 1966. In the fall of that year, he had landed a small role in the new Broadway musical *The Apple Tree*. It was during this same period that Robert reconnected with a Second City alum named David Steinberg. Despite having been rivals in Chicago, it was at David's urging that Robert give stand-up another try at the Improv.

ROBERT KLEIN:

Steinberg was just so brilliant. He had been at Second City for a while by the time I arrived, so he was the big star of the place. One night not long after I got there, David invited me up to his apartment, and Sheldon Patinkin, who was one of Second City's principal directors, was there. He took me aside and said, "Be careful of David."

Then David told me, "Watch out for Sheldon."

Anyway, David wiped the floor with me. I was talented but raw, so when he eventually left the company and went to London, I was relieved.

DAVID STEINBERG:

Basically the feud with me and Robert—and we talk about it a lot—wasn't about us. It was about our friends because we were both coming up at the same time and they'd say things like, "He's better than this and he's better than that." However, we were never in a conflict about the work itself. I don't mean this in a good way, but if anything, I was just so intimidating at Second City—that and the fact that I'd been there for a couple of years before he arrived. But then not long after, I went to England with the company and that's when he blossomed.

ROBERT KLEIN:

With David, it was never an issue of whether we worked well together or whether or not I respected him. What I thought about him back then, and what I still think of him now, is that I've never seen as good an improviser anywhere. However, there was also a period of dislike when I kind of resented him for giving me a crisis of confidence—even though it never showed up in our performances per se. He was famous for stealing the stage and I had to toughen up in a hurry. By the time we were heading to New York with Second City in 1965, I had ulcer symptoms because he was still making sure he had all the best scenes.

But that was pretty much that, because by this point I had gotten pretty good at holding my own and doing what I did. Actually, the show ended up closing after only five months and years later David apologized. Even before that, we had already begun mending fences by the time I landed my first Broadway role in *The Apple Tree*. I had also started toying with the idea of trying to do stand-up again—and that's when David told me about the Improv.

DAVID STEINBERG:

By the time I got to the New York company of Second City around 1965 or '66, I had already been in England. Then Second City wound up closing in New York after only about five weeks. About six months later, Bill Alton, who had been a founding member of Second City and was the one who told me about it, approached me about putting an act together. He'd been living in New York for a number of years by this point, and Bernie Sahlins from Second City arranged for a producer from *The Merv Griffin Show* to come and see us at the Improv. The setup was that I played a very nervous stand-up comedian coming onstage for the first time and Bill played a drunk heckling me from the audience. We ended up getting on *The Merv Griffin Show*, which suddenly jump-started my career—all because Budd knew enough to let us do it because we were sketch comics and stand-up was where everything was headed. He was always willing to take chances.

Then I became a regular at The Bitter End in Greenwich Village. So one night, Robert dropped in to see me not long after he'd gotten *The Apple Tree*, which was at the Shubert Theatre, right around the corner from the Improv. We were friends at that point, which we always were more than adversaries. We got to talking about him doing stand-up again and that's when I told him he ought to try and get on at Budd's place. The Improv just seemed tailor-made for Robert, and I think I told him to do something musical.

Even before he did whatever he did onstage that night, Robert made an immediate impression as soon as he came in and introduced himself to me. I vividly recall saying to myself right then and there: "Wow, he's a tall, good-looking Jew from the Bronx who went to my high school. How bad can that be?"

ROBERT KLEIN:

Even though I was gradually easing back into stand-up at this point, I had never heard of the Improv until David told me about it. For starters, I wasn't a bar guy and I never hung out in them. And I wasn't what you'd really call an "uptown" guy either. I mean, I was living at 108th Street and West End Avenue, which wasn't the greatest neighborhood in those days.

Anyway, I believe that it was in the fall of 1966 when I first started at the Improv. It was after the reviews of *The Apple Tree* had come in and I knew I was going to have a job for a while. I wound up staying with the show for seven months. I was making $200 a week and I had just bought a Volvo. I think the word on the street was that the Improv wasn't a hootenanny the way a lot of these clubs down in the Village were.

My memory is that David told me Budd would definitely love to have me because I was in a Broadway show—this, and that it seemed very uptown, even though I wasn't, like I said. But it was also such a dive that I used to do this bit where I'd say: "The Improv is the kind of place where you put toilet paper on the men's room door before you went in." When I went there, it was the only place of its kind and it was still equally music and comedy.

There was this short redhead whose name I forget who could belt it out. And then I saw, or maybe I heard, that Liza Minnelli had been there to try out something. I also saw comedian Jackie Vernon coming through to put the finishing touches on his next Ed Sullivan appearance. What was great was that there were a lot of stars around but also a lot of fringe show-business people like managers and people who came in because they lived in the theater district. It hadn't caught on with tourists yet and it was about as hip as a late-night audience could be where there'd be an incredibly eclectic hodgepodge. You'd see regulars who had their favorites, alcoholics, people who had money, and eccentrics, who came in overdressed wearing gloves and things. There were also bums who'd peep in from 44th Street.

To the club's credit, this is one of the reasons why I had to write so much material. I'd had that improvisational training at Second City to begin with, but then having the same people in the audience every night at the Improv forced me to keep building things up and changing them around. One of the first comics I met there was Richard Pryor and we wound up doing some improvs together in a group.

On my first night there, I arranged to have the entire cast of *The Apple Tree* with me. That impressed Budd. I already knew when I walked in that I wasn't just depending on, "Gee, will he put me up?" And then I just killed that night.

Budd was good to me right from the beginning in part because I'd been in *The Apple Tree* but also because of how well I did. However, I'll say this about him: There were plenty of times after that when I saw him dealing with other people, including comics and singers, and he wasn't warm and fuzzy. I guess I was lucky in that sense because he never gave me any problems. Over time, I came to admire him all the more because he's one of three people who have told me some pretty intimate tales of combat. Ever see that scar on his leg? That always impressed me, and this is a guy who was never afraid to confront somebody who was out of line because his own life had been in mortal danger in Korea.

But as much as I love Budd, I'd be remiss if I didn't mention that he had a pretension about him when he'd introduce me. He would even sometimes take my lines. I'd say something and then he would go: "Ha, ha, ha." I'd be like, "Get your own material, Budd, please." I wasn't as offended as I would have been if another comic had done it, but he would, and it kind of annoyed me. Basically, though, we always got along fine and if pretentiousness was part of the package, you pretty much accepted it because it was also part of his charm.

Back when I had my goatee, I liked to refer to myself as "your charming bearded host" and the "benevolent dictator," even though there were plenty of people who took issue with that. Robert was never one of them, though, and I used to love stealing a line or two from him as I was bringing him up, which I still liked to do even when we had another emcee. If he ever got pissed about it, it didn't show. The other thing about Robert is that he's always had a very charismatic presence both on and offstage and he never lost his composure.

But putting aside his ability to connect with any audience and how talented he is, the other thing that has always impressed me about Robert is his passion for the work to the point of perfectionism. He'd have this humongous reel-to-reel Wollensak tape recorder with him. It was probably a foot and a half long and probably even wider. It weighed a fucking ton. Not only would he tape every performance; more importantly he would listen to it.

He said Joan Rivers told him to do it, but he was the first guy I knew who taped his acts. He'd call me up asking to go on, and he invariably did because he could do absolutely no wrong. If Rodney Dangerfield had been the king of the Improv, then Robert was definitely the anointed prince. He always went to the head of the line. Hardly anybody ever questioned it either because he was that good and he always had something to say.

CARL REINER:

My introduction to Robert was through my son Rob. He called me up one day and said, "I just saw this guy who was so different than anybody else I've ever seen." After I went to see him for myself, I instantly knew what he was talking about. Robert Klein informed every comedian who came after him.

ALAN ZWEIBEL:

We all kind of felt like Robert was God, and that's what it was like whenever he came into the club—an encounter with God. I remember being there one night when Robert came in with his manager, Buddy Morra. Robert was getting ready to record an album and he came in and just killed. I'm talking annihilate here. Afterwards, they sat down at one of the booths in the back and he started writing stuff down on a bunch of napkins with a red felt-tip pen. Then he left and I noticed one of the napkins that he had sort of discarded. It was crumpled up and smudged, but I took it anyway because it had Robert's handwriting on it. I was just this kid in awe because I'd seen what he could do with stand-up.

MARVIN BRAVERMAN, writer and comedian:

I used to be in this doo-wop group with Buddy Mantia and Robert. We'd sing backup for him. The idea originated at the Improv. Robert always inspired me with his comedy. Whenever I saw his act, it was so smart and funny that it pushed me to become better. He wasn't always easy to be around and he wasn't always nice, but when he was, he was great. The other thing I remember about Robert is his technique. Some people pushed through their material, but he blasted through his.

LENNY SCHULTZ:

Without fail, Robert was always brilliant onstage and I think he's one of the reasons I started taping my acts. He was also a bit of a loner, and I don't remember him ever being one of the guys who would go out with us for breakfast at four in the morning. However, we all respected him.

JERRY STILLER:

Robert came to the Improv a little after Anne and I did, but once he was there, he kind of became the nucleus of the place. He was instantly likable. And he was always very intelligent and literal. Then he started talking about his own connection to comedy and the fact that he was Jewish, which was something that I could easily relate to.

MIKE PREMINGER, screenwriter and comedian:

Interestingly enough, Robert and I grew up four blocks from each other in the Bronx and my mother knew his mother. We could have lived four hundred miles from each other, but it just so happened that we lived four blocks apart and we went to the same high school and the same junior high school.

But we never once laid eyes on each other until we got to the Improv. Robert was there a few years before me, and by that time he was a big star, so Budd pretty much gave him the run of the entire place and he'd come in and do these long sets. He was fabulous, but again, we never talked. And then one night, I guess he'd either seen me perform or he'd heard about me somehow and he kind of walked up to me out of the blue and said: "You're next. It's going to happen to you soon." I'm not sure if we said much else after that, but it was the supreme compliment he paid me.

DICK CAVETT:

Klein makes me laugh inordinately—I mean, unmeasurably. It's like when he starts, I just start laughing. You can be badly fooled that way in show business sometimes, but I knew from the moment I first saw him that he was somebody I would probably like. And I've felt that way about him ever since. He's never disappointed me.

LIZ TORRES:

No doubt about it—and I think rightfully so—Robert was Budd's fair-haired child and he always had the main spot. Whenever he came in, you knew that the show was on. He was still a teacher even though he'd left that world professionally, and he used to bring me to *The Tonight Show* with him because he liked the way I laughed.

FRED WILLARD:

Bob Klein and I probably go back more than fifty years. The first time we met was at the William Morris office in New York when were both up for Second City. Flash-forward a couple of years: We were no longer at Second City by this point. He was back in New York and I was living in LA, but I had gone to see him in *The Apple Tree*. After the show, I went backstage and I asked him if he was doing stand-up again, which I knew he wanted to. He looked at me and said, "It's funny you asked that. I just got signed by Jack Rollins [the same manager who eventually represented me], and I've been working out at the Improv." Then he said, "Why don't you come down and watch me tonight?"

And so in an odd serendipitous twist—the same kind of six degrees of separation scenario that Bob had had with David Steinberg just weeks earlier—I wound up going there because of Bob. About a year or so later, I also began performing at the Improv after I'd joined The Ace Trucking Company improv troupe.

SHELLEY ACKERMAN:

The best way to describe it is to say the waters parted when Robert came in. But he was an acquired taste, too, because he could do so many things and there was such an incredible level of intelligence. With guys like Andy Kaufman and Robin Williams, it's like you accepted their zaniness at face value, and then you could just follow along and get stoned. But with Klein, it was a different trip. First off, he's funny, he's New York, and he's Jewish. Then he's political and then he becomes musical. He morphs into all these different things, so it's a different kind of journey that requires an appreciation of history and cultural context. With Klein, it's kind of like watching *Jeopardy!*. Both have been around for a long time, but not everybody gets them without a certain level of refinement.

JIMMIE WALKER:

The waters parting is an accurate description. And the clouds, the moon, and the sun, too, for that matter, because Robert was *the* guy and he pretty much got to do whatever he wanted whenever he wanted. It's like you'd be standing there and Budd would say, "Okay, Walker, you're next." But then, Robert would come in unannounced and you knew what was going to happen next because Budd would always say, "Okay, let's push you back."

It really didn't matter who else was there or how long you'd been waiting to go on either. There were definitely some periods where that caused some friction and resentment among the other comics, because at first you thought he was only going to do ten or fifteen minutes and then he'd wind up being onstage for an hour and a half. But there was never any doubt that he was the Improv's anchor—or that he would kill every time.

JOHN DEBELLIS:

Robert was another comic who was a generation before me, but whenever he came in to do a guest spot, you wanted to watch whether you were on that evening's lineup or not. My writing is totally different from his, but for some reason he took a shine to it and he tried to get me on a television show once. It didn't happen for whatever reason, but then another time he was doing *The Tonight Show* and he recommended me to Johnny Carson during one of the commercial breaks. I mean, how many guys would do that? But Robert did. Every time I see him to this day, he is always a class act.

RICHARD LEWIS:

It's understandable why Budd loved Robert so much, because he ruled the roost and he should have. Robert was just phenomenal. I'm sure all of us who were Budd's favorites aggravated the other comics who weren't. I guess I was one of the lucky ones and it later dawned on me what a powerful gig Budd had.

JUDY ORBACH:

Budd had Robert's album *Child of the 50's* hanging on the front wall of the New York club right by the door so you saw it as soon as you walked in. I had this massive crush on him at the time because he was so sexy, not to mention brilliantly funny and smart. One night in the late seventies or early eighties, we had this birthday party for him and I still have pictures of them bringing up the cake while he was onstage performing.

Robert loved me because he's got the musician side of him with the harmonica and I'm a singer, too. A lot of times, he would wander in after we'd already closed when the chairs were going up on the tables and we'd get up and perform together. Most of the time, it was just us. He'd play the harmonica and I'd play the piano and sing.

He used to call me "singer girl." We were always friendly, but we don't talk all that often because he's still in New York and I live in LA now. But one day about ten or fifteen years ago, I happened to be at a taping of *Hollywood Squares* and Robert was one of the panelists. He might not remember this, but either before or after the taping, we ran into one another backstage. As soon as he saw me, he came up to me and said, "Singer girl, you haven't changed a bit." Of course I had, but I'll never forget that day. It was like déjà vu.

TOM DREESEN:

I've always thought he was a very interesting character by equal measure as much as he has material out the yin yang. He was a major influence on me comedically even though we're around the same age and our humor is completely different as far as styles go. Early in my career, I remember sneaking into this little club in Chicago called the Quiet Knight and just being completely blown away by how conversational and off the cuff he was.

I'm paraphrasing here, but he went on and did this ten- or fifteen-minute bit about cars. The setup went something like, "I was on my way over here and I'm standing in between two parked cars and this guy blows his horn." I forgot what the punch line was, but the crowd went wild, although at first I kept thinking his act was all ad-lib. A couple of hours later, he did his second show, which I'd stuck around for, and I heard him do the bit again, which was basically exactly the same. That's the essence of Robert Klein's brilliance—and something I always told comedians from then on—that it's a conversation and not a presentation. I mean, of course it's your act, but it's your job not to make it look like it is.

It was such a fundamental lesson in comedy and I've never forgotten it. There's also a certain dichotomy about Robert and his humor. I don't mean this in a bad way, but it's just a fact and I'll give you an example. Robert always used to score well on *The Tonight Show*—I mean, I don't think he ever had a bad set in his life. But he's never done well in places like Las Vegas, Reno, Tahoe, or Atlantic City. I didn't realize just how true it was at the time, but one night I was working at Harrah's in Lake Tahoe when this guy came up to me afterwards and said, "I just saw Robert Klein across the street and he didn't get any laughs."

I was like, "You've got to be kidding me. He's one of the best comedians in the country."

The following night I went across the street, and as it turned out, this guy was right—Klein didn't score. As a fellow comic, it was very painful to watch. This is when it occurred to me that he's a former schoolteacher who sometimes uses words that most people don't in their everyday conversation. At first, I was thinking to myself that maybe Robert was just too intelligent for his own good. But then I saw him on *The Tonight Show* a few weeks later and he absolutely fractured the audience. That's another important lesson I think he taught me and a lot of other comics: the importance of finding the right audience and playing up to them.

JOE PISCOPO:

Robert's influence really didn't come to bear on me until I began doing stand-up in the midseventies and I went to the Improv. The funny thing about being a comic when you're just starting out is that you sometimes don't feel like you can be as funny if you went to college. I know that sounds like an odd statement, but it's true—especially since some of the best guys in this business barely made it out of high school. It's not like having a formal education gives you an edge, which in some ways it does. But I went to college and so did Robert, who went to the Yale School of Drama, even though he didn't graduate. The point is, he went to an Ivy League school and was at the top of his game. Watching Klein at the Improv was like seeing the first "educated" comic and that was a huge influence on all of us—especially somebody like me.

SEVENTEEN
Locking Horns
with David Brenner

As much as I loved Robert Klein I can't say the same about David Brenner, who was also starting to break out around the same time.

In fact, he's the one comedian whom I never got and still don't get to this day. Do I ever look back now and think, "Maybe I missed something about David?" Never, but I will say that he was probably one of the most generous comics who ever lived. He was largely responsible for Freddie Prinze and Jimmie Walker getting their own sitcoms, and I think you'd be hard-pressed to find many people in the business who have something bad to say about him. I'm not trying to take anything away from that or diminish what he did either. For me, though—and admittedly, a lot of it has to do with my own personal taste—I just didn't get him.

Not only did he never strike me as being funny at all, in many ways I always felt David was almost too intelligent for his own good. One of the things that used to bug me the most was this obsession he always had about taping his act. Not that there's anything wrong with that. I mean, Robert Klein did it and that was fine. But David always made this big fucking issue out of taping his act. He used to say, "Robert Klein tapes his act. I'm going to tape mine." And boy, did he tape it. I also used to say, "I bet David has all of his tapes in order."

Though we never got along, what cinched things was one night in the early seventies when he stormed into the club demanding to be treated like Robert Klein. I was absolutely livid and it was all I could do to keep a civil tongue.

Still, I calmly tried to explain to him that Robert always called to ask if he could go on before he even came in, which was true. But David wouldn't hear anything of it and he'd already been filling in regularly for Johnny Carson, so he just looked at me and said, "Fine, I'll go someplace else." Then he stormed out of the club. After that, he went uptown to Catch A Rising Star, which had just opened, and literally made that place.

I will get back to Catch, and I don't hold any animosity towards the owner Rick Newman either, although at the time I thought David was doing it just to get back at me. At any rate, about three or four weeks after I'd opened the LA club in 1975, David came in just as Freddie Prinze was about to go on and asked that I put him on first. Not only was Freddie starring in *Chico and the Man*, which was one of the top-rated sitcoms at the time, he was also an investor in my new club. But that was beside the point. I wasn't about to kowtow to David, especially after what had gone down in New York.

Nevertheless, it was a very polite exchange, probably the most courteous we had ever had. In fact, David seemed like an entirely different person. He said, "Let's let bygones be bygones." I was all for that, and I was completely open to giving him a second chance. But then when I tried explaining to him that Freddie was there and we also had another improv group called The Credibility Gap auditioning, it was the same David all over again. He just looked at me and said, "Never mind." Then he walked out and that was basically that, although in the years before his death in 2014 we did see each other a couple of times in New York. Once was at the Plaza Hotel where I was staying with my wife, Alix. The second time was at a Friars Club roast and we were always cordial. But no, David and I never got along and he never came back to the Improv.

TOM DREESEN:

I remember being at the LA Improv not long after Budd opened and David coming in when he was guest hosting for Johnny Carson and asking to go on. I'm paraphrasing here, but Budd basically looked at him and said, "I'm filled up tonight." Well, everybody knows that when a major star walks in, you make room for them. That's one of the biggest gripes of all comedians—like, "Hey, I was supposed to do a set the other night and this other guy walks in and the fucker does an hour and a half." Budd actually turned Brenner down, so I can certainly understand him getting upset no matter what their history had been.

MARVIN BRAVERMAN:

I'll tell you the backstory of the history between David and Budd, because I was part of it. I'm the one who begged Budd to put David on in the first place and David conned me. I know he's gone now, but whenever I'd do a television show he'd say to me, "How come you only did five minutes? I did ten." I didn't like his cocky attitude. Whenever I'd see David at the Improv or wherever, he'd always be writing his material out on a notepad. I don't know if this was intentional or not, but the script was so tiny you could barely read it.

Years later—several days before Johnny Carson died in 2005—we were both in Cedars-Sinai hospital at the same time. I was there having a procedure done, and one morning around 4 AM, I wheeled myself upstairs to the eighth floor where Johnny was staying. No one was at the nurse's station, so I rolled myself into Johnny's suite, which was down at the other end of the hall.

Johnny was fast asleep, but I tried to talk to him anyway. I said, "Johnny, how do you feel? It's me. Marvin Braverman. Do you remember me? I did *The Tonight Show*."

A few seconds later, he opened his eyes and said, "No, I don't remember you."

I said, "I have a question for you."

His voice was barely audible, but he managed to get the words out that he was going to call security if I didn't leave immediately.

I knew he didn't have the strength to do it, so I said, "I'll pull your drip out."

That's when he muttered, "Okay."

"Why did you like Brenner and not me?" I asked.

There was a brief pause and then Johnny said, "Because he wasn't funny and I could be funnier than him."

To which I replied, "Thanks, Johnny!" And then I left. True story!

ROBERT KLEIN:

I was never around David and Budd at the same time, so anything I ever heard about their feud was secondhand. I will say that I always respected David even though we only met a handful of times. One occasion that comes to mind was sometime in either the mid or late seventies. I was doing this PBS show where I played a chef of some sort cutting up a pie and David happened to be the associate producer. I think we were filming it at WNET, which is the local PBS affiliate in New York.

Even though we were both established already, David came up to me afterwards and said, "You know, I'd love to be doing what you're doing." He was very nice about it and he had a warm smile on his face.

I said, "Really?" That was about it. I just remember that he struck me as this quiet, kind of studious guy.

ED BLUESTONE, screenwriter and former comedian:

I never had a problem with David personally, but I was never crazy about him either. He could talk about himself endlessly— especially if he'd just done a halfway decent set someplace. You'd think his appearance had been the equivalent of the bombing of Nagasaki or something. He'd just go on and on and on about himself and I found it a bit annoying. David wasn't a bad guy. He was just egotistical.

LIZ TORRES:

I witnessed David and Budd butting heads almost from the first moment he ever came into the Improv. The reason they fought was because Budd wouldn't put David on during prime time for whatever reason, and David resented that. I was privy to his anger, and whenever he came in, he'd just sit over in the corner and brood. David and Budd barely ever spoke to each other.

Maybe it was because I'm a woman, but all the comics felt they could confide in me. David was no exception and he would start complaining to me about whatever particular gripe he had with Budd, but then he'd stop because he knew he shouldn't be discussing this with me. And then the next day or whenever he came in again after that, he'd start complaining to me all over again.

DANNY AIELLO:

Years later, after I became an actor and I was doing *Gemini* on Broadway, David came to see the show one night and I was fuckin' stunned. But when I was at the Improv and I'd be filling in for Budd as the emcee, Budd would say to me, without any equivocation, that he didn't want me putting David on during prime time. Sometimes I'd do it anyway because I felt terrible if David was there when I was substituting and there was an opening. It wasn't that I was trying to go against Budd's wishes necessarily. I just thought that if he didn't know, he wouldn't mind.

MARTY NADLER:

Not knowing very much about the ins and outs of their personal history at the time, I always thought it was a bit of a mystery why Budd and David didn't get along. It was a mystery because whenever David *did* go on, he would do very well, but Budd still wouldn't put him on during prime time. From our vantage point, though, Budd was like a God—and, of course, he was still the key for the rest of us getting on, so we never questioned it. I mean, we were never going to go up to him and say, "Why aren't you giving David better spots?" But in the back of our minds, we were always wondering why, and to this day I'm not exactly sure what his reasons were. It very well could have been that Budd simply didn't think David was funny.

JIMMIE WALKER:

Brenner was the guy who first told me about the Improv. Regardless of whatever happened between him and Budd, I loved Brenner. He was my mentor and I wouldn't be where I am today without him.

The other thing about Brenner was that he always had plans. None of us were really like that when we were starting out. It was just about getting stage time, or getting better and getting chicks, or whatever. Brenner had a plan—and he had the exact dates of when he was going to do whatever he was planning to do—things that never really occurred to guys like me. We'd hear him talking about this stuff and we'd be like, "What is this guy talking about?"

Don't get me wrong, Budd and I also had our issues, but if I had to guess, I think Budd may have felt a little intimidated by David for whatever reason. David was a few years older than all of us and he knew more than we did. But I also think he thought he knew more than Budd, and Budd may have been insulted by that.

DANNY AIELLO:

David was the guy all the comedians came to for advice, and I think that might have been part of the beef Budd had with him.

Here's another thing about David, and it's really interesting. Once I was at his apartment and he showed me these metal filing cabinets he had. Then he opened the drawers and pulled out these index cards, with each one detailing the date he did a certain performance, the exact time of night he did it, and people's reactions to a specific joke. It was the most amazing thing I had ever seen.

RICK OVERTON, screenwriter, actor, and comedian:

I gave Brenner a tag line that he used in a joke once. The joke was, "Did you ever notice that when a guy sticks a coat hanger into a car door somebody will ask, 'Did you lock your keys into your car?'"

I threw him the tag line where he added, "Thank God the top was down or I never would have gotten in." I came up with that, Brenner used it, and it worked on one of the late-night shows, so he's responsible for the first time I ever threw a guy a line and it worked on television. He gave me the confidence to think that somewhere down the line I'd do this again—some variant of that—and I did. It was all because of Brenner.

JEFF FOXWORTHY:

I never met Brenner personally, but I remember watching an interview with him somewhere not long after I started doing stand-up. He was telling this supposedly true story about how he'd done a show in Las Vegas and two ladies in the audience didn't laugh. So he went back to his hotel room, wrote a new act, and then the next night the same ladies were there and they still didn't laugh. This went on for like four or five nights in a row and the punch line was that they didn't laugh because they didn't speak English. Well, even at this point—as young as I was—I knew Brenner was full of shit. I knew there was no way he could be writing a new act every night because I knew how difficult writing stand-up was.

ALAN BURSKY, comedian:

I never will forget a night back in 1975 or 1976 when David took me, Freddie Prinze, and a bunch of other comics out to eat. It was at this place in LA called Chez Deni that used to be Dean Martin's restaurant in the sixties. Basically, it was this upscale diner where you could go and have eggs at one in the morning. Anyway, David took us there and it was right when Freddie was at the peak of his fame on *Chico and the Man* and David had just done a TV pilot that hadn't been picked up.

Keep in mind that David and Freddie had been great friends, but on this particular night, David was absolutely seething about all the success that Freddie was having and he wasn't. I remember what he said like it was yesterday. He said, "Freddie needs to fall down a flight of stairs. He's getting awful cocky." I think it drove David crazy that Freddie became such a big star overnight.

Right up until the day he died, David always had a big chip on his shoulder. I remember hearing a story that, just before he got sick, Robert Klein's manager wanted to package Robert in a show with David. But David didn't want to do it because he said that Robert's audience was too old. When I told Budd this, he said, "David Brenner is delusional to the end."

EIGHTEEN
Richard Lewis

T hough I may have had a rocky relationship with David Brenner personally, his generosity towards other comedians ultimately benefited us in many tangible ways. One of the biggest acts was Richard Lewis. Not only did David lend him $1,000 so he could quit his day job to pursue stand-up full-time, he's also the one who first told him about the Improv—and advised him not to try and get on until he was ready. When that time came, Richard was another one of my favorites from the beginning, even despite having a less-than-stellar second set his first night.

RICHARD LEWIS:

I forget which, but I'd either read about the Improv or heard about the Improv. When I finally decided to become a stand-up comedian, I decided to go check it out, which is when I was befriended by my pal David Brenner. He became my mentor, and he told me this was *the* place. Then he forbade me from going on there during open mic night until he thought I was ready.

We became best friends instantly after that and I took about six months playing every conceivable dive you can imagine. I was so driven that sometimes I'd drive a hundred miles round-trip and I must have performed 340 nights that first year.

Basically I worked at any place that had a microphone, but then there were better ones. The Champagne Gallery down in the Village where a lot of other Improv guys worked was my favorite, and it was the first time I ever went onstage.

By the time I started doing stand-up, I knew Lenny Bruce's albums. I also had Richard Pryor's and Robert Klein's routines memorized by heart and I'd watched every comedian on Ed Sullivan and *The Tonight Show*, so I knew what the craft should be and I knew what the high bars and the low bars were.

After about five or six months of doing hundreds of shows anyplace I could—and where I was head and shoulders above everybody—Brenner came to see me one night. He had a gig someplace nearby, and after watching me do my set, he walked me outside and said, "You're ready."

I'd been there before to watch, but I want to say that my first night performing at the Improv was sometime in the fall of 1971. I'll never forget this, because after my set, Budd walked onstage and he put his arm around me and said: "We have our new 1971 Rookie of the Year." It was a defining moment in my life—and an educational one—because the regular show started at ten o'clock and Budd informed me that he was bringing me up again.

This particular open mic night, I think, was on a Monday, and I had an incredible set. What I should have done is just gone home afterwards with my college girlfriend or tried to dig up enough change for a glass of wine at Mama Leone's around the corner, but when Budd asked me if I wanted to go on during the regular show, of course I said yes. What ended up happening was that I didn't go on until two o'clock in the morning and I bombed.

A total of four people were there and it was an impossible audience, which was the high and the low of it, but Budd still made me a regular. The exact way he phrased it was, "You can come here and perform anytime you want to." I knew that to become a regular at the Improv meant that I had made it. After that, I didn't even think of turning back.

Richard came in to audition for me on one of our Monday open mic nights in 1971, and completely unbeknownst to me he brought in some of his friends to watch him make his big debut. When a new comic does this in order to get laughs, we typically call these people "bringers." In fact, many comedy clubs today even have a standing policy where they'll only put a new comic on if he or she brings a certain amount of people, which is something that we've never done at the Improv and is a practice I personally abhor. I've always felt it was unsavory just on basic principle. Moreover, I think it dilutes things. My feeling has always been that if a comic can't get an honest laugh in front of a group of complete strangers—no matter how raw or inexperienced they are—it's usually a pretty sure sign that there's either something wrong with their act or they're not ready to go on.

This isn't to say they won't get better, because plenty of comics have. One particular case in point is Eddie Murphy, whom my first wife, Silver, turned down in New York years later for being too vulgar when he first auditioned for her, as I probably would have done, even though he eventually performed at the Improv in LA. While I'm sure there are many readers who will take exception with this, the truth is that I've always found Eddie's use of the F word to be excessive and often without merit. Nor have I ever particularly been a huge fan of his stand-up either, although I do think he's one of the best impressionists and comedic actors of all time hands down.

I'll also admit that I didn't like Chris Rock at first either. As a matter of fact, when Chris first came to my attention in the late eighties, my initial reaction was that he was little more than an arrogant Richard Pryor rip-off, although when he came back about a year later he absolutely blew me away, and from then on I've been a huge fan.

But in Richard Lewis's case, I could tell he had the goods immediately, plus he was never dirty. What's more, he had great delivery and timing, even if some of his material was slightly underdeveloped. When he went on that first time, it wasn't just his friends who were laughing. He had almost the entire room in stitches, something that I quickly became very highly attuned to early on after we began using comedians and I learned how to gauge an audience.

When Richard got done performing, I told him to stick around for the next show, which started at ten o'clock. The only problem was that none of his friends decided to stay, and so his second set that night wasn't as strong, and the later audiences weren't nearly as responsive as the first, although it wasn't until a while later that he finally told me about having his friends there during the first set.

Richard and I became pretty tight after that, which we've remained over the years. In fact, just as I was getting ready to embark on my move to Los Angeles in early 1975 to open up a West Coast branch of the Improv, Richard co-wrote and starred in an NBC movie of the week called *Diary of a Young Comic*, where one of the characters was a "Budd

Friedman type" that he invited yours truly to play. Although I only had a couple of lines, it was a blast. But then when we got done filming my scene, one of the production assistants came up to me and asked me to sign a release, which meant I wasn't going to get paid, so I said, "What about my union?"

When she asked me what union I belonged to, I told her the Screen Actors Guild, which I didn't, but I was also determined not to let Paramount, the production company that was producing Richard's film, get away without paying me, even though I still wasn't paying my own comics by this point. I also went out that same afternoon and joined SAG for $500. The amount I received for basically playing myself in Richard's movie was $365. Even so, doing the film was a joy for me— just as it always has been working with Richard Lewis.

NINETEEN

The Hippest Room in America

ALAN ZWEIBEL:

In 1973, I was this Jewish kid working as a deli clerk in Queens and writing jokes for these Catskills comics for seven dollars a pop. When I was working at the deli and we weren't busy, I would scribble down jokes on the backs of little grocery sacks they used to sell cigarettes in. Then what I'd do is go home and type them up at my parents' house on Long Island where I was living at the time.

But slicing meat in a deli got old pretty quickly, and when I went to an employment agency in Manhattan to look for another day job, I told the guy who interviewed me that I wrote comedy and he asked me if I'd heard of the Improv. I hadn't, but not long after, I took my then girlfriend and we went as customers. That very first night on the same lineup, I saw Richard Lewis, Elayne Boosler, Jimmie Walker, and Gabe Kaplan.

I remember immediately thinking to myself that these were my peers. Richard Lewis was frenetically hilarious. Elayne back then was real sort of sexy looking, although she scared me a little bit. She had this loud voice, but she was really funny and smart. She had a woman's point of view that was different than I was used to from the women on *The Ed Sullivan Show*. It wasn't the ugly girl who couldn't get a date.

Instead, she talked about guys who were inadequate in bed, which was a stark contrast to the guys I was used to writing for in the Catskills. They were always about: "My wife wouldn't fuck me because she had her hair done today." But here at the Improv, Elayne was talking about men who wouldn't satisfy her. It was guy stuff from a woman about guys.

I forget what Gabe Kaplan did that night, but my girlfriend and I were seated at a table that was pretty close to the stage.

I remember Jimmie Walker asking me what I did for a living, but I didn't have the balls to say I was a comedy writer. Number one, I didn't really consider myself one yet even though I'd had some minor success. And number two, I didn't want to be ridiculed by him. So I told him I was a dentist and he did some really shitty dentist jokes about me.

BOB "UNCLE DIRTY" ALTMAN:

Budd and his first wife, Silver, saw me perform at the Café Au Go Go down in Greenwich Village in the late sixties and they immediately asked me to start performing at the Improv. Being there was like being a child wrapped up in a big security blanket every night—women, free booze, and adulation. How could you resist that? You went in dressed in Levi's, a T-shirt, and a pair of comfortable sneakers, and then you just got up in front of a mic and started bullshitting in front of a bunch strangers. It was the ideal gig. You didn't have to get dressed up; you just told everybody what was on your mind and they treated you like you were important. It was a fucking dream, man.

Even as we continued to live hand-to-mouth financially, the early 1970s would be magically artistic years for us. It also wasn't long after Richard Lewis's arrival in the fall of 1971 when I began to realize that, by extension, the Improv was slowly being recast as the progenitor of a new kind of showcase comedy club that hadn't existed before. While we never officially stopped presenting singers who remained paradoxically popular and would continue to perform into the next decade, inevitably their once-dominant presence would be significantly diminished and eventually ended.

A lot of that had to do with the fact stand-up itself was undergoing a radical metamorphosis and becoming hipper in the wake of America's political social upheaval in the mid to late 1960s. Added to this was the other fact that comics—most of whom were having a difficult time finding live audiences to work to at old Greenwich Village hangouts that were either closing or switching to mostly rock 'n' roll formats—needed a place to go and came to the Improv.

First, there were the already-established and soon-to-be-established regulars and semi-regulars like Robert Klein, George Carlin, Lily Tomlin, Stiller and Meara, Rodney Dangerfield, Richard Pryor, Professor

Irwin Corey, Jimmy Martinez, Ron Carey, J.J. Barry, Martin Friedberg, and Steve Landesberg, as well as newcomers Gabe Kaplan, Marvin Braverman, Ed Bluestone, Lenny Schultz, Billy Saluga, Marty Nadler, and Mike Preminger.

After that, and in no particular order, this list would go on to include Jay Leno, Richard Lewis, Freddie Prinze, Bob Altman, Jimmie Walker, Bob Shaw, Bruce Mahler, Elayne Boosler, and Andy Kaufman, as well as such popular comedy teams as Overton & Sullivan and Weeden, Finkle & Fay, who wrote a parody to commemorate our tenth anniversary. In what was often compared to a high school for humor, each year's incoming class of cutups and freshly minted graduates would both collectively and individually permanently catapult the Improv into the American pop culture hall of fame.

The press also began to take notice, beginning with a profile by Calvin Trillin in *The New Yorker* and a five-page spread in the New York *Daily News* Sunday magazine on November 29, 1973. It ran with the headline, "Let's Hear it for the Improv."

After that, there was seldom a week that went by when someone wasn't writing something about us—and me—after I became one of the hosts of music impresario Don Kirshner's nationally syndicated NBC variety show, *Don Kirshner's Rock Concert*, which premiered that same year. This was in addition to the Improv's occasional big-screen cameo appearances such as in the 1977 film version of Neil Simon's *The Goodbye Girl* starring Marsha Mason and Richard Dreyfuss.

It's notable that several years before, we got another major boost when director Michael Blum filmed what would be Richard Pryor's first—and comedy's first ever—recorded stand-up special called *Richard Pryor: Live & Smokin'* at the Improv on April 29, 1971. Shot in black-and-white, it was first seen in a 1985 VHS release. At the time, Richard was still several years away from becoming America's biggest comedy superstar. But in the four years since his self-imposed exile in Berkeley, California, following the notorious 1967 incident where he stormed off-stage during the middle of a performance at Las Vegas's Aladdin hotel, he had also long moved away from doing clean, innocuous material towards an act that was dirtier and rawer than anybody had ever seen. More importantly, though, he had never done his act on film. He talked about growing up in a brothel ("That's where I first met white dudes—they used to come to our neighborhood to help the economy"), race, and experimenting with homosexuality. Almost by default, this pretty much became the template for all other comedy concert films that followed.

As a result, the dynamic at the Improv would get even more competitive as the years wore on, albeit a lot funnier. This was especially evident on Mondays when I held auditions for our open mic nights. The way we did it was through a lottery system where each comic would put his or her name on a little piece of paper that would go into a fedora. Some days I almost couldn't get through the front door because there were so many people blocking the entrance. There would literally be hundreds of young hopefuls lined up around the block.

And so it went, although everybody was pretty much just another face in the crowd when they first got to the Improv. And they all have war stories, particularly the comics. Undoubtedly, my three most favorite are Jay Leno, Freddie Prinze, and Andy Kaufman. Actually, Jay and Freddie auditioned on the same night. There was also the time that Larry David, who had never done stand-up before and was in the audience as a customer, came up to me out of the blue and asked if he could go on—all of which I'll get back to. But first, here are the stories of a couple of other comedians because they are also interesting.

TOM DREESEN:

Man, do I remember my first time at the Improv and meeting Budd Friedman, who later became one of my dearest friends. I grew up in Chicago, and back in the late sixties I was part of America's first—and last—biracial comedy team. This was over forty years ago and there's never been one since.

I had been an insurance salesman and I joined the Jaycees, a civic group in my neighborhood. I wrote a drug education program where I taught grade school children about the dangers of drug abuse, with humor. That's how I met my future comedy partner, Tim Reid, who was also a Jaycee. Tim later went on to major fame playing the hipster disc jockey Venus Flytrap in the late-seventies CBS sitcom *WKRP in Cincinnati*.

While we were in the Jaycees, we began doing funny bits together during the lectures that were very well received. One day after the lecture, a little eighth-grade girl said, "You guys are funny. You ought to become a comedy team." We took her suggestion and developed our act and we rehearsed and rehearsed it. The only problem was we had no place to do it, so we'd volunteer to provide the entertainment at any charity we could find. And then we'd wander into all of these little jazz clubs around Chicago asking the musicians if we could go on after they finished. Sometimes they would even say, "We're going to take a break, but we've got a little comedy team who are going to entertain you while we're gone." Usually, the people would get up and leave. But it still gave us an opportunity to try out our material until I wound up starting Chicago's first comedy club at a place called Le Pub on Lincoln Avenue.

Meanwhile, I'd either heard or read about this club in New York called the Improvisation where you could work every single night even though it was for free. Around that same time, Tim wrote a letter to Craig Tennis who was the talent coordinator at *The Tonight Show*. (Later, he changed my life overnight after putting me on in the early 1970s.) Craig's a great guy who was very approachable, which was extremely rare even back then considering all the power he had. The even more incredible thing was that he wrote Tim back telling us to come see him if we were ever in New York.

Needless to say, we were on a Greyhound bus that same night, but when we auditioned for Craig the following afternoon at his office at NBC, it didn't go well. Craig, being the guy he is, was very nice about it. He said, "Look, there's a guy named Murray Becker who handles George Carlin. Let me see if I can get you an appointment to go see him."

So we did, and Murray couldn't have been nicer. He said, "Craig sent you over and you're the first black-and-white comedy team. That's interesting. Where can I see you work?"

When I told him we were going back to Chicago, that's when he offered to call Budd to see if we could get on at the Improv that night. I remember meeting Budd and just completely being taken aback by how insensitive he was that first time. I'm not even sure if we shook hands, but when Murray introduced us he was like, "I've got so-and-so and so and you'll follow so-and-so and so-and-so."

The bit we were planning to do that night was a spoof of *The Dating Game*. The setup was that I played the announcer and Tim played the bachelor. Then I'd put a wig on and I became the girl, which required two stools. But when I asked Budd about it, he gruffly informed me that he only had one. And when I asked him if he had two microphones, he absolutely bit my head off. He said, "Two microphones! What the hell do you need two microphones for? What do you think this is, Radio City Music Hall or something?"

It was just awful—and so was our performance for this big-shot manager that night. Since we only had one microphone, we had to pass it back and forth, which made things awkward and completely screwed up our timing.

Just as bad was the fact that he gave us a chair and stool instead of the two stools the same size that we needed, so Tim wound up sitting high and I was seated low. The whole thing was an absolute disaster, and Budd was as sympathetic as a doorknob that night. Like I said, he's since become one of my dearest friends, but back then he didn't give a fuck if you bombed.

MIKE PREMINGER:

I can't put a specific age on it, but I always liked stand-up comedy and I wanted to be a comic from as long as I can remember. What sealed it for me was watching *The Steve Allen Show* as a kid and seeing all those guys he had, like Don Knotts, Tom Poston, Bill Dana, and Louie Nye. To this day, I don't think there's anybody who can talk and work an audience better than Steve Allen could. He made it look so easy but also enjoyable, and that's what made me want to do it.

After high school, I flunked the New York City College entrance exam and joined the army because they were going to draft me anyway. I spent a year and a half in Korea, and after I got back, I got a job at NBC giving studio tours in New York. It was great fun, but there really wasn't a lot to show because in those days the only things being produced there besides *The Tonight Show* were the news, soap operas, and the musical-variety show *Hullabaloo*. The tours were about an hour, but mine were an hour and a half to an hour and forty-five minutes. The reason was that I'd do stand-up in between each stop and the tourists just loved it.

But the executives at NBC didn't—even though I later got a job in the advertising department, which I hated. This was 1969 and I had a big birthday coming up, so one day I decided to start doing stand-up professionally. When I gave my bosses at NBC my two-weeks' notice, they couldn't get rid of me fast enough. They liked me, but their response was, "Just get out of here. Go away." So I cleared out my things, and that very same night I went down to this little club in Greenwich Village called the Champagne Gallery. It was a weeknight and it was slow, but they had about fifteen people there—including a table of four guys in the back who looked to be about fifty years old, maybe more.

So I'm sitting there when one of them from this group gets up onstage and starts telling jokes, although you couldn't really call them that because it was the worst stuff I'd ever heard. It was absolutely horrendous—just the most sophomoric things like, "I went to the store and the milk fell over on my head." But these guys were all doubled over laughing like he was Don Rickles or something. At first, I was like, "Gee, I guess comedy's not all that hard if these guys are laughing." But as it turned out, they were all friends and it took me another four times of going back before I finally worked up enough courage to ask the owner if I could go on, which I did.

In the meantime, I'd also heard of the Improv, which was the place to go in 1969. I remember thinking to myself that if I could ever get on there then I'd have reached the top. By the time I finally went there myself, it must have been at least two or three months later. And it was another two or three months after that before I even spoke to anybody, much less tried to go on. I just sat there like a piece of furniture watching the other comics until one night around two thirty in the morning the guy who was the emcee came up to me and said, "You're on next." Even though I hadn't said a word, somehow somebody must have tipped him off that I was a comedian. That somebody was Danny Aiello. At first I resisted, but then he almost physically grabbed my hand and I did just fine.

In the weeks and months that followed, it didn't make things any easier when it came to persuading Danny's boss Budd to put me on earlier. The thing about going on late was that there was hardly much of an audience, so you'd always have a much tougher time getting laughs and gauging your material. This didn't faze Budd in the least, and I'm not exaggerating when I say that this went on for months and months and months and months. It didn't even matter what time I got there. Let's say I arrived at nine o'clock; Budd still wouldn't put me on until two-thirty or a quarter to three in the morning, by which point he usually wasn't even there, so there was no way for him to tell if I was getting better or not.

But that was how I learned the craft, and on a good night there might be seven people—mostly a couple of hookers, their pimps, and a few drunks from out of town. They even used to put me on when the waitresses were putting the chairs up on the tables and this guy named Hy was delivering the next day's bread order.

But that was my stage time. Afterwards, we'd all go over to this all-night coffee shop around the corner called the Camelot for eggs—where just as they were delivering the order, one of the waiters would almost always decide it was time to start mopping the floor. Ever eat eggs with the smell of ammonia around your feet? It kind of ruins the taste. But that was the life of an Improv comedian back then. And we all loved it because we'd say to ourselves, "This is what I do and I'm with my peers and we're all struggling and we're all going to eat eggs at four in the morning until Budd gives us better spots."

MARTY NADLER:

I love Mike, don't get me wrong, but he was always a little bit of a whiner—especially when it came to ordering eggs at the Camelot, which was almost always our destination of choice after the club closed. The Camelot was open all night. Sometimes we'd go even later and here's what would happen. We'd sit down, open the menu, and even though he'd order eggs practically every time, he'd still say, "Eggs! I have eggs at home."

We'd all go, "Here they cook them for you, Mike. They bring them out and they even clean the plate afterwards." The other thing was that he was always the last one to order, so we'd have to wait, which drove us all insane.

On one particular winter evening after we'd finished eating, none of us wanted to leave because it was freezing out and we would've had to walk over to Columbus Circle to catch the D train back up to the Bronx where we all lived. So instead, we huddled into the vestibule inside the entrance of the restaurant waiting for somebody to make a move, when all of a sudden Mike looked out and saw a police car pulling up Eighth Avenue. There were two officers in the front but no one in the back so Mike goes, "Why can't we get a ride with the cops?" We all started to laugh our asses off like a bunch of hyenas, because none of us could get over the fact that Mike actually thought they would stop and pick us up.

It was just about then that the car stopped and one of the police officers rolled down the window and said, "What are you, a bunch of comedians?" After this, he got really pissed, because his comment made us laugh even harder and now he thought we were making fun of him. It was hysterical.

As far as getting stage time at the Improv went, every night you'd go down and it was like being a longshoreman waiting at the docks to see whether you'd get on the boat or not. Sometimes you did and sometimes you didn't, but that was the deal and you either bought into it or you didn't buy into it.

I still wasn't scheduling any formal lineups. The system was very simple. If a comic walked in and there was nobody there, usually I'd put them on next. But if Rodney Dangerfield came in, I'd go, "Oops, you're on after him." And then if Robert Klein, Bette Midler, or someone else of equal stature happened to come in while Rodney was on, the lowest man or woman on the totem pole that night usually wouldn't get on until probably three in the morning. I'll be the first to admit that it was no democracy. It was the furthest thing from being a democracy without being a totalitarian state.

ED BLUESTONE:

God knows I paid my dues as much as anyone else, but you know something—one of the things I respected most about Budd was that the Improv was always a meritocracy compared to most other places.

To Budd's credit, if you were one of his regular performers and you'd worked your way in and he believed in your talent, by and large he wouldn't knock you off just because a guy who was on some television show walked in. Of course, there were exceptions when it came to the big marquee names like Robert Klein, Rodney Dangerfield, or Bette Midler, where he had no choice, but he was basically very loyal.

TWENTY
The Improv's Gentle Giant

B esides all of the wonderfully gifted performers we've had over the years, I've also had the great fortune of having some equally terrific people working behind the scenes, one of whom was actor Danny Aiello. Danny was the New York Improv's bouncer from the late sixties until the early seventies, and like many of the other good fortunes I've had in my life, both meeting and hiring him were complete flukes.

As I've said before, I've always loved sports, so when the club was presented with the opportunity to have a unisex softball team in the Broadway Show League in 1968, I immediately jumped at the chance. Established in 1955, as the name suggests it originally started as a way for cast members of the various Broadway and Off-Broadway shows to informally gather and blow off steam between the Wednesday afternoon matinee and when they had to return to the theater for their evening performance. By the late 1960s, however, the league had begun to relax its rules and started admitting people who were on the fringes, meaning that they had some sort of affiliation with the theater—which the Improv did, not only because we were located in the theater district but also because of the kind of club we were.

Not only were we invited to join, I'm also enormously proud to say that the team endured long after I moved to California in 1975 until the original New York club closed in 1992, and that during that time, it boasted a list of players that included Larry David, Jerry Seinfeld, Paul Reiser, Paul Provenza, Joe Piscopo, Sarah Silverman, Judy Gold, and Dave Attell, just to name a few.

During the years I was still there, I was the pitcher, and while we never set any world's records, we had a blast. Our seasons typically ran from mid-spring until early summer, and our games with the various Broadway shows that were currently running were played at the Heckscher Fields just east of Columbus Circle in Central Park.

One of our first opponents, believe it or not, was none other than Woody Allen, who was then starring in a play on Broadway called *Don't Drink the Water*, which ran for two years and had 598 performances. I'm not sure if Woody ever swung a bat, but his show had a team and we played them. He was also there on the day of the game, and so was my mother, although she was more impressed by the fact that one of my guys was an actor on *As the World Turns*, her favorite soap opera.

I don't remember who won or what the score was, but as we were warming up, I noticed Danny Aiello, whose face I vaguely recognized because I'd seen him at the club a few times. On this particular day, he happened to be in the park tossing the ball around with someone from one of the other teams. He had an incredible pitching arm and we must have needed an extra player because the next thing I knew I went over to see if he wanted to join us. The only problem was he wasn't affiliated with the Improv other than as an occasional customer, and I wasn't about to risk being thrown out of the league for having a ringer, so the first thing I asked him was if he had a job, which he didn't. In fact, he'd recently been fired, and he was expecting his fourth child at any moment.

As soon as we began talking, I could immediately tell how down on his luck he was. I also had the sense that he was an extremely likable guy who was probably dependable and so I offered him a job as the Improv's bouncer. I said, "Look, I'm the bouncer and we don't need one, but I'll hire you anyway." Needless to say, he accepted and we had another player that day, although the even more astonishing part was that I offered to pay him $190 a week, which was more than I was making at the time.

I don't know why I offered to pay him so much—especially since he would have probably accepted anything—but the dividends have been enormous because in the years since, Danny has never forgotten to mention me and the club whenever he's doing an interview about his life.

He started working for me that same night and he stayed for the next three years. At the time, though, I don't think he had any particular goals other than being able to support his growing family—and certainly a career in show business was likely the furthest thing from his mind. Nevertheless, he liked to sing and he had a very rich voice, so when he wasn't guarding the door, he'd often get up and perform a lot of times with Robert Klein, who is also extremely musical. They'd do these impromptu songs, making the lyrics up as they went along and eventually joining The Untouchables, a doo-wop group with Robert, Marvin Braverman, Bobby Alto, and Buddy Mantia.

Danny also had acting ability, something that quickly became apparent not long after I began letting him emcee late at night. Like me, he loved it. I also think it's pretty safe to say that the audiences loved him more than me because not long after, he began reading these wonderful monologues, which caught the attention of a struggling young playwright from Hoboken, New Jersey, named Lou LaRusso. Lou ended up writing a play for Danny called *Lamppost Reunion*, a barroom drama that centered around stars who achieve fame and ordinary people who don't, that would change both of their lives.

After that, Danny starred in another play called *The Knockout* that eventually went to Broadway. Talent aside, though, the biggest thing I'll always remember about Danny is how much everyone liked him. He's an absolute teddy bear, and he's never forgotten what I did for him. To me, our friendship is priceless.

DANNY AIELLO:

I don't remember the specific date I first went to the Improv, but it must have been around 1968 or 1969 while I was still working at Greyhound, because I sometimes used to stop in after my shift ended over at the Port Authority Bus Terminal. Even though I had no idea whatsoever that I would or could become an actor, the thing besides the comics that fascinated me most was when they'd announce this character actor named Charles Dierkop, who occasionally performed there and later went on to minor fame in the 1970s TV series *Police Woman* starring Angie Dickinson. At the time, he'd already appeared in a film with Robert Downey Sr., and when they brought him up onstage, I thought it was the biggest fucking deal in the world.

But again, I had absolutely no idea that I would or could become an actor when Budd and I first formally met. I had recently been fired from Greyhound, where I also worked as their union president. Besides hustling pool and some other activities I'm not proud of, I occasionally got work unloading trucks at the New York Coliseum across from Central Park, now the site of the Time Warner Center.

When I wasn't unloading trucks or out looking for other work, I'd go over to the park where I frequently got recruited to play on one of the softball teams even though the use of ringers was against the rules. Through a friend of mine who had connections, the first team I played on was for CBS, alongside football legend Frank Gifford, New York Yankees shortstop and announcer Phil Rizzuto, and a local news anchor named Jim Jensen. For a while, I was also on a team fielded by Sparks Steak House. As much as I lived for those games—and relished the notoriety of being called "Tree City Danny" because of my ability to swing for the tree in left field from 275 feet away—I was literally at the end of my ropes as far as the rest of my life was concerned. God knows why he did it other than the fact that he needed an extra player that day, but Budd Friedman saved me. Years after I left, he also gave my son Ricky a job as a bouncer in New York and later at the club in LA. When I say that my life began at the Improv, I'm not exaggerating.

The even more amazing part was that Budd let me be the emcee when he wasn't there, despite the fact that I was terrified and didn't have any idea what I was doing, especially when I was talking off the top of my head. That's why I've always admired comedians so much, particularly monologists, who can get up there and talk about practically anything. Whenever they were on, I would look at them with admiration and I'd be like, "How the fuck do they do that?" Although there were a lot of them I enjoyed, one of my favorites, like Budd, was Robert Klein.

ROBERT KLEIN:

Danny's Italian and I'm Jewish obviously, but he had that New York way about him so I understood him. Plus, he had gone to my high school, DeWitt Clinton, along with Budd, although we were all there at different times. Nobody knew how talented Danny was or that he'd become who he'd become, although we did sing doo-wop together at the Improv. After that, I didn't see him for a while and the next thing I knew he was doing a show Off Broadway.

Danny was always this gentle giant, even though he came off like a tough guy. Everybody liked him, including Rodney Dangerfield, who used to take families out to Sunday dinner and always invited Danny to come along. When it came to being the Improv's bouncer, Danny was a wonderful one, too. He wasn't like a lot of these macho guys you see today walking around with earpieces bullying people. The way it sort of went down is that whenever somebody started trouble, there'd be five inches between his fist and the intestines of the guilty party—at which point Danny would show them the door and that would be that.

MARVIN BRAVERMAN:

Danny definitely knew how to handle the troublemakers when he had to, but he didn't always show them the door either. One night in the late sixties or early seventies, I had gotten to the club very late, around 2 AM. I'm sure Budd had left already. By that point, the audience was comedied out and they were laughed out, but I got onstage anyway, and Aiello was working the door.

It was brutal and I started doing my material, which was bombing. About halfway or maybe two-thirds into my second or third joke, this big German guy in the audience turned to me and said, "What makes you think that you're funny?"

As any good comic will tell you, one of the first rules of dealing with a heckler is to simply ignore them. A lot of times, they're just like a little kid causing a scene in the middle of a store for attention, but if you don't give them any, they usually stop.

Well, not this guy. He just kept going on and on, and the next thing I knew he started screaming. He said, "You're not funny. I'd like to come up there and break your legs." Now, I normally don't scare easily, but the combination of this guy's enormous size and his German accent was really starting to make me afraid, and so I turned to Danny and said into the mic, "Did you hear that, Danny?" But Danny just started laughing and I ran out of the club as fast as I could.

DANNY AIELLO:

Both Marvin and Budd were up onstage, but when the heckler started his drunken tirade against Marvin, my initial reaction when he asked me if I was going to do anything was that the guy was talking to him and not me.

But then, this son of a bitch kept making these terrible remarks about Marvin—I mean, literally calling him every anti-Semitic name in the book—until we finally ended up throwing him out.

BUDDY MANTIA:

To this day, Danny is as good a friend as I could ever have. He's loyal to a fault and he'd give you the shirt off his back, although there was this one incident at the Improv where I saw him have to drag somebody out of there. I'm not sure who the person was, but it was a celebrity of some stature, and someone in the audience was either pestering him for an autograph or getting too close and Danny threw them out, although he wasn't violent about it. He would never hurt a fly.

DANNY AIELLO:

Except for once. Probably the most noteworthy heckler story—and one that did involve violence, which I also wrote about in my memoir—was the night we had this loudmouth in the audience named Doug Ireland, who as it turned out, was none other than the press secretary for Bella Abzug, the most outspoken liberal female politician of the day.

But this had absolutely nothing to do with politics. For starters, Ireland was drunk as a skunk, on top of which he was this massive guy who could have easily weighed 450 pounds. Making matters worse, he was there with a group of equally inebriated staffers from then New York mayor John Lindsay's administration.

Despite his lofty position, Ireland wouldn't shut up. In fact, I think it was his power that made him think he had the right to be an asshole. He just became louder and louder with each act we brought up until finally I walked over to him and calmly warned him to settle down or else. He was having none of it, though, so I went back over to his table and sternly said, "All right, out you go"—and he just looked at me arrogantly and replied, "Do you know who I am?"

By this point, I was absolutely livid and impulse took over, because I said, "Yeah, you're the loudmouth prick who's leaving this club."

That's when all hell began to break loose because the next thing he said to me was, "Does your fucking mother know you talk like that?"

I tried to remain calm even though it took everything I had to restrain myself. "What did you say to me?" I said.

"I said your mama—" That was when I grabbed him by the neck and punched him in the head before he could finish his sentence. I did it with such force that when I hit him, he fell forward and split the concrete tabletop in two.

I'm not sure where Budd was at first, but when he found out what had happened his face turned bright red and he came running over screaming, "What the fuck did you just do?" Then he said, "Those are Mayor Lindsay's people. They'll close my fucking place."

I think there must have been about ten of them there, and let me tell you, after I hit this cocksucker you never saw a group of drunks sober up so fucking fast in your life. They were all just speechless. Nobody said anything—except for Budd who shoved me outside and ordered me to take two weeks off. But then when I explained what happened and how this guy Ireland had been insulting this one female performer in particular, Budd suspended me with two-weeks' pay. I learned an incredible lesson in crowd control and employee fairness that night.

MARTY NADLER:

I'm not sure if it was the same group, but I also had issues with members of the Lindsay administration. One of the performers I wrote for was an actress and singer named Lynne Lipton, and we'd often go over to the club to test things out. We happened to be there one night when, just as Budd was about to put Lynne on, one of the other comics came up to me and said, "Be careful about that table in the back. They're a bunch of assholes and it's so hard to perform with them around. We just wanted to give you a heads-up."

I was like, "Thanks, but what am I going to do about it?"

Anyway, Lynne went up, and sure enough, the moment she did, this table started talking. They weren't even heckling her. Basically, they were just talking among themselves, but it was still rude, so I told them to shut up. Well, when Budd heard me from wherever he was standing, he went absolutely ape shit.

The next thing I knew, he had me by the collar and he was dragging me out of the club going, "Do you know what you're doing?" I didn't really care, though, because the bottom line was these people were in the wrong no matter who they were, plus they were talking while Lynne was doing *my* material. So I said to him, "Do you know what *you're* doing? Do you know how to run a nightclub with people talking while the show is going on?"

When I said this, that's when Budd really got his nose bent out of joint, because it was Lindsay's people and apparently these people here were the ones who issued the licenses and permits, so I guess he had reason to be concerned. He wouldn't put me on for six whole months after that. He essentially ignored me every time I came in. So Danny wasn't the only guy who had problems at the Improv because of Mayor Lindsay's people. Danny was great. He taught me a lot about humanity.

JERRY STILLER:

Even though he wasn't a comedian, Danny was very funny and he was always very connected to his background. He was also extremely protective of the other comics when it came to hecklers trying to disrupt our acts while we were onstage. He was literally like the Godfather in the sense that he would rear his presence. He would rarely ever do anything violent, but the minute they saw him, they'd usually shut up and so he was good to have around for that reason.

BETTE MIDLER:

He was this big, burly Italian guy and he welcomed basically everybody. Everyone felt comfortable around Danny and you never got the feeling he was going to hurt anybody or throw anyone out—at least I never saw him do it. He also never came out and said, "I'm an actor," even though he obviously became one, and he'd take Budd's place at the mic from time to time. Later on, after he made it big in the movies, I was always so proud whenever I'd see him on-screen.

BUDDY MANTIA:

Danny also loved Bette and I think they had a mutual appreciation for one another's talent from the start. He was the first one I heard say, "She's going to make it big." When I asked him why, he said, "Because she's smart, she knows where her audiences are, and she gets them."

JOE PISCOPO:

Danny's one of my dearest friends now, but we didn't work at the Improv at the same time. Later on when I was there, though, he'd come back in as a customer and I was always in awe. It was the same thing with Robert Klein. I'd be like, "Wow, these guys both came out of the Improv and look where they are now." It was New York show business at its finest.

TWENTY-ONE

The Improv and
The Tonight Show

J ust as I knew I could always count on Danny to look after everybody's best interests inside the Improv, I was also very fortunate to have another strong ally by the name of Craig Tennis on the outside. Born in New York and raised in the Midwest, Craig was a former public relations executive who had joined *The Tonight Show* in 1968, where he quickly rose to become Johnny Carson's talent coordinator for the next eight years.

Needless to say, *The Tonight Show* was, and still is, a very important part of all our lives. It was the peak of the highest mountain that nearly every comedian wanted to climb. The first guy we had who got on was a Catskills comic named Howard Mann. What made it especially meaningful was that Howard had been a struggling comedian for nearly thirty years before he finally got his big break, and it made me feel like a proud father even though I was nearly nine years younger than him.

As has often happened when one of our comics has made their first appearance on *The Tonight Show* since then, Howard invited me to the taping. On the appointed evening, I and several others from the club were waiting with him backstage at NBC when this gorgeous woman dressed in a long evening gown came into the green room. Howard, being the archetypical, always-ready-with-a-line comedian he was, sauntered right up to her and said, "Hello, my dear. My name is Howard Mann, the comedian. What do you do?"

The woman couldn't have cared less. She just looked at him and said, "I'm Myra Breckenridge and I'm a producer." Then she turned and walked away. What none of us knew at the time was that this woman was actually Raquel Welch.

Anyway, Howard had a pretty decent set that night, although I'm not sure if he ever did *The Tonight Show* again. But regardless, Craig Tennis became our man there. While he handled many aspects of scheduling guests for the show, principally his job was auditioning new comedians and getting them ready for their appearances. He also had the formidable task of anticipating whom Johnny would like. It was never a precise science, although when it came to trying to exact the right formula, no one had a better track record than Craig. This, of course, made him an invaluable asset to us.

CRAIG TENNIS:

Johnny Carson was born in Corning, Iowa, and raised in Norfolk, Nebraska. I grew up in Sioux City, Iowa, which was halfway between those two cities. So I knew exactly how to talk to Carson because we grew up with people who had the same sense of morality, values, and economy.

If I was on the phone explaining a sketch or something before a show, he'd say, "Tell me about it." Then he'd say yes or no and just hang up. I grew up with people like that, who never wasted words. So I became a surrogate Carson—and I think it's because I came from the same heritage as he did that I became very good at anticipating the kinds of comedians we should have on the show.

Never in his life did Johnny say, "Have a good afternoon. I'll see you on the set for rehearsal." That never came out of his mouth. What also never came out of his mouth was, "How's the wife and kids?" He never said that to anybody because he didn't give a shit. If Johnny didn't know you, he couldn't care less.

Early on, I learned to talk to him on a very abbreviated level, which was just fine with me. There were no wasted words and we got along great, but it wasn't like he was going to invite me out for cocktails. By the same measure, I think our senses of humor were very parallel, so I would try to anticipate what he would like and that spilled over to my relationship with Budd, which was very symbiotic, because when I went to the Improv, it wasn't just to catch one act. Usually, I would go in and spend the entire evening to see who was a comer, who I should keep an eye out for, who I should stop and talk to, and whether or not they were receptive to my suggestions—stuff like that.

I would often see a lot of comics months, and sometimes even years, before they were ready. When I was there, they were aware of it. They were also aware that they were going to see me multiple times a week, or sometimes just once a week. The Improv was the place where I went to watch them get better or disappear, so it wasn't something where I'd go in specifically to see just one person, although there were definitely instances when I might.

It was my job to use the club as an educational tool for both me and them. I would know pretty much the twenty minutes they would do so that we could cut them down to six. My rule was you'd better have that second appearance ready and it better be better, because Carson was going to want you back in ten days and you had to score that second time. The third time meant that he was going to start looking at you as a potential threat, and if you could get past a fourth and fifth, that meant you were going to be okay.

Budd always understood what I was there to do and we made each other laugh. He also understood what I could do for the Improv, and I always made damn sure that the club got mentioned whenever we had a comic on *The Tonight Show* who was a regular there. We understood that we were helping each other out. Were we ever going to hang out? Probably not, and we never really did, but it was a mutually beneficial relationship from the get-go.

The Improv has happily always had a terrific relationship with *The Tonight Show*—and perhaps even more so in recent decades for sentimental reasons since both Jay Leno and Jimmy Fallon started with me. Certainly in the beginning, though, one of the biggest advantages we enjoyed was the fact that, like *The Ed Sullivan Show*, it was taped in New York, just blocks away from the club.

However, by the spring of 1972—less than a year following CBS's cancellation of Ed Sullivan after twenty-six seasons—both the Improv and the New York entertainment community were dealt a serious blow when NBC also made the unprecedented announcement that it was relocating *The Tonight Show* to Burbank, California. Though it would eventually be a major catalyst for my decision to open a second Improv in Los Angles in 1975, which I'll get into later, at the time—especially given the predominance of comedians on both shows and with both shows now gone from New York—it felt as if the rug had been ripped right out from under me.

A classic case of not fully appreciating what you have until you no longer have it, what especially worried me about *The Tonight Show*'s departure was how many comics had been plucked from us directly under Craig Tennis's watch and that many of my best acts might leave now that the balance of comedic power was shifting to the West Coast. Another thing that puzzled me was why Johnny Carson had chosen to relocate in the first place, although as I later discovered, the decision had not entirely been his.

CRAIG TENNIS:

There was so much shit that went down. NBC was telling us that they were going to build us our own high-rise building in Burbank to house *The Tonight Show* offices. It was going to be this wonderful and luxurious state-of-the-art office building. But when we got out there, there were these two modular units—basically a couple of double-wide trailers with bad air-conditioning and Formica walls like you'd find at a construction site. It was terrible.

Virtually everybody on the staff was invited to go, but it was also a good excuse to get rid of some people. Johnny had this assistant at the time whom he loathed, and a friend of mine later told me that the reason he left was just so he could get rid of her. I have no idea if it was true, but it's an amusing story. To tell you the truth, I don't think Johnny was all that anxious to go other than the fact that he could get away from his most recent ex-wife. Plus, Johnny had a great apartment at the UN Plaza and could get into the best restaurants in Manhattan if he wanted to, even though he rarely did that.

If anything—and this has all been well documented—I think it was Johnny's executive producer, Freddie de Cordova, who pressured him into moving. A big part of that had to do with the fact Freddie had a lot of social status in Hollywood, but in New York he had almost none.

There's no doubt that Johnny adjusted fine to Los Angeles after he got there, but relocating definitely wasn't a priority with him. As for getting acts, we never had trouble flying people in to New York from LA, or vice versa. That was never an issue then, nor is it an issue now for Jimmy Fallon. It was still the show to do and the publicists knew exactly how to work *The Tonight Show* with the major stars. What they'd do is fly you to New York and then maybe they'd fly you down to Philadelphia to do Mike Douglas. There wasn't anybody who wouldn't get on a plane. The West Coast move was strictly for other people's convenience other than Johnny's.

TWENTY-TWO

A Tale of Two Comedy Clubs

As I was slowly adjusting to the loss of *The Tonight Show* on top of my unsuccessful attempt to launch a sister club in Greenwich Village called the Improvisation Two, which never caught on despite our notoriety uptown and only lasted a few months, I was faced with yet another potential bump in the road when Rick Newman decided to open a competing club called Catch A Rising Star on the Upper East Side on December 18, 1972.

Rick was always a terrific, affable guy and he's as salt of the earth as they come, although when I first learned that he was opening Catch, my initial impression was resentment and that he was stealing my idea. But then very quickly after that, we became friends, which we've remained. Back then, we even helped one another out on evenings when we didn't have enough comics. Another unexpected benefit was the press we received, because whenever somebody wrote about Rick, they'd also have to mention us since we were there first.

RICK NEWMAN:

Before I started Catch A Rising Star in 1972, I ran a bar called Danny's Inferno in Queens. When Danny had to leave New York unexpectedly, he asked me to take it over for him. The deal was that he gave me a free pass to run it any way I wanted, plus he said I could keep all the profits as long as I paid all the bills, which was great, even though I didn't know the first thing about running a bar.

Anyway, I had the bar for a few years and I wound up tripling the business because I put in entertainment on Thursdays,

Fridays, and Saturdays, when I had a piano player and a few local comics. None of them ever made it and this was long before people were concentrating on comedians, but the point is that I knew how to book comics. Then after about two years, Danny came back and he suggested we open something up in Manhattan.

The place we found had been called Lester's Bar & Grill on 31st Street and Third Avenue. It was a dive, but I redecorated it and I turned it into a singles' bar called the Clan 1890s. It became so successful that we literally had to wait for people to leave before we could let others in. But then after a few years, I wanted to do my own thing and so I started looking for another location. This time, it was on First Avenue between 77th and 78th Streets, which eventually became Catch A Rising Star.

JAY LENO:

As far as I know, Budd and Rick always got along fine, although I also think that initially Catch was a bit of a thorn in Budd's side. The great thing about doing Catch was that you got a meal and you got cab fare, which was unbelievable. But you also had to be kind of careful. You didn't want to say, "Budd, can I get on early? I have to go on at Catch." You didn't want to say any of that stuff and rock the boat, but eventually things worked themselves out.

MAX ALEXANDER, comedian and actor:

Everybody jockeyed back and forth between the Improv and Catch—and later on the Comic Strip and the other clubs, too— myself included. It was never a rule that you couldn't, and nobody ever tried to stop you, although I always kind of had an issue with the comics who would advertise it. I mean, what was the point of rubbing their noses in it and making waves?

JIMMIE WALKER:

As far as club owners go, Rick Newman is one of the best guys in the business, just one of those people that everybody loves and you almost never heard anyone say a bad thing about.

MARTY NADLER:

Oh my God, Catch A Rising Star was the changing of Budd because before that he'd been the only game in town. As standoffish and aloof as Budd could be, Rick was like your uncle because he'd welcome you and give you food and a drink, plus he was also paying for people's cab fare.

One analogy I can give you is that when you're starting out in this business you're panning for gold, meaning that you're trying to get discovered. And not only were you panning for gold at Rick's place, you were being greeted warmly. It was like night and day, and it really got Budd to be more giving because he knew he had to be. It was an amazing transformation to watch and it was great to have another place to work.

RICHARD LEWIS:

Budd is one of the most important figures in my life career-wise and he's always been like family to me. But so has Rick, and when I started working at both places, Budd was totally fine with that. Before they started giving us cab fare, one night about six of us hitched a ride over to the Upper East Side to do a set at Catch with a comedian who had a car. But before we left the Improv, we saw Budd and one of his best friends—who I think was an agent or a producer—standing outside in front. Surrounding them was this group of nefarious-looking guys who looked like they might be up to no good, which very well might have been the case, because in those days Hell's Kitchen was an absolute shit hole. They weren't carrying any guns or anything like that, and Budd and his friends didn't look like they were in any imminent danger, but as a ruse, I immediately knew what I was going to say to the other comics once we got in the car.

After about twenty minutes, we were driving towards Eighth Avenue about to take a left and make our way through Central Park when we stopped at a traffic light and I decided to start my riff. With a completely straight face, I said, "I think Budd and his friends are going to be murdered. This is horrible. What are we doing leaving? We've got to go back there and see if we can help."

"They'll be fine," the others said.

But I protested and said, "No, no. How are we going to feel if they get murdered? These guys look really dangerous and we should go back."

Well, just about then I looked out the window and noticed a couple of mounted police officers on horseback. I rolled down the window and said, "Look, officers, I'm a comedian. I just came from the Improv. It's on the corner of West 44th Street and Ninth Avenue. You've got to do me a favor. You've got to go back." By this point, the other comics were totally buying into it and they thought I was saying this because I was genuinely concerned about Budd's safety.

That's when I delivered the punch line. Still with a completely straight face, I said, "And find out who Budd Friedman is. When you do, tell him that Richard Lewis wants to work both shows this Saturday night." With that, the guys started just laughing their asses off. I swear to God, it was maybe the biggest laugh of my career.

SHELLEY ACKERMAN:

I'll tell you how picking up the acts' cab fare between the two clubs started. One night around the end of 1972, not long after Rick opened, I got a frantic call during prime time one Saturday night from Bill Mahru who was emceeing up at Catch. We were pretty friendly and he said, "Shelley, I'm stuck. The house is packed. I need acts."

So I said, "Will you give them cab fare?"

"Yes," he said.

Then I added, "And dinner?"

"Yes."

That was all it took. I got Marty Nadler, Jimmie Walker, and about two others, and I sent them uptown. This is what started the shuttle between both clubs and the comics getting fed. Once Rick started doing it, we did, too.

RICK NEWMAN:

The night I opened, I threw a fiftieth birthday party for boxer Rocky Graziano just to get the press there. He had absolutely nothing to do with the concept, but it created a buzz. Comedian Jackie Kannon, a friend of Rocky's who had a place in the East Fifties called Jackie Kannon's Ratfink Room, was there, and it got us a ton of ink. Syndicated columnist Earl Wilson wrote me up and there was also a big piece in the show-business trade *Backstage*. So the press was plentiful, and in the weeks leading up to the opening, I took out these little square ads in all the New York papers like the *Post*, the *Daily News*, and *The Village Voice* that said: "Catch A Rising Star Is Opening." It included the location and [a note]: "For producers, studio executives, network people, managers, and agents—we are going to pre-screen and pre-audition all the major talent, so you can come in and rest assured that you are going to see the best of the best."

I also told talent in the same ads that we were going to have network people, talent people, managers, and talent scouts.

All I did was play both ends against the middle, and it was the perfect storm because everybody came on a very regular basis from the get-go. I also wasn't paying attention to what was happening over at Budd's place. I just wanted to get them into mine.

Look, he might have felt, "Well, you opened what I did," but I can honestly say that was never my intention. I opened a performance club and then when there were comedians we were both using, I started to call over to the Improv because my shows kept up all night. People kept coming in and the acts would leave, so I'd call up Budd and go, "Do you have anybody you can send over?" It became a regular thing for us to pick up the phone and call each other. Some nights he was busier and some nights I was busier.

It also didn't bother me in the least to give the comics cab fare or give them free food and drinks. I thought nothing of it to give them a soda, or a hamburger, or a steak sandwich on the house. What a lot of them did was wrap the food up in a napkin and take it home or they'd pocket the cab fare and ride the bus instead, but I was just fine with that.

CRAIG TENNIS:

I always liked both of them—and I'm not sure what their relationship was—although I have to admit that when I found out that Rick was opening a similar club to Budd's, my first impulse was that it wouldn't work. I thought Budd had a lock on it, which he did, but the other reason I thought Catch wouldn't work was because there were already a couple of other comedy rooms out on Long Island and they seemed to be struggling.

As it turns out, I was obviously wrong because the Upper East Side was a neighborhood you wanted to be in, whereas Hell's Kitchen was one that when you left at two o'clock in the morning, you were taking your life into your hands. I also thought the emphasis would be more music than comedy, and when the comedy part took off I was surprised. To say that I didn't think that Rick had a prayer in hell presenting comedians would be kind of extreme, although if he had asked me to invest in the beginning, I probably wouldn't have.

Also, when it comes to the difference between their personalities, it was like night and day. If I remember correctly, Rick was more of a table hopper. He wanted to make sure his customers were happy. That was never Budd's intention. In other words, he wanted people there, but he wasn't the type to go out of his way to keep them happy. There were many times when he'd get up onstage and berate the comics and

Publicity photo of the New York Improv
taken shortly after the club opened in 1963.

Very early photo of the New York Improv
show room in the 1960s with a chalkboard menu.

Actors Michele Lee, Rudy Vallee, and
Robert Morse at the New York Improv in the early 1960s.

Budd with Rodney Dangerfield and actor-comedian
Ron Carey at the New York Improv in the 1960s.

Judy Garland and her son-in-law Peter Allen,
Liza Minnelli's first husband, at the New York Improv in the early 1960s.

Group photo at the New York Improv, around 1980.
Courtesy of Judy Orbach.

Comedians at the New York Improv from the late 1970s to the early '80s.
Courtesy of Judy Orbach.

Jerry Seinfeld
and Barry Diamond

Paul Provenza
and Rick Overton

Paul Reiser

Budd with *Laverne & Shirley* stars Cindy Williams (left)
and Penny Marshall (right) at the Hollywood Improv in the late 1970s.

Budd at the Hollywood Improv after the 1979 fire.

Budd and comedian Phil Silvers
hosting *An Evening at the Improv* in the 1980s.

Budd with former *Tonight Show* bandleader Doc Severinsen and
talent manager Bud Robinson at the Hollywood Improv in the 1980s.

Budd with Andy Kaufman at the Hollywood Improv in the early 1980s.

Budd and his oldest daughter Beth with comedians Tom Smothers (left) and George Carlin (center left) at the Hollywood Improv in the mid-1980s.

Budd with his family in the mid-1980s.

Budd with daughter Zoe and wife Alix
at the Hollywood Improv in the early 1990s.

Budd and Bette Middler at the Hollywood Improv in the late 1980s.

The 1989 Hollywood Free Clinic Roast of Budd. Front row (left to right):
Bette Midler, Budd, Garry Marshall, and Paul Rodriguez. Back row
(left to right): Dale Gonyea, Brandon Tartikoff, Wil Shriner,
Harvey Korman, Danny Aiello, and Pat McCormick.

Budd with Oprah Winfrey and Robin Williams
when Oprah hosted her talk show at the Hollywood Improv in 1989.

Exterior shot of the Hollywood Improv in the early 1990s.

Budd with Merv Griffin and Donald Trump at
Griffin's Resorts Casino Hotel in Atlantic City in the 1990s.

Jerry Stiller and Anne Meara in New York City in the 1990s.
Courtesy of Stiller and Meara Enterprises.

Budd with Freddie Prinze Jr. and Jay Leno
at the Hollywood Improv in the early 1990s.

Budd with Paul Giamatti, Jim Carrey, and Danny DeVito
on the set of Andy Kaufman's biopic *Man on the Moon* in 1998.

Adam Sandler at the Hollywood Improv.
Photo by Mike Carano.

David Spade at the Hollywood Improv.
Photo by Mike Carano.

Bill Maher at the Hollywood
Improv. *Photo by Mike Carano.*

Richard Lewis at the Hollywood
Improv. *Photo by Mike Carano.*

Jimmy Fallon at the Hollywood Improv.
Photo by Josh Paul.

Budd with Mike Myers, Helen Hunt, and Kevin Spacey
backstage at the Las Vegas Improv in 2002.

Budd and Alix with Lily Tomlin in
Washington, DC, at the Mark Twain Awards in 2003.

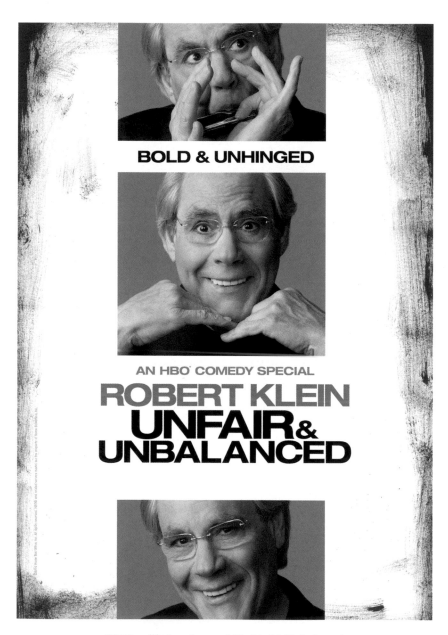

2010 publicity photo of *Unfair & Unbalanced*,
Robert Klein's ninth HBO special. *Photograph courtesy of HBO®*.

the cook and do jokes at other people's expense. That was just who Budd was and you accepted it. I don't remember Rick Newman ever getting up on the mic, although he may have.

But Budd would get up there and he'd just rip people. Like if somebody would come from the bathroom, he'd say, "Sit down, I'm talking. I'll let you know when you can go to the restroom." It wasn't mean-spirited, although I think Budd wanted to do stand-up himself. Of course, it wasn't going to happen except in his club, and he seized the opportunity whenever he could. Everybody just said, "That's Budd." Again, though, I don't think that anybody was ever offended unless they were from Omaha.

MICHAEL GOLDSTEIN:

Besides all of the ways that Catch ultimately benefited both Budd and Rick, I think the biggest way it helped was that it definitely forced Budd to be nicer because both clubs were competing for comedians and they were fighting for loyalties.

MIKE PREMINGER:

One night I was up at Catch and Budd was there also. Rick came up to me, whispered in my ear, and asked me what I wanted to eat. I thought he was joking, and before I could think of how much it was going to cost me, he said, "It's all on me." Then he said, "I'll tell you what, I'll bring you a steak." And true to his word, which Rick always was, he brought me a steak and it was delicious. I hadn't eaten all day and I was starving. But I was also shocked because the only other place I had ever worked at that point was the Improv and Budd had never offered me so much as a piece of bread before. I was dumbfounded.

A day or two later, I was at the Improv and the first thing Budd said to me was, "Hi, what would you like to eat?" And I was like, "Son of a gun!"

When Catch opened in '72, it was great for me personally because now I had two clubs. There were many nights—and when I tell people this they still can't believe it to this day—but there were times when I'd do a nine-thirty spot at the Improv, then get a cab and go on at Catch at ten-thirty, then head back to the Improv for the twelve-thirty show, and finally fin- ish up the evening around two-thirty in the morning at Catch. I was doing as many as four shows for free some nights, but I loved it and I was in heaven because this was what I wanted to do.

SHELLEY ACKERMAN:

I was a singing waitress at the Improv from 1971 until 1980. Budd gave me my first job and I'll always be grateful for that. But soon after it opened, I also eventually wound up singing at Catch. I think Budd was initially a little threatened even though it turned out fine for both clubs.

I began singing at Catch through a comedian friend of mine named Cassandra Danz who died in 2002. She was part of a singing-comedy-improv group called The High Heeled Women before becoming a solo act and writing two books. She also did segments on *Regis and Kathie Lee* called "Mrs. GreenThumbs." Cassandra told me about Catch and she recommended I start singing there. At first I was like, "What do I need that place for when I have the Improv?" But then I did, and it quickly became clear to me that something was brewing. Rick had this wonderful publicist named Gene Weber, and between the Improv and Catch I started getting all of this press. I didn't realize that my being a singing waitress and nineteen years old at that time and a rabbi's daughter from the Lower East Side was really that interesting, but I guess it was.

BILL MAHER:

I'm guessing I was around eight or ten when I first realized I wanted to become a comic, although I never said anything because I was basically a shy kid and I didn't really grow up in the era when everything was about pumping up a kid's self-esteem. I also think that a lot of kids today have too much confidence, if that's possible.

We were just the opposite in my era and so the idea that I could reach such a lofty height never really crossed my mind. Also, when I was a kid, becoming a comedian was a rare thing. It became a lot more common just as I was starting out with the explosion of comedy clubs—and largely because of the Improv and Catch. But for me, in the era I grew up in, it was just a crazy dream, so I kept it to myself.

The way I first found out about the Improv was reading about it in the newspaper when I was in high school. Of course, as somebody who was interested in comedy, I'd started thinking about it in practical terms of how I was going to go into comedy even though it never crossed my mind not to go to college. I mean, it was sort of expected of me and I wanted to go. But even so, I was never thinking for a minute, "Oh, this is going to get me a job." All I was thinking was, "I'm wasting precious time when I should be doing comedy."

When I was a student at Cornell University in Ithaca, New York, in 1975, there was no place to perform. But I actually forced myself into performing once. There were these weekly poetry readings on campus, and I wrote what I thought was some funny stuff and basically tried to do a comedy bit because there was an audience. Not surprisingly, it didn't go great because I was new. I didn't really know how to do it and it was a fucking poetry reading.

After that, I started checking out the New York club scene while I was in college. I auditioned for Catch during college, but before that I rode the bus into Manhattan from New Jersey just to see the Improv as an audience member. By this time, both places were getting a lot of press—you know, the new comedy club scene and how you lined up on Monday nights to audition. I remember reading about that and I lined up at Catch. This must have been around 1977 and I remember talking about the Yankees, who were in the news a lot. There were some stories floating around about them growing marijuana in the outfield and I think I did some riffs on that. There was also a heckler in the audience who I got some laughs off of. Whatever it was, the emcee, who I believe was Larry David, passed me. He told me that I could come back and start hanging out, but I still had college to go to. All I could think about was how I needed to cash in this chit, and then, like a year and a half after I graduated, I went back and said, "I'm here. I'm ready to hang out."

Not long after that, I started working at both clubs, as well as the Comic Strip, and Rick Newman eventually made me one of his regular emcees at Catch. Being the emcee was like being God because you had the power to pass people. You also didn't have to fight city hall to get stage time because you were city hall, which meant you basically got as much stage time as you wanted, plus you got paid and you got free drinks. If the crowd sucked, you just brought the next comic up, but if the audience was great you did ten minutes.

At the time, I think we all had the same idea in our head: You got your shit together in New York, where you got good enough to do a bunch of *Tonight Show*s. Then you moved to California and got a sitcom.

CATHY LADMAN, comedian, screenwriter, and actor:

Bill Maher was always incredibly generous to me and he took me under his wing almost immediately. Not long after I auditioned for Budd's former wife, Silver, at the Improv, Bill arranged for me to audition with Rick Newman at Catch.

The exact date was September 5, 1981, and I remember this because this was the day my nephew was born and I was just about to go on when my parents called to tell me the news. This immediately took the edge off things, so I wound up having a great set and I became a regular.

I'd been doing stand-up for a while and I did fine after that, although it wasn't until sometime in 1982 when I got the call for my first prime weekend spot because another comedian, Gilbert Gottfried, didn't show up. It was like being called by Hollywood, and it was great because back then the only other place you could see stand-up was on late-night television. Comedy club audiences were also for the most part well educated and hip, which meant that you were going to be able to cover intelligent ground with a receptive crowd that was quick on the uptake.

RITCH SHYDNER:

Thanks to Gilbert Gottfried, I had a similar experience to Cathy's at the Improv, although it was kind of the reverse of hers. Back in the seventies and eighties, the clubs used to stay open until three or four in the morning. You'd get on, but the goal was for somebody not to show up so you could get on earlier, which is what happened the night I was meant to follow Gilbert, and when I realized how desperate people got when they didn't have enough comics. You'd literally see the owner or whoever was running things getting so panicked that they'd stand outside to see if another comic was going to drive up in a cab. Well, on this particular evening, they didn't have anybody and they put me up, which is how I became a regular after that.

BUDDY MANTIA:

For the most part, we all had each other's backs. This was true at both the Improv and at Catch, even though I was at the Improv more in the beginning. A lot of times we'd also come up with a line and say, "That's not right for me, but it would work for so-and-so."

PAUL REISER:

In the seventies and early eighties, the Improv was always viewed as the purest of the three New York clubs. I played all three and the Comic Strip was my home club if I had to rank them, but it was also the new kid on the block so it never had the same prestige. Catch had a bit of sexiness to it because Pat Benatar, who Rick Newman managed, and stars like Mick Jagger, David Bowie, and John Belushi came through there a lot just to hang out at the bar. So, Catch had this kind of show-biz, rock 'n' roll vibe about it, like Studio 54 and Elaine's.

Budd's place, on the other hand, was more organic because it was there first. This made it feel different. I remember watching an episode of *Seinfeld* once where he was at a comedy club, and they were clearly modeling it after the Improv because the stage entrance was on the other side like the Improv's. The actual portal that you walked through to get up and do a set was only about twenty inches wide, although it was huge contextually because it meant you were in show business.

The other cool thing about the Improv was that being on Ninth Avenue with all the junkies and prostitutes had a nitty-grittiness about it that the others lacked. I remember when I got the audition with director Barry Levinson for *Diner* in late '80 or early 1981, he came to see me at the Improv. What made it so special was that the Improv had been the DNA of my comedy career.

JOE PISCOPO:

Like most guys back then, I kind of jockeyed back and forth between the two clubs, but I was definitely more of an Improv guy because I was also the emcee and the doorman. I'll tell you how it happened for me at both places. After I graduated from college in 1974, I was kind of in a catatonic stupor for a year or two—you know, what am I doing, where am I going, am I going to law school like my father? That kind of thing. Then I heard about the Improv, probably through Robin Williams or Billy Crystal.

This was February of 1976. I put together five minutes of God-awful material, and on a bitterly freezing Monday night, I got into my 1972 Cutlass Oldsmobile and drove through the Lincoln Tunnel and over to the Improv. I swear, there must have been two hundred or three hundred people, and after taking one look at the line, I chickened out and went home.

I decided to go back the next week. I'd talked to some people beforehand and they told me to get there at noon. So I got there at the stroke of noon for an eight-thirty audition. By this point, Budd had already moved to California, and Chris Albrecht and Judy Orbach were running things. Anyway, I got passed, but guys like Larry David and talk-show host

Alan Colmes were already there and they were ahead of us. Because we were all new and they still weren't doing strict lineups on Monday night, the other guys and I would sort of draw straws as to who would get up first because nobody really wanted to.

It was all very random, and on nights when the club was really crowded, we'd all wait in my car because I was the only comic who had one, and it was freezing out. Then we'd go in and go on and you know the drill—it was bad, but it wasn't that bad. It was like I held their attention, but didn't get many laughs. This went on for two weeks at the Improv before I finally had the nerve to go over to Catch and try that also. I always did okay there, and by week three or four, I got on my feet and the laughs came.

BILLY CRYSTAL:

In New York, I was mainly a Catch guy. Part of that had to do with the fact that I was living on Long Island and Catch was closer to the 59th Street Bridge. Plus, my wife, Janice, was supporting us, so Rick was always great about giving me earlier spots so that I could get home in time to get a couple of hours of sleep before I had to get up at six-thirty with our eighteen-month-old daughter.

Beyond the logistics of getting there, I was also a little bit intimidated by the New York Improv. Not by Budd, who was always great to me, but by the club itself, which had this reputation as *the* place. I remember the first time I went there was in late 1972 or early 1973. It was a rainy Monday night, and Bette Midler came in dripping wet and sang "Danny Boy." I'd gone there with an improv group called 3's Company that I was in.

We did well, but I was always more of a Catch guy in New York. As others have said, Catch was more of a show room whereas the Improv felt like Kronk boxing gym in Detroit. It was the place where all of the heavyweights went to work out.

TWENTY-THREE
Meeting Jay

I n between my initial concerns about *The Tonight Show*'s departure and Catch A Rising Star's arrival, even more unexpected surprises came my way in the early seventies. Fortunately, they were mostly happy ones. One of the best occurred when a shaggy-haired young man from Boston came into the club on a chilly fall evening in 1971. He was dressed in a wide-collared, open-neck shirt and bell-bottom jeans with a gigantic turquoise-studded buckle securing an oversized leather belt. It wasn't so much his physical appearance that made an impression on me as it was the curved tobacco pipe he clutched in his right hand.

This young man was Jay Leno. Without a doubt, Jay is one of my favorite subjects to talk about. He was twenty-two when we first met, and in the years since, we have enjoyed one of the most incredible friendships in the history of show business, both personally and professionally. While practically all our comics have been special to me in one way or another, when I think of Jay, I always have to add the word "extra" and I can never stop bragging. One of my proudest moments was when he invited me and my second wife, Alix, to see him accept the Mark Twain Prize for American Humor at the Kennedy Center in Washington, DC, in 2014. It was comedy's highest honor, but it represented so much more than just an award. When he mentioned my name and invited me to stand at the end of the ceremony, I nearly choked up as the cameras panned towards us on national television.

My relationship with Jay had something of a roundabout beginning. Born in New Rochelle, New York, and raised in the Boston suburb of

Andover, Massachusetts, Jay, the son of an insurance salesman, struggled academically in school while dreaming of someday becoming a stand-up comic. After briefly enrolling at the Bentley School of Accounting and Finance, he transferred to Boston's Emerson College, the nation's only four-year college dedicated to communications and the performing arts, where he majored in speech therapy.

JAY LENO:

Now they even have an entire major devoted to stand-up comedy, but back when I was there, there really were no comedy classes at Emerson. I was pretty much the only comic I knew in Boston.

Most of the classes were just drama and I wasn't interested in that, so I didn't apply myself. I did have a comedy team for a while with my friend Gene Braunstein, and after that I joined a comedy troupe, Fresh Fruit Cocktail. I remember that we had a lot of fun and it was great training and all that. The problem was that it wound up being one of those deals where some people wanted to work and some people didn't. Basically, their attitude was, "Oh, we worked last weekend, so let's take this weekend off." I wasn't like that and I wanted to work, so I decided to go solo.

I obviously didn't know Jay yet, but I later found out that he took any gig he could find. Hospitals, retirement homes, Kiwanis clubs, strip clubs, and even prisons, you name it; by the time he got to the Improv he'd done just about everything. One of my favorite stories was how he used to walk into local bars, give the owners fifty bucks, and ask to do a set, telling them that that they could keep the money if he bombed.

JAY LENO:

Basically, I was just trying to get spots pretty much any place I could. Although Boston had a fairly fertile underground scene, it was still kind of an odd time. Lenny Bruce, who'd been dead for about four or five years by this point, was sort of a mythical figure to all of us, and Albert Goldman's best-selling biography, *Ladies and Gentlemen—Lenny Bruce!!*, had just come out.

One of the places Jay worked was a jazz club called Lennie's on the Turnpike on Route 1 in Peabody, Massachusetts, where he opened for acts like Linda Ronstadt and Kris Kristofferson. I also knew the owner, Lennie Sogoloff, and had booked Bette Midler there a couple of times when I was managing her.

JAY LENO:

Lennie Sogoloff was a wonderful guy who was very good to me. Unquestionably, next to Budd, he was one of my biggest supporters early on, and I got to meet all of these incredible jazz musicians like Buddy Rich and Miles Davis. But let's face it, Route 1 was obviously not where show business was, so I drove down to New York to try and get on at one of the places where you could do comedy. At the time, there really weren't very many other than the Improv, and they were still using singers, although it was also becoming known as more of a comedy room by this point.

Besides comedy I had another reason for making frequent trips down to New York because my day job was prepping cars for a Rolls-Royce and Mercedes-Benz dealership called Foreign Motors in Boston. It was great and sometimes they'd fly me to New Jersey and then I'd pick up the car and drive it back to Boston. Which reminds me, one of my craziest—and scariest—Improv stories was the night some guy gave me $34,000 in cash for a Rolls-Royce. That was how much they cost back then. I delivered the Rolls to this guy and he gave me the biggest wad of cash I'd ever seen in my life. Then I picked up another car, but instead of going back to Boston, I impulsively decided to drop in to the Improv and do a set. I got there around 8:30 PM, but there were a lot of other comics there and I wasn't an established regular yet, so I just hung out at the bar until I went on at one-thirty in the morning. I also distinctly recall bringing the money into the club with me and holding on to it until it came time for me to go on. This is when I put the money on top of the piano.

Then I did my set—and it was probably one of the best I'd done yet—because I was absolutely on cloud nine. Afterwards, I got back into the Rolls, which was parked on the street and thankfully hadn't been stolen or vandalized, and drove off. As soon as I got out of Manhattan, I began listening to my set on the tape recorder I always carried with me, still on this incredible high from how well I'd done. I was driving along, replaying the tape over and over, until I made it all the way up to Greenwich, Connecticut, which is where the tollbooth was. When I reached into my pocket to take out some change for the toll, it suddenly hit me that I'd left the envelope with the $34,000 in it on top of the piano at the Improv.

Immediately, I turned the car around and drove back. My mind racing along with the car, I must have gotten there within the hour. I wasn't exactly sure how to handle it, because I knew there was a fifty-fifty chance that somebody had made off with it. All I could think of was how I was going to explain to my boss that I'd lost thirty-four grand. It was horrible. But when I parked the car in back of Dykes Lumber Company and raced back into the club, to my complete surprise the money was still on top of the piano. There were about eight people left in the audience and a young woman was onstage singing. Relieved but still shaken, I made a beeline for the stage and said, "Excuse me, I forgot my lunch." Then I took the envelope and left. God, it was scary.

Here's another scary but true story. A lot of times, instead of driving back to Boston, I'd finish up at the Improv and sack out in the backseat of whatever car I was driving, which I usually parked in the alley of Dykes', adjacent to the back of the club. On this particular night, I was exhausted and I remember being just about to drift off to sleep when suddenly this prostitute brought one of her clients into the alley and they started doing whatever they were going to do. Suffice it to say that there was a lot of moaning and groaning going on, and it was one of the grossest conversations I've ever heard. I can still picture it like it was yesterday. I remember thinking to myself, "Is this what show business is all about?" It was pretty depressing.

So was being refused a room by two hotels on the same night. I don't recall the exact year, but it wasn't long after I started at the Improv, and this will give you an idea of how different things were back then. On this particular evening, I had a late set and it was too late to drive back to Boston, so I went over to the Plaza on Fifth Avenue, where they wanted twenty-eight dollars for a room. Then I went next door to the Hotel Navarro, which is long gone, where they charged twenty-three dollars. But I only had eighteen dollars and when I asked if I could stay for just two hours, they still said no and I wound up sleeping in my car again.

Before I became friendly with the other comics and we sort of developed a trade-off where they'd stay at my place in Boston and I'd crash with them in New York, I slept in my car a lot. I also got into the habit of letting comics I didn't know, like Billy Crystal and Freddie Prinze, crash at my apartment in Boston. When word got out that I was doing this, people used to call it "Leno Arms."

MIKE PREMINGER:

When I first met Jay, I was living a half a block from Central Park on West 70th Street and sometimes he'd stay with me. I'd also stay with him in Boston and it was great, because I'm a few years older and he was like a kid brother to me.

We each had our own keys to one another's apartments, and one of the things I remember most was the time Jay was staying at my place while I was out of town on a road gig someplace. Trying to be a hospitable host, I'd gone grocery shopping the day before I left and bought a few things for him to have. When I got back a day or so later, I opened up my refrigerator only to find that Jay had literally eaten me out of house and home. I was like, "Couldn't you at least leave me a soda?"

But then, the next day I opened up the refrigerator and Jay had stocked it with every kind of soft drink imaginable. I'm not talking about a few cans here, I'm talking cases—Coke, Pepsi, Sprite, root beer, ginger ale—you name it.

It was just incredible and so was his appetite. I don't know how he did it without ever gaining a pound, but let me tell you this boy could eat. Once we were having Sunday dinner at my parents' house in the Bronx, and when my mom brought out the roast beef, Jay tried to eat the whole thing.

Not only could Jay eat, he ate fast, too. I remember another time when we went to McDonald's and Jay ordered three hamburgers. Then I placed my order and Jay went to find a table for us. By the time I sat down a couple of minutes later, he'd already eaten everything. When it came to food, Jay didn't chew. He inhaled. I swear, I don't think his teeth worked for chewing.

Jay was definitely one of the ones I never had any qualms about in terms of raw talent and his ability to always deliver. But the most interesting part of all of this—and there's a direct correlation here between cars and comedy—is that by the time I finally put him on that night in 1971, he'd already driven back and forth from Boston three nights in a row.

When he told me this, I couldn't believe it. I said, "Wait, you're telling me that you drive all the way down here, four hours, don't get on, drive all the way back, and then turn around and come back the next day?" As soon as Jay said yes, that was all it took. I immediately said,

"You're on next." And after a quick five-minute set, I told him he could come back anytime.

JAY LENO:

Even when I didn't have a place to stay, I never really minded it too much because I was getting great spots at the Improv. Budd treated me well. He was a character, but he always had a good heart.

SHELLEY ACKERMAN:

I was working the night that Jay auditioned for Budd, and besides the fact that he'd come down from Boston three nights in a row, maybe one of the other reasons Budd put him on immediately was because he needed an act. It's very possible that it served Budd at that point to say, "Okay, here he is. I need someone now."

Regardless, Jay was always a very nice, hardworking guy from day one. This never changed even after he began making it. He always had his eye on the prize and he never got involved in meaningless shit. He would do these hysterical bits where he'd say things like, "There was another senseless killing on the Upper West Side today." And you'd be sitting there saying to yourself, "As opposed to what—a very sensible killing on the Upper East Side?"

SILVER SAUNDORS FRIEDMAN:

I'm not sure where Jay stayed when he was in New York, but I had a lot of fun with him once or twice. One blizzardy New York night in the early seventies, I went home at about two in the morning so I could get some sleep and be up in time to take our kids to school. Budd was still at the club and asked Jay to drive me back to our apartment, which was on West 76th Street and Broadway.

At first, I hesitated because it was pouring snow and I knew that Jay's car was one of the Rolls-Royces he'd driven down from the dealership he worked for in Boston. But Jay, being the consummate gentleman he always was, didn't mind. We got in, and when he started the motor, of course it didn't move because there were eight-inch drifts and we were stuck. So Jay said to me, "I'll tell you what, Silver. If you go out and sit on the back of the car, I'll gun it and it will move."

I looked at him puzzled and said, "You mean I'm going to be the leverage that makes it jump out of the snow?"

When he told me yes, I somehow made my way through the snow, which was all the way up to my knees, and began pushing the car. Sure enough, it did the trick and while we were driving up Broadway I asked him why he didn't do any material about cars in his act. He didn't have an answer and then we dropped it, but I always sort of found it ironic since cars are one of his trademarks.

ZOE LANE FRIEDMAN, comedy producer and Budd and Silver's daughter:

My parents didn't bring the comics into our home a lot, but they both adored Jay and he was one of the ones who sometimes used to sleep on our couch. Even though he's a well-known carnivore, when we were growing up, my parents used to tell my sister and me that we'd wind up with a chin like Jay's if we didn't eat our vegetables.

Obviously, I never regretted my decision to put Jay on that first time for one minute. But beyond the fact that I'd been so impressed when he'd told me that he'd driven round-trip from Boston three nights in a row, the other thing that bowled me over was his uncanny ability to take the most mundane subjects and make them hilarious by putting his own spin on things. Of course, I'd seen Robert Klein do it before, and later there'd be guys like Seinfeld, Paul Reiser, and others who are all brilliant. However, Jay was always in a class by himself.

One of my favorite early routines he did was this thing about McDonald's, where he said, "You can eat there and then you can take three showers and someone would still be able to tell three days later." While he always killed at the Improv, one of the most transcendent incidences in my early association with him occurred when I went to see him open for the legendary drummer Buddy Rich at Lennie's on the Turnpike.

At the time, I was considering managing him and I wanted to see how he could do outside of the Improv where the audiences were usually a lot different than ours. So I drove up to see him, and because Buddy Rich was there, Lennie's was packed. I ended up standing in the back at the bar when the first thing I noticed was Jay onstage. In between his act, he was dancing and literally hopping from one foot to the other. It was one of the craziest things I'd ever seen, and at first I couldn't figure out what was going on.

JAY LENO:

It was my first paid gig ever. When they said, "Please welcome Mr. Jay Leno," some guy in the audience yelled out, "We hate him."

I remember saying to myself, "How can they hate me? I haven't been anywhere. Do they know my parents?" I was a kid and the audience was a bunch of men with cigars. It was the most intimidating environment you could possibly imagine.

Even so, Jay held his own, true to form. What I learned afterwards was that there was a guy seated next to the stage who manufactured cymbals for Buddy Rich. And for some unknown reason, he was either trying to work the audience up for Buddy or deflect attention from Jay by pounding on Jay's toes. Nevertheless, he handled it masterfully and that's when I decided to become his manager, which I was for the next two years.

Not long after, I also crossed paths with Murray Becker, a former navy buddy of comedian Lenny Bruce's, who later went on to a prominent career managing such acts as George Carlin and Jack Burns in addition to being the road manager for Dick Rowan and Dan Martin, the hosts of NBC's late-1960s sketch-comedy-variety series *Laugh-In*. At the time I met Murray, he was the booker at the Hollywood Playboy Club. He was also moonlighting for another manager who handled country music singer Eddie Arnold when he came up to me one day and said, "Why don't we go into business, Budd? You discover them, I'll develop them, and when we need it, I'll go to Mr. Bigshot and he'll help us get them to the next level."

As much as I liked and respected Murray, I must admit that I wasn't all that keen on the idea at first. While I would go on to manage a number of other singers and comedians over the years besides Jay and Bette Midler, being a personal talent manager was never something that I was ever particularly comfortable with, mainly because I quickly found myself assuming more of father figure role at a time when I already had two young daughters of my own. However, this realization didn't really occur until a number of years later, so Murray and I briefly worked together.

There were parts of being a manager that I found very fulfilling, particularly with clients like Jay. Even after that aspect of our relationship ended, Jay, needless to say, has never ceased to amaze any of us at the Improv. He was—and still is—the consummate comic's comic.

ROBERT KLEIN:

By the time Jay came along, I wasn't really an Improv regular anymore, but I still used to drop in from time to time to do a set and he'd be there. He had long hair that hung down to his shoulders, and with the round glasses he wore, he kind of reminded me of Thomas Jefferson. On my wall at home, I still have a terrific black-and-white picture of me with Budd and Jay, and Jay is literally looking up at me, which is very flattering. A couple of years before the picture was taken, I had bought a Mercedes at a place called Foreign Motors in Boston, which Jay had prepped for me, although I didn't know it at the time because the salesman had driven it down.

From the moment I first saw Jay at the Improv, I liked him. What resonated most was that he was intelligent and we both sort of spoke the same language humor-wise. Like mine, his wasn't borscht belt and so I always considered him to be a cut above everyone else.

JERRY SEINFELD:

Robert Klein and Jay Leno were my two biggest influences. They were always guys I looked up to and wanted to be just like because they were so strong and sharp. They had a crispness to their comedy, which I just loved.

AL FRANKEN:

We were sort of kindred spirits because Jay was coming down from Boston and my comedy partner Tom Davis and I were, too, so we had that in common. I remember that Jay used to do this hysterical routine about a bee getting caught inside a screen door. It was just this very funny sound effect that only

Jay could do that became a staple of his act for a while. Of course, it wasn't anything remotely like he ended up doing, but it was something he did really well.

RICHARD LEWIS:

Budd's told the story a million times about how Jay used to commute back and forth from Boston just to do sets at the Improv. I don't think I was there the first night he did it, but after I found out about it, I remember it impressed me because we both shared a similar work ethic when it came to stand-up. And he was also a great stand-up—just an amazing thinker. He was definitely one of the brainier guys from our group. When I say great and brainy, what I mean by that is that he was always a terrific observational comic in between the Robert Klein and Jerry Seinfeld years.

Also, he had long hair and wore glasses and he had a pipe, which made him this kind of hip hippie. The other thing was that his material was a lot more intellectual than the typical observational comic in those days. None of his bits ever started off with, "Hey, did you ever notice?"

ALAN ZWEIBEL:

The Improv was Jay's place. Case closed. Even on the menu, Budd had something called the Leno Burger, whatever the hell that was. When I was there, he used to come down from Boston on a motorcycle. He'd get up onstage and just rock the place.

BOB ZMUDA, writer, comedian, producer, and creator of *Comic Relief USA*:

Back in New York, Leno had this broken-down motorcycle that he would drive down from Boston in the winter. The thing was a piece a shit and the chain would always come off. Every time Jay came into the club, his hands would be filthy and Budd would say, "Here, I've got a jar of Lava soap for you. Clean your hands before you go on."

PAT BUCKLES, talent executive and former New York Improv waitress and manager:

During the famous New York blackout in the summer of 1977, Jay's motorcycle really saved us when he drove it into the club and parked it up onstage with the lights on so we could see while the show was going on. Practically everyone got drunk that night.

JACK KNIGHT:

I don't know how he managed to pull it off, but Jay actually drove into the LA Improv, through the show room, and up onto the stage with his motorcycle one night. It was right during the middle of another comic's set when all of the sudden there was this tremendous roar followed by the stench and cloud of exhaust smoke everywhere. Needless to say, the audience absolutely went nuts and afterwards he turned the bike around, left the club, and sped off down Melrose Avenue.

WILLIAM KNOEDELSEDER, former comedy reporter for the *Los Angeles Times* and author of *I'm Dying Up Here: Heartbreak and High Times in Stand-Up Comedy's Golden Era*:

Beginning in late 1977, I started covering the local comedy scene for the *Los Angeles Times*' Calendar section. It was the best gig in the world because we were the first newspaper in the country that ever had a comedy beat and I was the only guy covering it. I can remember that when I first saw Jay at the Hollywood Improv around 1978, he could literally get up and go on for an hour.

The other amazing thing about Jay, in contrast to guys like Robin Williams, was that he didn't go on flights of fancy. Robin sort of took it to a whole other stream of consciousness, as did Richard Lewis. But Jay was more of a traditional comic and the others admired that. He could play off the headlines and he could play off something that happened that morning. He was all over the place and he really hustled. It was like he did one thing and this was it.

HOWIE MANDEL:

I didn't start doing stand-up until the early 1980s, which was a good decade after Jay. I was also strictly an LA guy when it came to the Improv and these other clubs, and my perspective then was the same as it is now. We were all kids who were just trying to have fun and hone our craft, which Budd basically identified and said, "Hey, spend fifteen minutes, or ten minutes, or six minutes, and do it on my stage."

We did and then we saw so-and-so's voice, so-and-so's sensibility, and so-and-so's sense of humor becoming internationally known right before our eyes. Maybe if we were lucky enough, we'd be one of them. Then it got to the point where the ones who became stars became synonymous—like it was Jay Leno before and now it's just Leno. People like him were the ones filling the room each and every night back then. I mean, it wasn't like you had to run and go see them even though you knew how great they were. You had no idea the kind of impact they'd make or how lasting their talent would be.

BOB SAGET:

Like in every profession, there are certain minefields to be avoided in comedy—one of them being that you never wanted to go up after Jay Leno had just killed.

PAUL REISER:

Yes, but the truth was that Jay needed the Improv and the Improv needed Jay. When I first arrived in LA in 1983, Jay wasn't *Jay* yet, but he was probably the number-one touring act in the country and he would just knock it out of the park.

RITCH SHYDNER:

He didn't do this with everybody, but if you were a new comic in LA and you had some heat, Jay was like the one-man welcoming committee. He'd help you buy a car and he'd have you over to his house. He was really terrific that way.

PAULA POUNDSTONE, comedian, actor, and writer:

One of my greatest, greatest nights at the Hollywood Improv was with Jay back in the mideighties. Although we weren't what I'd call buddy-buddy yet, we'd met a couple of times before, plus Jay is a Massachusetts boy and I'm a Massachusetts girl so we had that in common.

One night, he pulled up in front of the club on this huge motorcycle he drove and came inside. We said hello, and then after realizing he needed to pick something up from the drugstore, he asked me if I wanted to come along for the ride. Naturally, I said yes, and so I climbed onto the back—and to this day, I'm sure I still have hip problems I don't even know about from straddling the back of it. It also had this massive sound system. So I got on, Jay cranked up the Beach Boys on the stereo, and we went cruising around Hollywood for the next hour looking for whatever he needed, with my hair blowing in the wind. It was as if I had fallen through some magical portal in Massachusetts and come through this astounding world on the other side.

BOBBY KELTON:

I'm thinking that 1978 or thereabouts was when I first met Jay at the Hollywood Improv and we became very friendly as the years went on. He hooked me up with his then managers Helen and Jerry Kushnick, which was a complete fiasco, but whenever I'd do *The Tonight Show* with Johnny Carson, the first call I got after my spot always came from Jay.

I wasn't ever on again after he became the host, but sometime in the mideighties, he asked me to fill in for him at a corporate gig he had in Hawaii. Despite the fact that it was at the last minute, there was no way I could refuse because he said, "It's day after tomorrow. The money is great. You can bring anybody you want. Everything is paid for."

I decided to invite my brother, and we flew over the next day. The only catch was that because Jay called me on a Thursday and the gig was on a Saturday, they couldn't change anything. It also meant that I had to use his name, which Jay told me to, and I flew to Hawaii as Jay Leno. This was before the days when people were hypersensitive about security and you had to present IDs everywhere, so when I got to Hawaii they rolled out the red carpet for us. Everything was comped and we stayed in the best hotel and ate at the finest restaurants with me posing as Jay.

A week later, I was scheduled to appear on *The Tonight Show*. I'd been telling everybody in Hawaii this, which I thought was okay, especially since I figured that most people there didn't watch *The Tonight Show*. Well, the night I was scheduled to go on after I got home, I was at NBC in Burbank when it suddenly occurred to me that when Johnny Carson announced me, everyone tuning in back in Hawaii was going to say, "Wait, that's Jay Leno!" I would have given anything to be a fly on the wall that night. To this day, I still often wonder what their reaction was.

EDDIE BERKE:

Somebody once told me a story about the time they'd gone with Jay on his private plane to perform somewhere. It was in a smaller city and after the gig on their way back to the airport, Jay wanted to get some food. The only place open was an ampm or a 7-Eleven, and when they stopped and the other comedian offered to go in, Jay told him he wanted to go instead. The reason why is because he wanted to let them have their moment. Jay wasn't being arrogant about it at all. He simply wanted to give the people working there a chance to meet a celebrity because they probably didn't have an opportunity to meet one that often.

BARBARA MCGRAW, college professor, attorney, and former Improv singer:

Jay never took off as an actor because he wasn't that great, but he's probably the best comedian there ever was when it comes to turning an audience around. There's just nobody like him and when he got *The Tonight Show*, we were all like, "Of course!"

Although I was already an attorney by this point and we'd lost touch, I remember writing him a letter to congratulate him and getting a call in my office a few weeks later. It was completely out of the blue and I was totally shocked, but when I picked up the phone his voice was unmistakable. He said, "Barbara, this is Jay. You didn't put your number down and I had to call all over town to reach you."

Keep in mind that this was 1992, which was before the Internet even existed yet. I just remember being absolutely floored that someone as important as Jay had gone to such lengths to track me down just so he could thank me for what seemed like such a small and well-deserved gesture.

But that's the kind of humble and unassuming guy Jay is. The last time I saw him was at a car show in Southern California several years ago. By this point, I'd gained about thirty pounds and was sporting a different hairdo. But Jay recognized me immediately. He came right up to me and said, "Hi, Barbara. How are you?"

DANNY AIELLO:

Let me tell you something about Leno. By virtue of when we were both there, I didn't know him that well at the Improv, but by the time he was hosting *The Tonight Show* we were pretty close. I was also a fairly frequent guest, and several years after he took over, I was on one night not long after my daughter Stacey had gotten married. Now I don't get offended easily, but all through my segment, Jay kept needling me about my daughter's wedding and asking whether or not we served meatballs at the wedding reception because I'm Italian. He just wouldn't stop, and for a long time after that I held a grudge against him. I really resented him talking about my daughter like that on national television even if he was just kidding.

But a few days after my son Danny passed away from pancreatic cancer in 2010, Jay did the most incredible thing. I'll never forget this and I still get choked up just thinking about it. Three days after my son's funeral, I was sitting in my house in Saddle River, New Jersey, not in the mood to talk to anyone when the phone rang. It was Jay, and on top of being in mourning over my son I was still pretty upset with him about what he'd said about my daughter on *The Tonight Show*.

However, I took the call anyway, and when I picked up the receiver, he said, "Danny, this is Jay. I just want to remind you of something. I saw a beautiful, blond-headed little boy hanging with you and watching what you did at the Improvisation so long ago. I just wanted to remind you that that boy was your son, Danny." I'll tell you I was speechless. Any ill feelings I might have had towards him just instantly faded away. He went way back up on the totem pole with me after that.

JUDD APATOW:

When he was hosting *The Tonight Show*, Jay used to accept unsolicited jokes for his monologue and I submitted some. Comedian Kevin Rooney was a buddy of mine and he'd written for Jay, so he recommended me. This was in the early nineties, not long after he'd begun hosting the show, and I was still living with my mother and grandmother at the time. So one night around midnight, the phone rang and my grandmother answered. It was Jay and my grandmother came running into the room to tell me. She was like, "Jay Leno's on the phone!"

At first, I couldn't believe it, but, sure enough it was Jay. He said, "I read your jokes and they're close." Then he explained why they weren't right. Of course, I was disappointed, but I also remember how incredibly kind and encouraging he was while saying my jokes weren't right for him. It was a huge thing for me.

PAUL PROVENZA, comedian, actor, writer, producer, and TV host:

To me, Jay was always one of these Oh My God! comics. When I first started going to the Improv around 1975, he had already moved to LA so he wasn't there that much. But as it just so happened, he was the emcee on the first open mic I did in New York. He probably did twenty minutes at the top and five minutes in between everyone else.

The way it worked back then was that the manager or one of the waitresses came in around six or seven to start getting ready for that evening's show. If you were a comic, they would hand you a number, which was the place you were on that night's lineup. And you didn't dare leave for any reason, because if you did you'd lose your place. At the time, I was still a teenager in high school living at home with my parents up in the Bronx, which was a good hour's commute by subway, and I had school the next day.

Even so, I wasn't about to miss my first shot at doing the Improv. But because I was a rookie I wasn't scheduled to go on until 3 AM. By this point, I was starting to get antsy and I was exhausted, so I went up to Jay and said, "Mr. Leno, I know it's not my turn for a couple of more numbers, but if there's any way I could maybe get on now it would be great because I've got class in three hours." Well, Jay just thought that was hysterical and he brought me up next. The best part of this story is that I got to retell it to him on *The Tonight Show* twenty-five years later.

JUDY ORBACH:

Jay and I used to have these great, really esoteric conversations about comedy. He used to say to me, "You know, Judy, there are a hundred jokes. Everything else is a finger off of that. It's only a hundred."

I'd be like, "Thanks, Jay. That's good to know."

TWENTY-FOUR
Producing My First Show

As much I enjoyed the newfound success and notoriety the Improv was bringing me, I never lost sight of my original goal of becoming a Broadway producer. In some ways, my dream burned brighter than ever—even in spite of the fact that by the early seventies, Manhattan's theater district, like the rest of the city, was in the midst of a precipitous and steadily escalating period of urban decay and economic decline that would nearly force New York to declare bankruptcy in 1975.

Of course, Times Square, where most of the Broadway theaters were not far from the Improv, has always had a seedy side. At the time, however, it was facing its worst crisis since the Great Depression. Practically overnight, the place once dubbed the "Crossroads of the World" had turned into a veritable potpourri of drugs, prostitution, and crime.

Even so, the 1970s ushered in some of the most acclaimed shows in Broadway history, particularly musicals. *Godspell, Jesus Christ Superstar, A Chorus Line, Hair, Sweeney Todd, Pippin, The Wiz.* These were just some of the names that lit up the marquees back then.

And now with my bank account and network of contacts expanding thanks to the Improv, I was clamoring to get a piece of the action any way I could. However, I still didn't have any sort of a game plan aside from occasionally attending opening-night parties, reading the show-business trades, and voluntarily holding multiple backers' auditions at the club.

Though most of the time my efforts were for naught, little by little I became savvy enough to know what was involved. I was also so excited whenever somebody tipped me off about a new show that I'd invariably take time to check it out no matter how busy I was, which is how I found out about a musical revue that was holding backers' auditions in the winter of 1972.

When I arrived at the stately prewar apartment building on Riverside Drive where they were being held not far from where I lived, I was immediately struck by a breathtaking blonde fashion model from Athens, Georgia, who was trying out for the lead. Not only did she have one of the most beautiful singing voices I'd ever heard, hitting every note pitch-perfectly, I also loved her genteel southern accent, which was sweetly tinged and foreign to me, and only added to her appeal. Her name was Kim Basinger.

The only downside was that she was still a completely unknown entity, and I worried that casting a novice would be too big of a risk. Having already worked with hundreds of young singers by this point, I had become highly attuned to what makes a person "ready." So with Kim, as much as I liked her personally, I just couldn't take a leap of faith—especially with my own money at stake. However, I was so enthralled with her otherwise that I might have been willing to overlook her lack of experience had it not been for one of the other producers telling me that I had to use her because she had a wealthy boyfriend who was only willing to invest if I did. Although I was as polite as I could be about it, I decided right then and there to tell him no. And while Kim would, of course, go on to become an Academy Award–winning actor, it turned out to be the right decision because the show never got off the ground.

It wasn't long, however, before I got another opportunity—and actually did produce my first show even though it never made it to Broadway. This time it was an anti–Richard Nixon political satire called *What's a Nice Country Like You Doing in a State Like This?* Originally conceived as a comedy album, it was written by Ira Gasman and Cary Hoffman. Aside from ripping apart Nixon, whom I loathed—and coming to my attention just as the Watergate scandal was about to explode—the other major selling point was that I'd known Cary ever since he started coming into the Improv to sing shortly after we first opened.

Not only that, our lives ultimately took similar paths. Like me, Cary had worked in advertising, although he wrote jingles and he was never on the account management side as I had been. He also later became a talent manager for singers and comedians—most notably for the late R&B legend Luther Vandross and comedian Zach Galifianakis—plus, he wound up owning a comedy club called Stand Up NY on Manhattan's Upper West Side. By the time I found out about the new show he had written and convinced him to let me produce it, we had known each other for nearly a decade.

CARY HOFFMAN, singer, talent manager, and composer of
***What's a Nice Country Like You Doing in a State Like This?*:**

Maybe it was 1964, '65, or '66, Cary Hoffman's name was Cary Ross and I was a struggling Frank Sinatra impersonator. Nobody told me that there was a pretty good real-life Sinatra and that I didn't have a chance. The only place I could sing was at the Improv—all because Budd Friedman used to introduce me and he liked me as a boring crooner. But make no mistake about it: I was a boring crooner. I couldn't lift my hands from my side even at the end of a song.

But Budd liked me, and I would come in with this other comic named Howie Mann who he loved, so he would put me on followed by Howie Mann. This went on for several years until I decided to give up singing to write advertising jingles. Then I got a call one day from a close friend of mine named Ira Gasman who also worked in advertising. Ira had been approached by somebody at another agency about writing the lyrics to a comedy album about Richard Nixon.

The premise was basically along the lines of the *First Family* album about the Kennedys, which had been a monster hit during the JFK administration. Ira asked me to write the music and so we collaborated on this comedy album called *Let Me Sing One Perfectly Clear Make* that was sold to Septa Records and recorded. One of the performers on it was Luther Vandross, whom I later signed and became his first manager and producer.

But then not long after, Septa discovered that Richard Nixon was putting together an enemies list and that anybody who went against the Nixon administration could get in trouble. This pretty much put the kibosh on things until Ira played a master copy for a woman named Miriam Fond who ran a small theater company out of a church in New York and convinced us to turn it into a live show, which we spent the next six months writing. When we finally opened, we had a lot of luck with it. It got a great review in the *New York Times* and eventually moved to the American Palace Theatre.

I went to see it not long after I read the review in the *Times*. Then when I discovered Cary had written the music, I immediately decided that I wanted to be involved. The premise was fantastic and the possibilities seemed endless because not only did it attack Nixon, it also went after H. R. Haldeman, John Ehrlichman, and John Dean, who were all co-conspirators in the Watergate scandal even though none of us knew how serious it was yet. I was so enthusiastic that I may have even called Cary the same night.

CARY HOFFMAN:

This had to be around 1972. Nixon had just beaten George McGovern in a landslide and been reelected president. Anyway, I got a call from Budd late one night. He said, "Cary, I heard about the show. I went to see it and I want to produce it."

Of course, I was thrilled because I always liked Budd and I never forgot the fact that he used to let me sing at the Improv. The only problem was that we were already in early negotiations with another producer who was planning to bring it to Broadway.

I told him that, but then I remembered that the other producer was also beginning to get cold feet because in a recent meeting he'd said, "Shows like yours belong in a cabaret, not a legitimate theater. You will die." Those were his exact words, [so I thought about it] and the very next day we cancelled our negotiations with this other producer and set up a meeting with Budd.

One of the reasons we decided to go with him was his enthusiasm. That was number one. Number two was the fact that I knew him, and I knew that he was a bit of a showman who could talk his way into just about anything. Plus, I knew how successful he'd been with the Improv. And he was funny, and he was a larger-than-life New York personality, which seemed like the perfect combination.

As much as I believed in the show, I also knew instinctively that it could never work in a traditional theater because it was a political satire and they rarely do well in this setting. My other concern was that the five-person cast was too small, and I also felt the audience was too specialized.

Still, my enthusiasm never waned and the woman who ran the Off-Broadway theater where it was playing was married to Sam Cohn at International Creative Management. Sam was one of the most powerful agents in America at the time. We were pretty friendly. We negotiated a deal where we were fortunate enough to get two then unknown actors named Betty Buckley and Priscilla Lopez. It was a major coup because they both went on to Broadway fame in *Cats* and *A Chorus Line*, although doing it at the Improv was out of the question because of our small stage and seating configuration, so I never even tried.

But as luck would have it, I was very friendly with two other guys named Sid Davidoff and Richard Aurelio, who had served as deputy mayors under New York mayor John Lindsay, who was one of the most progressive mayors in the US at the time. Sid and Richard had also recently become partners in a new restaurant called Jimmy's on West 51st Street around the corner from CBS. In the 1940s and '50s, the restaurant had been the site of Toots Shor's, a celebrity watering hole frequented by the likes of Jackie Gleason, Frank Sinatra, Orson Welles, and Ernest Hemingway. In its new incarnation, Jimmy's attracted a lot of politicos and media types.

Upstairs, it had a ninety-nine-seat theater. Plus, it was named after Pulitzer Prize–winning journalist Jimmy Breslin, who had originally been slated to be one of the partners. Jimmy was an ultraliberal who'd recently run for president of the New York City Council alongside onetime independent mayoral candidate and author Norman Mailer.

Its lineage and aesthetics notwithstanding, the way I saw it, putting on a show that took direct aim at Nixon at a place named after a left-wing journalist—and run by two of Mayor Lindsay's cronies—seemed like the perfect hook.

SID DAVIDOFF, lobbyist, attorney, and former co-owner of Jimmy's restaurant:

Richard Aurelio and I were the two principal partners of Jimmy's. Jimmy Breslin was supposed to be the other partner, but because of his contract with NBC they didn't want him owning a bar even though he was there all the time. Richard and I took it over towards the end of the Lindsay administration.

How Budd first approached us I don't really remember, but I'm sure he showed up one day with the idea of doing *What's a Nice Country Like You Doing in a State Like This?*, The arrangement we had was that he licensed the room for two nights a week. It was great because the show was topical and anti-Nixon. I'm also sure that one of the reasons he came to us was because we came out of the Lindsay administration, and many of our best customers were high-profile liberal politicians like New York governor Hugh Carey, Ted Kennedy, and Mario Cuomo. The deal we had was that Budd took the cover charge and we took whatever was left over on the food and drinks we sold.

The logo for the show was a pregnant Statue of Liberty, which I purposely chose because it made a statement, although after I'd already bought an ad in the *New York Times*, they refused to run it because they thought it was too controversial. In retrospect, I should have sued them because of all the free publicity we'd have received, and *What's a Nice Country* might have gotten a much longer shelf life if I had.

Still, we had a terrific run of nearly two years. It also received almost unanimously positive reviews, most notably from *New York Magazine*'s John Simon who called it "New York's Most Necessary Musical."

Though the show fizzled when it came to finding an audience in other cities—particularly Chicago where we closed after only a couple of months—after that, I continued to produce it elsewhere. One of those places was Los Angeles, where by mid-1974, I was also seriously contemplating opening a West Coast branch of the Improv.

PART THREE

TWENTY-FIVE
Expansion

Even though I was and will always consider myself a New Yorker, I'd been wanting to live in California ever since Easter weekend 1952, when six army buddies and I decided to drive down to Los Angeles from San Francisco while we were waiting to be deployed overseas during the Korean War.

I'm an avowed atheist Jew, but the thing that cinched it for me was when the USO invited us to attend Easter services at the Hollywood Bowl, and I heard the late actor Howard Keel—probably best remembered by younger generations for his role as Clayton Farlow on the 1980s TV soap opera *Dallas*—perform "Ave Maria" that evening. Howard's rich bass-baritone voice was so awe-inspiring that it indirectly planted the seeds of my wanting to live in California. On top of his incredible set of pipes, what made the experience so special was the equally spectacular setting. In those days, the band shell of the amphitheater had a concentric bowl-shaped set of arches, which made for unbelievable acoustics. Then there was also the famous Hollywood sign towering in the distance. The combined effect swept me off of my feet, and from then on I instinctively knew that I wanted to live in California someday.

But what mainly motivated me to make the move, once I finally did nearly two decades later, was that most of the entertainment industry, especially movies and television, had moved to the West Coast. Of course, there would be obvious exceptions like *Saturday Night Live*, which not only originated from NBC's New York headquarters at 30 Rockefeller Plaza, it also forever changed American comedy. However, at this point it hadn't even been conceived, and while the residual impact of *The Tonight Show* moving to LA in the spring of 1972 hadn't been nearly as bad as I thought and the club was doing better than ever, I could also no longer ignore the fact that many of my best comics were following suit.

But even as much as I wanted to make the move, I still had serious doubts about whether I really could. Moreover, I had never taken a single day off from the Improv in the entire time I ran it, plus everybody knew me, so the most pressing question was how it could survive without me. And shuttering the New York club and moving it lock, stock, and barrel to Los Angeles was completely out of the question, especially considering how hard I had worked to build it.

Fortunately, my answer would soon come in the form of an ambitious young man and future president of both HBO and Starz Entertainment named Chris Albrecht, whom I left in charge of the club for two weeks in the summer of 1974 while I took my first vacation to France.

At the time we first met, Chris was part of a two-man comedy team. Its formation came out of a chance encounter with a young radical named Bob Zmuda, who later went on to become Andy Kaufman's writing partner and occasionally played his alter ego Tony Clifton onstage and in television appearances. In addition, Bob founded Comic Relief USA, an annual event that raised money for the homeless in the United States beginning in the mideighties. He also worked briefly as a bartender at the New York Improv in the early seventies. He and Chris first met in Pennsylvania during the summer of 1973 where they were both performing in a summer-stock theater company.

CHRIS ALBRECHT, president and CEO of Starz Entertainment and former New York Improv partner:

I met Bob Zmuda for the first time on the day we got to Mansfield, Pennsylvania. It was kind of a meet and greet, waiting for this guy who was supposed to be the main character in this play we were doing, which was Bob.

After a few minutes, he finally pulled up in a car with this woman who was driving. He gave her a kiss and said hello to us. The woman was very attractive, which I immediately took notice of, and I asked him who she was. That's when he started telling us this story about how she had picked him up when he was hitchhiking and they'd been shacked up together for the past couple of days in a hotel where they had a wild, passionate love affair.

It turned out that she was his wife, Brenda, and he was lying, which Zmuda does habitually. However, we hit it off instantly anyway. There's a state college there called Mansfield University that had a tent theater, and we were doing a season of a bunch of different plays. I can't even remember them all, but Bob, who was graduating from Carnegie Mellon in Pittsburgh, had a comedy-magic act on the side. When I told him I wanted to pursue acting professionally, he told me that stand-up comedy was a great way to do it. A lot of comics like Freddie Prinze, Jimmie Walker, and Gabe Kaplan were getting sitcoms because they'd come out of clubs like the Improv and Catch A Rising Star. So Bob had this idea that we should move to New York—which he was already considering doing—and that we should be roommates so we could put together a comedy act that we could audition at these clubs.

I grew up in New York, so I liked the idea. But I also kind of filed it away for a while because at first I wasn't sure if he was serious about it, which he was. Eventually, we got an apartment together, as well as jobs working in the scene shop at the theater at Riverside Church. And in our spare time, we wrote.

Back then, comedy was a whole new world for me and I didn't have a better idea than Zmuda had, so I just followed his lead and we worked up some stuff in the living room—mostly bad advertising parodies. One of them was a takeoff on this TV commercial for some guy who had a hair replacement business where he said, "Hard to believe I'm bald. I know it is."

Basically, we inverted the premise, so I would sit on Zmuda's lap and he would put his arms through mine, pretending that I was a cadaver. Then I'd go, "It's hard to believe I'm dead. I know it is." It was just awful, but somehow we managed to get passed at both the Improv and Catch A Rising Star.

BOB ZMUDA:

I started out as a kids' magician, and then I went from that to being a ventriloquist and a stage hypnotist. I also put together my own theatrical troupe when I was sixteen or seventeen and then I hung out at Second City in Chicago. All of this is really important because the progression is totally relevant to Budd Friedman.

In the 1960s, I got caught up in politics with Abbie Hoffman and Jerry Rubin. I was the Midwest head of the Yippie Party in Chicago where my politics were pretty much guerilla street theater and doing put-ons with protesters. I finally left Chicago for Carnegie Mellon University in Pittsburgh, where one of my first jobs was in summer stock in Mansfield, Pennsylvania. I think the show we were doing was *The Drunkard*, which is how I met Chris, and we became fast buddies.

What drew us together was we were both pranksters. I always thought I was the Prankster King. When we first met, Chris was this great-looking guy who had a full head of hair. I showed up that day with my wife, but I didn't want anybody to know about it because I was trying to get laid that summer. All of a sudden, Chris came up to me and said, "Bob, I don't know much about you, but everyone is talking about what a great actor you are. I gotta tell you, you blew the roof off. You see that girl over there? She was just raving about your performance."

About ten minutes later, I went up to this girl. I'd had a few drinks in me and when I tried talking to her, she just blew me off. She hadn't even seen the show, and she thought I was just this obnoxious guy trying to hit on her, which I was. Chris had totally set me up and I was like, "You motherfucker!"

But we laughed our asses off about it and we became inseparable that summer. One of the things we talked about was our careers, acting-wise, although Chris still wasn't sure this was what he wanted to do. I think his backup plan was to become an accountant. But I urged him to try acting anyway. I said, "Look, why don't we pursue this acting dream of ours. We could go to LA and pursue it there, or we could go to New York."

So we both left college and headed to New York, where we got an apartment and tried to become actors even though we were totally green, stupid young kids. We actually thought we could get on Broadway in six months even though we didn't have Equity cards. The only things we could audition for were Off-Off-Off-Off-Broadway and our only saving grace was that we both had a little savings.

Meanwhile, there was this guy at Riverside Church, where we were working in the scene shop, who turned us on to this other guy named Dick Scanga, who was building a little dinner theater called the Little Hippodrome on the Upper East Side. It turned out to be the first dinner theater in America. It also turned out to be an ingenious idea because a night out on the town was so expensive between the cost of theater tickets, dinner, drinks, and a cab.

Dick's concept was to have it all under one roof, and he hired us to do the construction. All of the sudden, Chris and I were learning about how to do Sheetrock and all this other stuff, which was great. But then the theater started going under because he'd overextended himself. Not long after, Chris and I got evicted from this shit-hole apartment where we were living because we couldn't afford the rent, so we ended up living in the back of this theater where we were also waiters because Dick couldn't afford to pay us.

Now, this is where Budd enters into the picture. While all of this was going on, we were still trying to keep our acting careers going by the skin of our teeth. And one day—I'm not sure why—I was walking through Hell's Kitchen. I made a left instead of a right and that's when I came across this little club called the Improvisation. I'd heard it was the first comedy club in America. As soon as I walked in, the first thing I thought to myself was: "What the fuck is this?"

Chris and Bob were so bad as a comedy team they were funny. But I knew Dick Scanga, who had started the Hippodrome, which reminded me a lot of my original concept for the Improv. I was also impressed by the fact that Chris knew how to build things, which I did also, and so I hired him to do some carpentry work.

Then I continued to let the pair do their god-awful comedy act against my better judgment. At the same time, I could tell Chris was a go-getter and that he seemed like he could handle responsibility. This proved correct when I hired him to work the door during our children's cabaret on Sundays that Andy Kaufman hosted. So when my then wife Silver and I decided to go to France for three weeks for our first vacation in the summer of 1974, leaving Chris in charge seemed like a no-brainer.

CHRIS ALBRECHT:

I think Budd basically felt that if Scanga trusted us—and especially me—that he could let me run the club while he and Silver went away on vacation.

But it was also kind of awkward because Budd already had a young woman named Judy Orbach working the door. So there were people who were like, "Why is this guy coming in and why is Budd putting him in charge?" I think there was definitely a little resistance to me at first, although that smoothed out pretty quickly and we began to develop a rapport. I also listened to the people who worked there and everything ran fine during those three weeks. The waitresses didn't necessarily want to hear from me, and it's conceivable that most of my duties during this time were restricted to mixing drinks as the relief bartender.

Upbeat and confident by how well the Improv had done in my absence, I immediately began making plans to open a second location in Los Angeles not long after Silver and I returned from France. However, not everyone understood my reasons at first.

BOB ZMUDA:

Budd was looking to get rid of the New York Improv around then. He might tell you otherwise, but my take on it was that he thought he was going nowhere with this shitty little place he had in Hell's Kitchen—despite all the success it had had, which was a total fucking accident.

The other thing was that he still wanted to be a Broadway producer, or at least an Off-Broadway producer, at this point. He was always leaving the club to have meetings to mount some Off-Broadway production. He had no idea that he was sitting on a gold mine with the Improv.

Contrary to what Bob and others may think, getting rid of the New York club never even entered my mind when I decided to expand. I have always prided myself on thinking things through from every angle when it comes to making a big decision and I didn't do this hastily.

Nevertheless, as I began getting more and more serious about making the move, the person I had the most difficult time convincing was Silver. At the time, our marriage, which was never a happy one, was severely strained and we fought constantly. Beyond that, though, Silver was never a fan of Los Angeles the way I was—something that can be traced back years earlier when she struggled to find work as a young actor in Hollywood before we met—even though she now lives there with our daughter Zoe and her family.

Though this would ultimately spell the end of our troubled marriage, she reluctantly agreed to go. As I was starting to look for possible locations, the first person I called was my old friend Jack Knight, who eventually became a stockholder, and was then appearing opposite Dom DeLuise on the short-lived NBC sitcom *Lotsa Luck*.

JACK KNIGHT:

I don't remember all that much about it except that Budd called me one day out of the blue in the fall of 1974 and told me he was planning to open up a second Improv out here. I did later become an investor, which I still am to this day, but there was never any talk about that at first.

Budd wanted me because he trusted my judgment and because of all the work I had done with him in New York. We looked at several places. One of them was on Third Street near Cedars-Sinai Medical Center. The other one was a plumbing supply house on Melrose Avenue in West Hollywood. While neither of them was practical, directly across the street from the plumbing supply house was a former furniture factory that after that had been a folk music club called the Ash Grove. At the time we saw it, however, the current occupants were an improv troupe called the Pitchell Players.

One of the most important lessons I learned with the New York club was that location is everything. So when I was scouting places for the LA club, one of my requirements was that it had to be on a centralized thoroughfare that was easy to get to from any part of the city. I also knew that because we were a comedy club it needed to be in Hollywood.

Those were my stipulations, and the Ash Grove met them. I was also intrigued by the Ash Grove's lineage as I had been with the New York club. Located at 8162 Melrose Avenue, it had been steeped in show-business history ever since a UCLA alumnus named Ed Pearl opened it in 1958. Over the next decade and a half, it had become a folk and rock music club with acts including Pete Seeger, Taj Mahal, Roger McGuinn, Linda Ronstadt, Johnny Cash, Muddy Waters, and Country Joe McDonald. Most recently, it had been the home of the Pitchell Players improvisational troupe where Minnesota senator Al Franken—a soon-to-be junior writer on *Saturday Night Live*—had been performing with his writing partner Tom Davis. Al was the one who told me about it.

AL FRANKEN:

Don't quote me on this, but it was probably around 1972. Tom and I would perform there with the Pitchell Players and

another Improv troupe called The Credibility Gap, which is
how we got to know guys like Michael McKean, David Lander,
and Harry Shearer.

Anyway, eventually the owners of the Ash Grove were looking to sell and it just so happened that Tom and I were back in
New York. When Budd told me that he was starting a club in
LA, I said, "Well, the Ash Grove—the old Ash Grove—might be
up for sale." He didn't know that until I told him. I also know he
never paid me a finder's fee.

They weren't the actual landlords, but the lease to the building was con-
trolled by Joe Roth, a film producer who had been part of a comedy team
I'd worked with in New York, and an actor named Roger Bowen, who
played the colonel in the film version of *M*A*S*H*. At the time, they managed both the Pitchell Players and the building; although it was dilapi-
dated like the New York club was when I first found it, it had great bones.

The only problem was that the room wasn't available yet, so I continued my search in earnest when about three months later I got a call
from Joe. Joe had been there the night I went to look at it in LA and he
asked me if I was still interested in the building, which I was.

However, the deal Joe tried to make with me was $30,000 for a two-
and-a-half-year lease, which wasn't feasible. I told him that, but I was
still interested, so I immediately flew out to LA anyway to see if I could
bargain with him. On the afternoon of my arrival, Joe, Roger, and I went
over to the landlord's house, who was the same guy who had originally
owned the furniture factory.

The first thing I remember about him was that he looked like a clone
of actor Lee Strasberg in the film *The Godfather*. He was about eighty,
and at first his back was turned, concealing his face. When he finally
turned around, I immediately told him I couldn't buy a business with a
two-and-a-half-year lease, which I also couldn't afford. I added, "Why
don't you just sell me the place?" to which he replied, "I already turned
down $75,000 for the entire corner."

In spite of this, though, something about the way he said it made it
sound like a now-or-never deal, and not only did I get a ten-year lease
out of him that day—where we initially paid $1,500 a month—we've
been there ever since.

TWENTY-SIX
My Early California Adventures

With a deal finally inked for my new LA club, which I initially named the Hollywood Improvisation, the first thing I set out to do was find investors to help absorb some of the risk. Naturally, the first people I turned to were comedians like Jimmie Walker and Freddie Prinze, who were both starring on the hit sitcoms *Good Times* and *Chico and the Man*, respectively. In addition, I asked Liz Torres, who had been one of my first waitresses in New York and was now a successful actor in her own right, as well TV producer Ernie Chambers, screenwriter Norman Stiles, and actor-writer Stanley Ralph Ross.

All of them enthusiastically said yes. The reason I asked them was that I wanted to get people with names who had a following and could draw people in, most importantly from the film and television industry. My plan worked, too, because after a breakfast meeting organized by my attorney, Stand Handman, in the legendary Polo Lounge at The Beverly Hills Hotel, I wound up with fourteen limited partners owning 1 percent each for $2,000 a share.

One of the most promising prospects at the meeting was Carol Burnett's business manager. Though Carol chose not to invest, Harvey Korman, then one of the co-stars of her CBS variety show, did. At the time, Harvey's career—whose other highlights included being Danny Kaye's former sidekick, playing Hedley Lamarr in the 1974 Mel Brooks western satire, *Blazing Saddles*, and The Great Gazoo on the 1960s animated children's series *The Flintstones*—was at its peak thanks to his work on *The Carol Burnett Show*, for which he was nominated for six Emmy Awards and won four times.

My friendship with Harvey also dated all the way back to the early days of the New York Improv when he came in late one night and we struck up a conversation with two women even though we were both married. Afterwards, we decided to go out for breakfast at an Italian restaurant on Second Avenue that stayed open all night—and where, aside from the fact that we each had wives, we realized that nothing was going to happen as soon as we sat down. This was followed by about ten or fifteen minutes of almost complete silence until one of the ladies finally said, "We're going to go. I have a car. Can I drop anybody off?"

With that, Harvey got up and walked out, although I took them up on their offer and they drove me home. Although I didn't see Harvey again until he came into the club about a year later, the first words out of his mouth were, "Did you get any action that night, Budd?"

"Not a thing," I said.

"Thank God," he replied.

I'm sure if I had, he would have been furious with me, but Harvey turned out to be one of my dearest friends and most trusted confidantes in Hollywood right up until his death from a brain aneurism in 2008. I also valued his opinion when it came to other comics, particularly after he brought Johnny Carson in one night in the midseventies. They came specifically to see Jay Leno, which Jay credits for helping to get him his first appearance on *The Tonight Show*.

JAY LENO:

The night Harvey brought me in, Johnny gave me some great advice because I was a better performer than I was a writer. He said, "You have a great way of telling a joke, but they need to be stronger." He taught me that and it's true—in other words, if you have a strong joke on paper, and if you're a strong performer, you have a much better chance of it working.

A lot of performers write funny, but they don't have any stage presence, and vice versa. On the other hand, if you can really deliver *and* it's well written, it kills on both levels. I remember learning that from Johnny. The other thing he said was, "You can't shout your way through a set."

CHRIS KORMAN, marketing and branding executive and son of Harvey Korman:

Jay always acknowledges my father for helping him get on *The Tonight Show* because he got Johnny Carson to come see him that night at the Improv. I don't know how many investors Budd had in the beginning, or what their relationship was before that, but I know my dad was one of the first.

I also didn't discover this until I was about fifteen or sixteen, and he told me one night when he took me to the club dressed in a tuxedo. I remember that Connie Sellecca, who was starring with James Brolin on the ABC nighttime soap *Hotel*, was there, and I innocently tried to strike up a conversation with her in the parking lot until my dad interrupted me.

But as close as we were, my dad wasn't the kind of guy who went around talking business, particularly with me. I also didn't go a lot after that without my father even though Budd invited me to come in for free anytime I wanted. But I rarely took him up on that because I didn't want to take advantage. I can also say that from an investment standpoint, the Improv was very lucrative for my dad. He genuinely loved Budd and I truly think it was mutual.

As I was making the final preparations for my move to Los Angeles in late 1974, I was also making contingency plans for the New York club, including asking Chris Albrecht to become my successor.

CHRIS ALBRECHT:

Budd didn't ask me immediately. Right after he and Silver got back from France, that's when I went to work as a bartender at another place over on Eighth Avenue called Jimmy Ray's. I don't remember if Budd stopped by or if he asked me to come to the Improv, but whatever it was, the way he presented it was that he wanted to go to LA for a month and he asked me if I'd be willing to come back and run the club.

I was, like, "Sure," but not because I necessarily wanted the job. It just seemed better than being a bartender and staying up until five in the morning to close Jimmy Ray's every night. So I went back to the Improv, and Budd was gone for about a month, maybe less. When he returned, he told me that he'd found a club and was planning to move. Then he offered me a partnership because he said he wanted to have more than an employee in charge.

It all made perfect sense—especially considering the irresistible deal he was offering me: 25 percent of the club for $25,000. This was a fortune in those days, but he also allowed me to pay it out over two years. I was practically broke at the time, so my grandmother borrowed the money from her credit union at United Airlines. I think it came out to fifteen grand that first year and $10,000 the second year, or vice versa. Anyway, I managed to swing it and then Budd and Silver moved to LA.

One of his only conditions was that he wanted me to emcee because he didn't want to spend the money [hiring another one], which was fine. Then things slowly began to change. There was this old bookkeeper named Tony who'd worked for Budd who would come in during the day. As I slowly started learning more about the business side from Tony, we began to experiment with things a little bit, like the food. Also, a couple of people from LA started to come in and perform there.

JUDY ORBACH:

Budd didn't tell me much about the move at first. He just said, "All right, I'm going to LA to look for space for the new club and you're in charge." At that point, a few months went by before Chris came, so there were tons of nights when I was the queen of the kingdom with the keys. It was pretty fucking amazing to be nineteen or twenty years old and running a New York nightclub. All of us, including Chris, were under the age of twenty-five.

DAVID STEINBERG, film producer and talent manager:

We were all wet-behind-the-ears kids who used to party a lot and we were kind of nuts at the time. But Budd's decision to let Chris take over was a very astute one even though it wasn't like he was the boss. He had an incredible comedy mind, which always made him smarter than everybody else. The best analogy I can offer was that Budd was more of a father figure whereas Chris was a partner in crime.

STEVE MITTLEMAN, screenwriter, actor, and comedian:

Chris and I attended the same high school in Queens, which probably helped me out a little bit, although he also liked my material and we hung out a lot. We played cards together sometimes.

PAT BUCKLES:

I have warm feelings for both of them, but I also think it's safe to say that a lot of the less-established comics were kind of intimidated by Budd, who had already had a huge reputation in New York. I think his leaving may have opened the door for new talent somewhat.

Following a series of farewell parties, I officially left New York in December of 1974 while Silver stayed behind with our two daughters, who were seven and nine at the time, so they could finish out the school year. Saying good-bye to my family, friends, and colleagues was obviously very bittersweet, and so was leaving the city I'd called home for most of my life as everyone wished me well.

When my plane landed at Los Angeles International Airport, where Jay Leno picked me up in his Oldsmobile, I immediately became convinced I'd made the right decision—especially after buying my first car, a 1959 white Cadillac that came complete with fins on the back. It reminded me a lot of the car I'd driven across country with a couple of college friends from New York University the summer after we graduated, and I felt like a teenager again.

For the first six months, I stayed at the Magic Castle Hotel before finally renting a four-bedroom house in Beverly Hills in the summer of 1975. The owner, a local high school shop teacher, had built the house himself. It was a wonderful place with impeccably detailed craftsmanship, a large backyard, terrific views, and one major catch: It also came with a pet monkey who lived in an iron cage on the patio that I had to feed. Being the inveterate animal lover I am, I happily agreed, although the arrangement quickly came to an end one afternoon not long after I moved in when I reached inside the cage with a piece of celery and the monkey nearly took my arm off.

Meanwhile, in preparation for the new club, I began galvanizing my relationships with many of my New York comedians, particularly Jay, whom I enlisted to help me paint the ceiling, although mostly I wanted to entice them to perform there. We had a lot of fun getting it ready, too, even though we had our work cut out for us. Just as it had been in New York, the LA club was rustic, although the conditions on Melrose Avenue were definitely a cut above West 44th Street for sure.

That's the best way I can describe things. In addition to installing new lights and a small sound system, one of the first things we did was put in a bar in the front room, which turned out to be one of our biggest assets even though we only served beer and wine in the beginning. After that, we put in tables and chairs in the main show room, along with lowering the stage and adding a brick wall, which Jack Knight helped me with.

BONNIE BOLAND, actor and Jack Knight's wife:

It was an empty building at first and Jack turned it into a beautiful place because Budd let him do it. We lived in the Valley at the time and I remember going over every day with our two kids and watching it unfold.

LIZ TORRES:

When Budd first called me about being an investor in the LA club, we'd been on the outs for a while, but I still agreed and there was no further discussion about it. It was me, Freddie Prinze, Harvey Korman, and Jimmie Walker, as I recall, and I did it sight unseen.

I remember wondering what I'd gotten myself into the first time I saw the club because the neighborhood itself was kind of dingy. It reminded me of Greenwich Village with little mom-and-pop stores scattered all around, and there was nowhere to park. The LA club was sort of dingy also, although it had the funky vibe New York had, which made it fun. But unlike New York, there was hardly anybody in that LA neighborhood at night back then, which I found strange because it was a showbiz town.

West Hollywood was definitely an up-and-coming area in those days, but it was still in Hollywood—and one of the reasons I chose this location was because Hell's Kitchen was no great shakes either and we'd succeeded beyond our wildest imagination in spite of it. When we finally opened in March 1975, the place was mobbed.

TOM DREESEN:

The thing that stood out most to me about the opening night was that it was a big deal, and there were people lined up around the block. I don't know how he did it, but Budd got everybody he knew in the business there.

DAVID STEINBERG, film producer and talent manager

I didn't really arrive at Melrose until 1980, at which point I was an expatriate from New York who was still this kind of new kid on the block. The Hollywood Improv back then was like the local commissary. You used to go there, drink too much, and then complain about the food because everything tasted the same. It was crap food, but it was fun because everybody was funny. And we all shared the same common bond of being in the comedy business.

Star-wise, the biggest person we had in the beginning was Freddie Prinze. We also had other New York guys like Richard Pryor, Richard Belzer, and Richard Lewis, along with Byron Allen, Wil Shriner, and Michael Keaton, who were just starting out.

BYRON ALLEN:

When I first got to the Improv right after Budd opened, I was just fourteen years old, but Budd took a liking to me instantly. He literally treated me like I was his own son. He got me right on and off, and he always made sure that I didn't follow any of the dirtier comics.

WIL SHRINER, actor, comedian, writer, director, and game-show host:

I used to show these little 8 mm films as part of my comedy act. I don't remember the one I used the first time I went to the Improv. I do remember—besides the monocle Budd wore— that it was during a Sunday night showcase where he'd put comics up for about six minutes. Afterwards, he said to me, "Very good, very funny." He didn't come right out and tell me I was a regular, but I was after that first night.

Besides a plentiful and steady stream of talented and willing comics, another thing we benefited from in the beginning was having The Credibility Gap, an improvisational troupe that was a holdover from the Pitchell Players. Its members included Harry Shearer along with

Michael McKean and David Lander, who were a year away from starring as Lenny and Squiggy on the ABC sitcom *Laverne & Shirley*. Staffwise, I also hit pay dirt early on with actor Debra Winger working for me as a waitress, Danny Aiello's son Ricky as a bouncer, and future president of CBS Leslie Moonves, who was one of the Hollywood Improv's first bartenders.

TWENTY-SEVEN
Andy Kaufman Turns Stand-Up Upside Down

The story of how our early California years evolved wouldn't be complete without devoting a couple of full chapters to some of the comedians we had in New York who were beginning to gain notoriety around this same period. Many of them would eventually light up the Hollywood Improv as well, but I'd be remiss not to mention their beginnings back East first.

Of these, the one I'm still asked about most frequently is Andy Kaufman, who arrived at West 44th Street about six months after our tenth anniversary in the fall of 1973. An enigmatic provocateur whose unflagging penchant for pranks and controversy often blurred the line between imagination and insanity almost beyond recognition, he was a wonderfully colorful kaleidoscope of contradictions from the get-go.

Above all, he helped redefine the very notion of what it means to be a comedian. In large part, this is because he never considered himself one and openly hated telling jokes. And nothing—and this shouldn't come as any surprise—could have prepared me for meeting him for the first time. No other audition on either coast ever had the distinction of going from completely disastrous to utterly mesmerizing in a matter of seconds the way Andy's did.

The event leading up to it was a random call I received one afternoon from a local coffeehouse owner from Andy's hometown in the New York suburb of Great Neck, Long Island. At the time, Andy was twenty-three and still living with his parents in Great Neck. He had also recently been fired from his gig at the coffeehouse.

Instead of telling me this, however, the exact words of the same person who had given Andy the ax were, "You should see this guy. He's terrific." Other than that, I don't remember much else about the conversation except for taking him at his word and saying something to the effect of, "Send him in."

But while I agreed to let him audition for me, I didn't really have any expectations. Keep in mind that I had been doing this for nearly a decade by then and I'd been disappointed before. In fact, very early on, I learned to adopt a wait-and-see attitude to avoid disappointment. And when a new performer does exceed your expectations, the excitement of seeing them before the rest the world knows who they are can be exhilarating.

So waiting and seeing was what I decided to do with Andy. In this instance, it turned out to be the right decision. When he showed up on the same night I got the call from this guy on Long Island, Andy immediately tried to catch me off guard by doing "Foreign Man"—an early prototype for Latka Gravas, the character that eventually became the basis of his role as the goofball auto mechanic on the late-seventies hit sitcom *Taxi*.

Though I was suspicious before he even opened his mouth, I still reasoned that I should give him the benefit of the doubt. As I always did with a new act, I began the audition process by asking where he was from—at which point his voice became childlike and he replied in badly broken English, "An island in the Caspian Sea."

I couldn't believe what was happening, and even though I immediately realized there were no inhabited islands in the Caspian Sea, there was also something very seductive in the way he said it and I put him on anyway. As soon as I did, Andy went up and proceeded to stumble through a sophomoric series of bad celebrity impressions, all of them in the Foreign Man accent and each one worse than the other, while the audience either stared at him or giggled nervously.

Clearly, we were being had. I was becoming increasingly impatient, not to mention angry, although looking back now I consider that night to be one of the most important milestones of the Improv. I can't imagine what we would have been without Andy. That said, I remember being concerned at the time that there might be trouble if I didn't do something.

Then Andy proceeded to pull off what would perhaps be one of the most spectacular sleight-of-hand tricks in the history of comedy. Just as I was about to try to get him offstage without causing a riot, he announced in the same Foreign Man accent, "I would like to do the Elvis Presley," and turned towards the brick wall.

After that, five seconds passed, maybe ten. From there, Andy turned back towards the audience and launched into a spot-on impression of Elvis singing "Treat Me Nice" as the audience went wild and I stood there in disbelief. Though it took me a minute or two to absorb what I had just witnessed, immediately after this he became a regular.

And not too long after that debut, of course, Andy became a cult favorite whose manic energy and envelope-pushing routines (eating ice cream onstage, reading *The Great Gatsby*, lip-syncing the Mighty Mouse cartoon show theme with a record player, etc.) would quickly make him one of the most celebrated talents ever to appear on our stage—and at the same time—elevate the Improv to a new level of acclaim.

The ripple effect also grew beyond the Improv thanks in no small part to the premiere of *Saturday Night Live* on NBC in 1975 where Andy was a featured performer during its first season. But even so—and despite his almost immediate audience appeal—there was likewise still something of an adjustment period.

Especially when it came to his comedic peers, he confounded them as much as he astounded them. On the other hand, if others weren't also trying to emulate his style, at the very least they all wanted to catch a live glimpse. And of the later Improv contingent who never even met Andy, there were those, too, who would occasionally try to mimic his act onstage—usually with lackluster results.

JIMMY FALLON:

I think every comedian of a certain age wants to have their Andy Kaufman moment onstage. I tried one night at the Hollywood

Improv in the early nineties when there were people from the David Letterman show in the audience. I think HBO may have even had a showcase that night, too, although I'm not sure.

I wasn't on either showcase, but I was the first comic up afterwards, so I figured that if they hadn't left yet, then maybe I could catch them and get cast in something. Budd had told me they were coming several days earlier, so I decided to grow a beard. The only problem was that I'd only started about three days before and so it was pretty much stubble.

But I decided it would be a moment, anyway, if I shaved it off onstage during my act. So when I got onstage, I had a razor, a can of shaving cream, and a bowl of water with me, and throughout my entire set, I shaved. By the time I was finished, I was clean shaven, but the bit had nothing to do with the jokes I was telling and it totally bombed. In fact, it was embarrassing even though I thought it was avant-garde at the time.

Of course, the more I think about it now, the more lame it was—and here's the kicker. As I was leaving, I completely forgot about the shaving cream, the razor, and the bowl of water, so I had to go back onstage to get them.

JACK KNIGHT:

I saw Andy perform for the first time in New York not long after he started at the Improv. Because I'd heard about this thing he had for trying to pull a fast one on the audience to make them look like fools, I decided to take part in it just to see what would happen. The particular bit he did was where he repeated a song—something like "Monday potatoes, Tuesday potatoes, Wednesday soup."

The part I wound up doing was "Wednesday soup," and when my turn came, I did it in the voice of Gregory Peck. I'll never forget the look on Andy's face when I did it either, because he was like, "Fuck! He knows what's going on and he's going to do it again." I think he may have even shortened it because he knew I was on to him.

MICHAEL RICHARDS, actor, writer, and retired comedian:

Andy resonated with me from the moment I saw him. Somebody told me about him when I was performing in San Diego. His description was, "This guy who gets onstage and plays the bongo drums." At first my reaction was, "Yeah, and what else?" But when he said, "That's it," I was like, "Cool, great. I've got to check this scene out."

If I remember correctly, the first time I saw Andy perform he had a washing machine onstage with him and he was reading a magazine while he did his laundry. The audience basically got up and left, but I remember thinking to myself, "That's fantastic." I just loved the play—that he would set something up like that and be so committed to it. He was the ultimate trickster, but I got him right off the bat.

ALAN ZWEIBEL:

I got to know Andy a little bit during *Saturday Night Live*'s first season on the air. I remember the first time I saw him perform, thinking to myself that I had never seen anything like it in my life. I'd heard about him before that, although when I first started hanging out at the Improv, Andy wasn't there. He had a gig somewhere in Florida that didn't go well for him, which a lot of the other comics were talking about.

But having never seen him before at this point, I didn't really understand what they meant. And then that very first time I saw him perform—all in one fell swoop—he read *The Great Gatsby*, he played the bongos, and he lip-synced the theme from Mighty Mouse. I think the first thing I thought was, "Of course, they wouldn't understand this in Miami." I had never seen such control—and maybe even to this day such manipulation of an audience, going from where he could make them hate him, boo him, and curse him, and then three minutes later, they're laughing their asses off cheering him.

JERRY STILLER:

Though we're of different generations and we come from completely different schools of comedy, I still think Andy Kaufman was one of the funniest human beings on the face of this earth. The thing about it was that I never knew if he was real or not and I'm still not completely sure. However, the more I've thought about it as the years have gone by, the more I'm convinced that he wasn't putting us on.

AMY STILLER:

Back in the mid to late seventies when Andy was first becoming famous, he came to my parents' apartment once for

Thanksgiving dinner with his then girlfriend Elayne Boosler. But instead of turkey and dressing, all Andy wanted was a peanut butter and jelly sandwich and a glass of milk. It was the funniest thing—and, of course, we gave it to him.

KITTY BRUCE, writer, former New York Improv hat-check girl, and daughter of comedian Lenny Bruce:

I had no idea that Andy and Elayne were ever a romantic item, but I do remember this bit she used to do about ordering a steak or a lobster in a restaurant and then getting slapped. It was incredible and so was her timing.

I also remember seeing Andy perform at the Improv. At the time, I was living downtown in a loft, and I was in this new-wave punk band that was either called the Great Mistake or the Great Mustache, I forget which. Anyway, the place I was living in was a dive and the only thing that separated our rooms was literally a sheet. So one night after the club closed, I invited Andy over. I said, "Do you want to come down to where we live and rehearse?"

Well, that was all I had to say because Andy's eyes lit up as if he had just received an invitation to the White House. But when we got back to my place and Andy sat down on the sofa, my sound guy, who was also one of my roommates, lit up a joint, and Andy literally almost came unglued. He absolutely freaked out. He goes, "There's marijuana here. It's a drug." Then he ran out of there as fast as he could.

LENNY SCHULTZ:

As crazy as Andy could be onstage, he was as straight as an arrow when he came off. During the years we were both at the Improv, Andy was still living in Great Neck with his family, and my wife and I were living in Rego Park, Queens, which is nearby. To help him cut down on the commute, we used to drive him to our place and then he'd take a cab the rest of the way. With us, he was always very quiet.

BYRON ALLEN:

By the time I first saw Andy out in LA, he was already a major television star on *Taxi*. I remember he would just get up onstage and do all of these sounds and characters. It was like watching a cartoon.

FRED WILLARD:

I never met Andy personally, but the first time I saw him perform was at the LA Improv. He did the most unusual thing I
ever saw. He got up and started playing the bongo drums and
singing some song. Then he left the stage and walked out the
back door and all around the block while his musicians kept
playing.

After that, he came back through the front door, got back
onstage, and without missing a beat, finished the song. I was
like, "Wow, that's the weirdest thing I've ever seen." I even
told my wife about it and we went back about a week later.
Only this time, all Andy did was order a hamburger and a
glass of chocolate milk and eat it onstage. He did this for
about twenty minutes and my wife's response was, "What the
hell is going on?"

All I could do was apologize. "I'm sorry," I said, "I saw him
do the funniest thing a week ago."

**LYNNE MARGULIES, film editor, Kaufman's last girlfriend,
and co-author of *Andy Kaufman: The Truth, Finally*:**

What drew us together was that we were so much the same as
far as our tastes were concerned. The thing that a lot of people
don't realize is that Andy really wasn't that into comedy and he
didn't go to the Improv to hang out with the other comedians.
He didn't even call himself one. The comedy we liked and both
gravitated towards was actually this televangelist named Dr.
Gene Scott. By the time Andy and I first got together, Gene
had bought a television station that was on twenty-four hours
a day. He was a wonderful madman, and watching Gene was
one of the things we did that week. So Andy and I shared the
same sense of humor. I think the thing that drew me most to
Andy's humor was not letting the audience in on the joke and
getting them so upset. That's what he loved the most and I was
the same way. It was also the aspect of his work that I found
most fascinating.

BOB ZMUDA:

My very first night at the Improv, the first thing I noticed were
framed black-and-white photographs of all these guys who
now had their own sitcoms. It was the last show of the evening, and I was waiting for it to start when this guy with a
foreign accent walked through the front door carrying this big

suitcase. He went right up to Budd, they started talking, and I heard Budd say, "No, I can't put you on tonight. Mondays are when we have auditions."

So the guy said to Budd, "Oh please, sir. I come from the Greyhound bus station. This would be my dream."

Again, Budd told him no, and then he started the show and the guy disappeared. One hour passed, maybe two. Finally, at the end of the show, Budd said, "Ladies and gentlemen, I don't normally do this. I don't know if you saw him a couple of hours ago. He was asking to perform. We have auditions every Monday. He seems like a nice guy. I'm going to break my rule and have him on. His name is Mr. Andy."

But when the guy went up onstage, he was just terrible. He went, "Take my wife, please." And then he imitated some politician, but his voice didn't change. Well, the people laughed anyway because he was so pathetic—after which he said, "I don't think you're laughing with me. You're laughing at me." And then he started crying for real.

Things finally got so bad that one guy from the audience went up to Budd and said, "It's cruel you put him on. He's going to kill himself."

Then Budd started blinking the lights. It was the worst fucking feeling I've ever had in my life. Then the guy said, "I like to do this one last impression for you: the Elvis Presley," and I was thinking to myself, "Thank God, the guy is leaving the stage."

He put on his Elvis jacket and combed his hair. He looked exactly like Elvis. He turned around. He went into an incredible medley of three Elvis songs. Now, nobody was doing Elvis impressions at the time at all because he was basically a has-been. But this guy did—and he just hit it out of the ballpark. So I was thinking, "What the fuck?"

Afterwards he said, "T'ank you veddy much!" in the foreign accent again and there was a standing ovation. I found out later that other comics wouldn't go on after him because he killed. I was confused, and when I went outside that night, he saw me standing there while he loaded up his car. He had all of these props with him on the sidewalk—cymbals, puppets, a heavy 16 mm projector, Elvis stuff.

He said to me, "Excuse me, I have bad back. Can you help?" And so I did, and it took about fifteen minutes. Well, no sooner did I get the stuff in the trunk that he got in the car and said, "Thank you very much." Again, he said it in the foreign accent, but then his parting word was, "Sucker!" which he said in an American voice. So now I was blown away and he drove off. That was the first time Bob Zmuda met Andy Kaufman and Budd Friedman.

BOB SAGET:

I was also in the audience once when he did his laundry onstage. He had a washing machine and everything. Another time, I saw him at The Comedy Store in Westwood, where he had these toy soldiers and he pretended like they were fighting. It was like watching a nine-year-old kid who should be on Ritalin, although when Andy was on, he was the leader of the pack.

Of course, precisely where that pack might lead was anybody's guess.

PAUL PROVENZA:

By the time I had moved up the ranks to be one of the comics who always got on, Andy was already pretty well known. Not surprisingly, every comic who happened to be there whenever Andy popped in would jam into that little doorway between the service bar and the show room so they could see him. I was one of them, but I also remember not getting Andy the first few times I saw him.

And then one night—I don't remember how or when—I was watching Andy with a bunch of other comics and it was like somebody flipped on a light switch. All of the sudden, I went, "Now, I get it. This is genius. You can never stop learning about comedy. It just keeps changing and growing, and now it's a real art form."

HOWARD KLEIN, TV producer best known for *The Office*, talent manager, and former assistant manager of the New York Improv:

I just have these vivid memories of Andy coming in and wanting everyone to be pissed off at him—performance art meets comedy. He would get up and do stuff like sing "99 Bottles of Beer" backwards and people would start booing even though he was so unique. He would get to like seventy-five bottles and people would be like, "All right, we get it."

GILBERT GOTTFRIED, comedian, actor, writer, and voice-over artist:

I was there on one of the nights he did this. At first, the audience laughed, thinking it was the gag, but then he really did it. He sang from ninety-nine to zero. A lot of people just got up and walked out, but I thought it was the funniest thing I'd ever heard.

KEVIN NEALON, actor, comedian, and former Hollywood Improv bartender:

I didn't know Andy in New York, but I got to know him at the Hollywood Improv around 1980 because I was trying to do stand-up while I was working there as a bartender. If another comic didn't show up, Budd would put me on and I was lousy at both. I'd go from being a bad bartender to a bad comic and then back to being a bad bartender—where Budd would often be furious with me because there was usually a crowd waiting to be served drinks.

It was great because I got to talk to the other comics, and one of my most memorable conversations was with Andy. I remember it like it was yesterday. He was out front and I knew that he was into transcendental meditation, so we discussed that for about thirty minutes. I wasn't really paying that much attention, though. All I could do was stare at the mole on his face and think to myself, "I'm talking to Andy Kaufman."

PAUL PROVENZA:

Andy wasn't really a sociable cat. When he was socializing with people, it was usually with people he knew, and I really didn't know him that well. However, one night in particular when he was in from LA, there weren't many of his cronies at the club for whatever reason and so Andy just came up and started talking to the younger comics.

Afterwards, out of the blue, he asked us to walk him back to his hotel. The Improv in New York was at West 44th and Ninth, and his hotel was at 59th and Sixth. So me and about two or three other comics went back to Andy's hotel, where we continued shooting the shit with him in the lobby for the next several hours.

The other thing I distinctly remember is that as we were walking him back to his hotel—and it took me a few blocks to realize this—what Andy did every time he stepped off the curb was to change accents. He would suddenly be from a different country and he wouldn't acknowledge you unless you spoke to him in the same accent. You had to walk the whole way trying to figure out which accent he was doing and take it on—at which point he would talk to you like everything was fine. The entire time he was doing this, I just remember thinking to myself how hilariously odd the whole experience was.

Though he won my heart from the moment he imitated Elvis Pres-ley the first time, not everybody always felt the same way about Andy personally—even if they were still able to acknowledge his talent.

DICK CAVETT:

Kaufman came to see me once in a Broadway play I was doing called *Otherwise Engaged*. He came backstage afterwards with his girlfriend and we went out for a beer. He was amia-ble enough, but I thought he was a tremendous liar and very strange.

The way I came to this conclusion was because that night I told him a story of something that had happened to me once during an accidental meeting with actor Danny Kaye. I don't even remember the entire context, but Kaufman in his warped way decided to put me on by telling me that he had met Danny Kaye in the exact same coincidental way, which was bullshit.

He was just doing one of his things, and I thought, "That's not only not funny, it's dishonest. There's something wrong with you, boy." And I was right, as we later saw, but he was still wonderfully talented.

Once I did a thing for *TV Guide* that was supposed to be on national television—and I wish I had it, but it doesn't exist—where they took me to the set of *Taxi* and had me interview each member of the cast. When I got to Andy, he decided to alternate back and forth between Latka and Tony Clifton. Then he switched to being German and I did, too. After that, he switched to being French and I followed suit. I think I threw him because I knew both languages. But then he switched to something else to try to throw me and we had everybody panicked. The producers said they would get me a copy of the tape, but they never did and they never used it on the show.

ROBERT KLEIN:

It's not that he wasn't talented, but I also thought he was over-rated. I saw him at the Improv where he did Elvis and Foreign Man and I also saw him on *Taxi*, although I was never a faithful watcher. It was a funny character, I'll grant you that, but it was all a humor of impatience built upon grinding annoyance. I mean, if you read Proust to an audience who doesn't even know who Proust is for six minutes and they're going to start yelling, "Fuck you," what's the point? It just wasn't comedy to me.

As Andy's popularity continued to grow at the Improv—first in New York and later in Los Angeles—the stakes also grew higher, especially after his alter ego Tony Clifton began to surface more along with his growing fondness for wrestling women.

TOM DREESEN:

After a while, if you knew Andy's act, you knew he did Tony Clifton and you kind of learned to put up with it. But if you didn't know who Tony Clifton was, you'd hate the fucking guy. One night, I went to the Hollywood Improv to see Budd. I wanted to ask him something, and he was in the back of the room while Andy was onstage as Tony Clifton. There was also a heckler next to us at a table who was like Tony Clifton and kept saying, "This fucking guy sucks . . . this fucking guy sucks." At first, he was apologizing to these girls that were with him. But then he turned to Budd and said, "You usually have good acts, but this fucking guy sucks."

I just grinned and looked at Budd because we both knew it was Andy doing Tony Clifton. If you remember how he did it, a woman would start heckling him and pretending to be insulted. Then he'd start talking about, "I was with this broad." When he'd do that, the woman who was doing it with him and being a shill would say, "Excuse me, I don't like that term you're using"—at which point Andy as Tony Clifton would go, "What term? You mean broad? You don't want me calling you a broad?"

Then Andy would have her come up onstage, scold him, and then he'd give her a slap and say, "You want respect from me? I'll give you respect when you can beat me up, lady. Go home and iron clothes and have babies 'cause that's all you're good for."

After that, he'd pretend to slap her in the face using shaving cream and she'd turn around, grab his hand, throw him on the floor, and beat the shit out of him. She'd just bang his head on the floor and whip his ass while the audience was cheering.

Then when he got done with it, he'd stand up, wipe himself off, and say, "You want to try two out of three?" That was the bit. Well, on this particular night, this woman stood up and a man from another table said, "Look at this guy. Now he's going to pick on this girl and if he lays one hand on her I'm going to break his fucking back."

As soon as I heard that, I went over to him and said, "Sir, this is an act."

After I informed him of this, he just looked at me and said, "It's an act? It's a bad fucking act." Then he stood up and lunged towards the stage as Budd got up to grab him. The next thing I knew, we both fell on the floor. At the same time, the woman onstage was kicking the shit out of Andy and the guy was going, "Whip his ass, whip his ass!"

So we stopped the heckler from getting onstage, and the next day I told Andy what happened. But when you were talking to Tony Clifton, he wasn't Andy Kaufman, and when you were talking to Andy Kaufman, you couldn't reference Tony Clifton. He would just stare at you blankly like he didn't know what you were talking about.

"Tony Clifton was in here last night," I said.

With a look of devilish bemusement, he looked at me and said, "He was?"

"Yeah," I said, "and he almost got his ass whipped."

"What do you mean?"

"Well, there was a guy who was going to kick the shit out of him, and Budd and I stopped the guy."

Well, with that, Andy's eyes got glassy. This turned him on. His whole thing was getting some kind of reaction. When he heard that guy was going to charge the stage and whip Tony Clifton's ass, he thought that was the coolest thing in the world. That's how weird he was.

RICK OVERTON:

I'm the guy Andy first dumped an ice-cold pitcher of water on when he was prototype-testing Tony Clifton, although he didn't put on the getup that night because he didn't know if it was worth it yet. He was still just trying to figure it out.

On the night he did it, everybody in the New York club was instructed to act like Andy was really Tony Clifton. He'd done it a bunch of times already, although this was his first time using the water where he said, "I'll show you what fun is—get up here. You think that's a funny joke? I'll show you a funny joke."

This was the setup—and then *splash*—he dumped the entire pitcher of water on me and I was drenched from head to toe, at which point I was supposed to say, "What the hell?" I forgot exactly why I decided to do this, but I wound up giving up my normal spot that night.

At the original Improv in New York, they had this side door by the stage, which was sort of this quick vaudevillian exit where I could go out, come back, and wait at the bar until it was time to do my normal set. But there was no doing a spot after an Andy thing like this—and especially not this night.

While he was splashing the water on me as the audience was booing him, it was right about then that he began winning them back from the "You suck" phase. It was also the earliest terms of him really saying, "What's the addictive boundary I can push to reel you back on the boat again?"

Honest to God, he became this two-mile fly-caster guy that night like a river ran between him and the audience. The thing people need to understand is that back then the crowd was different and their endurance was different. They'd literally stay until their hands and stomachs hurt, but they didn't dare leave the club because they'd never seen anything like it before.

PAUL PROVENZA:

I had an amazing experience once in New York where I was onstage late one night, and I was being heckled by Andy in a very early phase of his Tony Clifton character. When I recognized who it was, I realized it was going to be funny, so I didn't freak out going, "Oh, my God. This guy won't shut up."

JACK KNIGHT:

One night in LA, Andy came into the club dressed as Tony Clifton, and when I tried to say hello to him as Andy, he corrected me. He said, "My name is Tony Clifton." Afterwards, we all went out to eat where he remained in character the entire time. He wasn't Andy Kaufman. He was Tony Clifton having something to eat.

GEORGE SHAPIRO, Andy Kaufman's longtime manager:

The way the Tony Clifton character evolved was from Richard Belzer, who was Rick Newman's longtime emcee at Catch A Rising Star. Richard had a reputation for sometimes being abusive to the audience, which Andy just loved. When it came to creating Tony Clifton, he just sort of ran with that.

BOB ZMUDA:

Tony Clifton was also based on the screenwriter Norman Wexler, who wrote the screenplay for *Saturday Night Fever* and *Serpico* and *Joe*, for which he received an Oscar nomination. Norman was this brilliantly talented but mentally unbalanced eccentric who would get into fights with people to the point where they literally wanted to kill him. Before I started working at the Improv as a bartender in New York, which is how I got to know Andy, I'd worked as assistant to Wexler and I used to tell these crazy stories about him at the bar.

Well, that was all it took to get Andy's attention, because each time I told them he got closer and closer to the bar so he could hear me. This went on for several days until late one night he finally said, "Is that all true about Wexler? Norman Wexler is a god. That's exactly what I want to do with audiences. I want to mess with their heads. I want that reality moment."

Andy would have never hired me to be his writer had I not worked for Norman Wexler. No matter what anybody else may tell you, Tony Clifton was a composite of Wexler as much as anybody else. Anyway, Andy did Clifton more on the West Coast than the East Coast. While he was developing it, he would take this nose putty and spend an hour making the Clifton nose. Then he'd put on a terrible wig and sunglasses. However, he never really did that at the Improv on the East Coast. It wasn't until we went to the West Coast that Tony Clifton took on a whole new life.

Nights like these when Andy transformed himself into Tony Clifton were some of our craziest and most memorable ever. However, as much as I truly loved Andy and always believed in his talent, even I couldn't deny that dealing with him at times was almost impossible. Then there was the Improv gaggle who simply avoided him altogether—either because they just didn't get him or they deemed it too big a risk to even try.

DANNY AIELLO:

I never knew who Andy was even after he'd been coming to the club for months. I think everybody thought he was nuts to some extent and I never had any sort of a relationship with him at all, which was perfectly fine with both of us. As a matter of fact, I think he was afraid of me. I think he was worried that I might beat the shit out of him if he came near me because I'm Italian.

BRUCE SMIRNOFF, comedian, writer, and former Hollywood Improv house emcee:

The only guys Andy evidently didn't put on were his writing partner Bob Zmuda, his manager George Shapiro, maybe sometimes Budd, and a guy named Mel Shearer, who supposedly worked for him. I just avoided Andy because I always knew where it was going, which was nowhere.

ED BLUESTONE:

You either loved Andy or you hated him. There were two divided camps and he pissed a lot of comedians off. He weirded a lot of them out, too. They just didn't know what to make of him. I think one of the main reasons was that he was never that approachable. He would start talking to you with one of his characters, and I guess people thought it was condescending. I didn't really give a shit. I didn't have any desire to talk to him. To me Andy Kaufman was much ado about nothing.

MIKE PREMINGER:

Andy Kaufman wasn't a comedian. I will fight anyone, anytime, anyplace who tells you he was. He wouldn't have known comedy if it bit him in the ass. I know he's considered to be one of the brilliant people of all time, but I never got it and I won't ever get it. To me, he was just some guy who went onstage doing stuff that you would do when you were four years old. You could never have a conversation with him.

The first time I met him in New York, he'd been there for a while and I walked up to him. I said, "Hi Andy."

"I'm not Andy," he said. "I'm Tony Clifton."

I don't know what I said back, but in my head, I was like, "Fuck you!" and I walked away. I mean, don't stand there and look me in the face when I'm trying to say hello to you. That's my whole Andy Kaufman story.

At the same time, though, as much as Andy and Andy-as-Tony-Clifton got under the skin of many adults, he also delighted kids.

SHELLEY ACKERMAN:

I don't remember how it all came about, but my mother paid Andy twenty-five bucks to basically come over to the community room in our apartment building one Sunday afternoon to do his act and entertain at my little sister's fifth birthday party in 1974. I think he did Mighty Mouse and played the bongos. He may have even done Elvis. The only rule he had was that none of the parents could be in the room while he was doing it, and it turned out to be this really special thing. My sister still has a videotape somewhere.

Andy also hosted our cabaret-style children's show on Sunday afternoons in New York beginning in late 1974, an effort that was sometimes assisted by my two daughters and child actor Danielle Brisebois, who later went on to appear as Archie Bunker's niece Stephanie on *All in the Family* and *Archie Bunker's Place*. For Brisebois, working with Andy was incredibly instructive.

DANIELLE BRISEBOIS, producer, singer-songwriter, and former child actor:

Andy essentially did the same act that he did for adults for kids, and I was the one who got picked from the audience to be onstage with him. This was before he became really famous and my job was to stand there and help him out with the props. It was great, and I thought he was funny, but then when he got well known, I was like, "Him?" I still didn't quite get it even though I loved it.

ZOE LANE FRIEDMAN:

Growing up around the Improv, I have all sorts of memories, but the children's cabaret was probably the first where what the club is became an imprint of who I am. It was stage time and I got to stand on my head while my sister Beth played the violin.

For a five- or six-year-old, there was no better comedian than Andy Kaufman. He had the most incredible imagination. He would just transform himself into all these amazing different characters. The best part was getting to choose what character he would do.

TWENTY-EIGHT
Dissing Larry David

Like Andy Kaufman, Larry David, who first came to the New York Improv about a year after Andy, was an enigma from the start. But while the curmudgeonly *Seinfeld* and *Curb Your Enthusiasm* creator would ultimately become a formidable presence both on our stage and off, his beginnings at the club, unlike Andy's, were anything but notable at first.

As a matter of fact, on the night Larry first came in with a group of friends and asked me to go on without having ever done stand-up before—which he later recounted in the 2013 EPIX TV documentary commemorating our fiftieth anniversary that my daughter Zoe produced—I told him no.

In my defense, my initial negative reaction had nothing to do with being rude or dismissive. I simply wasn't about to put an untested rookie on my stage during regular prime time. There were no ifs, ands, or buts about this, no matter how talented he or she was. I still wouldn't do it to this day either if I had the chance to do it all over again.

And, in all honesty, I felt completely blindsided. From wherever I was standing, I remember hearing him say, "I'm going over to that guy." Then, mistaking me for the emcee and not knowing I was the owner, Larry walked right up to me and said point-blank, without even introducing himself, "I want to go on."

In those days, he had a thick, frizzy mop of sandy-brownish hair, and on this particular night he was wearing a camouflage army jacket. His devil-may-care appearance looked like a combination of G.I. Joe and Larry from *The Three Stooges*. I was in no mood to make idle small talk either, so I asked him matter-of-factly if he was a comedian, to which he replied, "No."

Then I asked him if he had ever performed before. Again, he said, "No."

So I said, "And you want to go on like that? You have to audition."

After about half a second, he asked me why and then that was that. This is the way I remember it, but here's Larry's version.

LARRY DAVID:

Actually, I didn't intuitively know I was even interested in comedy yet. I always liked it, and on the occasion I could make my parents laugh I liked that feeling, but it was never connected to a profession. That didn't really happen until I was in my early twenties—at which point I was at pretty loose ends with myself after graduating from the University of Maryland, serving a stint in the National Guard, being girlfriendless and nearly homeless, and finally taking acting classes in between selling women's brassieres and driving a limousine to support myself.

I had taken one class with the famed acting coach Bill Esper, but what they were doing didn't really appeal to me until one day I had to deliver a speech that got a lot of laughs. It was from a book called *Spoon River Anthology* by Edgar Lee Masters. I could barely decipher what any of these people were talking about, but the assignment was to take one of the characters and put it into our words. So I did, and people laughed. And I remember saying to myself, "Yeah, that's for me."

At the time, I was living at the Manhattan Plaza, a federally subsidized housing project for people in the arts on West 43rd Street, which is right around the corner from where the original New York Improv was. One evening in 1974, I decided to go there with a friend of mine. We went in and as soon as we started watching the show, I turned to my friend and said, "This doesn't seem too hard."

Then I told him I was going to try to get on, and when I asked one of the waitresses who the person in charge of putting the acts on was, she pointed Budd out to me. It was on a Saturday night and the place was packed to the gills, but I walked right up to him and said, "I'd like to go on."

Budd just looked at me and said, "Who are you? Are you a comedian? Have you ever done stand-up?"

When I told him I hadn't, he informed me I had to audition, which came as a complete surprise. All I can say is thank

God he didn't put me on because I probably never would have gone on again anywhere after that.

I can't say that Budd's rejection was necessarily the catalyst, but it wasn't too long after that when I decided to begin pursuing stand-up. I found out where to go and I started doing all of these small clubs down in Greenwich Village like Gerde's Folk City and Gil Hodges's bowling alley in Brooklyn. After that, I eventually auditioned and got passed by Rick Newman at Catch A Rising Star. Then gradually, I began going back to the Improv, which was an easy transition, because by that time the comedians knew me.

I'm a bit fuzzy on the exact dates and I may very well have had one foot in California by this point. However, I don't think it was all that long after Larry came back to the Improv and became a regular before he was reunited with his childhood friend—and once-nemesis—Richard Lewis.

RICHARD LEWIS:

Interestingly enough, Larry and I were born in the same hospital room. We didn't actually come out of the womb there, but we wound up being in the same ward. I was a preemie and I had to stay an extra week in Brooklyn Jewish Hospital, which no longer exists. I was born on June 29, 1947, and Larry's birthday is July 2.

Our arrivals into the world kind of dovetailed one another, and then one summer when I was teenager, I went to a famous sports camp in New York State and Larry was there. He was a terrific athlete and so was I, but we hated one another. It was like oil and vinegar and we just didn't get along. But then years later, I began doing stand-up before Larry and he was a big fan. I wasn't at the Improv the night he tried to go on and Budd told him no, but he used to hang out there a lot because he had this dumpy little apartment a couple of blocks away.

By this point, I was already making a name for myself with guys like Billy Crystal, Jay Leno, and Freddie Prinze, and Larry and I became inseparable best friends at the Improv almost from the start. Then one night—I forget when or exactly where we were at the club—something happened. I looked at him and there was something about his face that freaked me out. Afterwards, we both realized we were the same teenagers who despised one another thirteen years before at summer camp. Ever since then, Larry and I have been bonded in some sort of mystical way. In those days, we used to hang out together all the time.

LARRY DAVID:

The way I remember it happening is that we looked at each other and he said, "There's something about you. You look familiar."

At first, I was like, "Yeah, you do, too."

Then he asked me my name and I told him, and he said, "David . . . David!"

And I said, "Lewis . . . Lewis!"

And pretty much that was that.

From then on—for a period on and off that spanned roughly the next fifteen years and simultaneously included writing and starring in ABC's *Saturday Night Live* knockoff comedy-variety series *Fridays*, one lackluster season writing for *Saturday Night Live* itself, and eventually cocreating *Seinfeld*—Larry was always a crowd-pleaser at both the New York and LA Improv.

However, he was equally as much of an agitator as well, especially in the beginning, and the stories about him are, without a doubt, some of our most legendary. Many, in fact, are downright bizarre. And taking nothing away from his prodigious talent, it's also not a stretch to say that at times—albeit in much different ways than Andy Kaufman—Larry was also an acquired taste, if not something of a provocateur.

LARRY DAVID:

As a comedian just starting out, you basically do whatever you can to get laughs. I was no exception, so I was just trying to figure out who I was and what I was supposed to say. Of course, I wanted to talk to the audience in the same way I was funny with my friends, but that wasn't always to be. I'd go up every night and experiment with different things. Whatever worked, I would keep.

Suffice it to say that it's probably a good thing I wasn't around very much in those days because when things weren't working for Larry there could be hell to pay.

LARRY DAVID:

Remember *The Gong Show* with Chuck Barris? It was at the height of its popularity at the time, and the audience at the Improv would often imitate what they saw in the show. If they didn't like you, they'd yell out, "Gong!"

I was very temperamental, so it's fair to say that if someone from the audience said "Gong" to me, it didn't sit too well. Sometimes I would yell at the audience and other times I would just leave. I simply didn't see the need for me to torture them—or them to torture me—any further, so I decided to part company. It's also fair to say that if I did well I loved it, and if I didn't do well I hated it.

This didn't just happen at the Improv either, although it did happen there with pretty regular frequency. One night up at Catch A Rising Star—and I've told this story many times—I looked at the audience and said, "I don't think so." And then I left.

Let me put it this way: Whenever I went on, the emcee didn't go very far.

ALAN ZWEIBEL:

When I first met Larry in 1974, I had never seen anybody who looked quite like him because he had this unkempt mane of wiry hair that resembled a giant Brillo pad. But he's my best friend now and we liked what each other did from the start. I can't remember what our first conversation was, although so many years later when I appeared with him on an episode of *Curb* our discursive banter was similar to every phone conversation we'd ever had.

On the handful of occasions when he went on during prime time at the Improv and I was scheduled to follow him—let's say it was on a Friday night, Larry was supposed to go on at 9 PM and I had a 9:20 spot—I would get there in time to go on at 9:01. I did this because if Larry didn't like the audience, he'd walk offstage after a minute.

JOHN DEBELLIS:

At the Improv in New York, Larry and I got together pretty quickly because we were the guys who usually went on at the end of the night, and we shared very similar views on comedy in the sense that we both wanted to do something different. Larry loved to shock people, so he'd always come up with different opening lines. One night, he'd say, "I hate my penis." And then the next night he'd say, "My penis has no friends." I was there once when Lily Tomlin came in with a bunch of female friends and Larry looked at them and said, "I don't like menstruating women. In my house, I make them stand on a newspaper." Not that it was necessarily directed at them, but Lily and these women were so offended that they literally ran out of the club.

I think the thing that bonded us the most, though, was that we were both huge Yankees fans, so a lot of our conversations were about baseball. Not long after we met, another comic from California named Bobby Kelton came along and the three of us became really close—almost inseparable. But then Bobby went back to the West Coast and it was just Larry and me.

Larry spent every holiday with me and my family in New Jersey. I used to take a bunch of the guys fishing at this lake out there and whenever we did this we always had luck, except when Larry came along. I never caught a single fish with Larry.

Later, when I was writing for *Saturday Night Live* and he was writing for *Fridays*, the producers used to accuse us of stealing sketches from one another, which was absurd. What made it so ridiculous is that mostly what we talked about was how bad both shows were at the time.

RICK OVERTON:

Larry had this giant thing of hair and I used to go visit him at his apartment at the Manhattan Plaza. That's where I met the real Kramer—the actual guy the *Seinfeld* character is based on—who was Larry's neighbor.

GILBERT GOTTFRIED:

We weren't great friends back then, but we were friendly. The only time I think I was ever in his apartment was when Larry had cable. There was a movie coming on with some actress we both liked that had a nude scene.

JOHN DEBELLIS:

A lot of times Larry and I had dinner together at his place, and we'd often have fish of some sort because it was cheap, nutritious, and there were a lot of fish markets in the neighborhood. The only problem was that Larry just had one spoon, one fork, one knife, and one plate, so we had to eat in shifts.

When we weren't discussing writing or baseball, most of our conversations were about women. I don't want to say we were afraid of them, but we were both painfully shy and so we'd talk about how much we got rejected. Larry would tell me his sad stories and I told him mine. Basically it was this mutual feeling we shared that we might get a woman or two, but if we did, they weren't going to stay with us or we weren't going to stay with them.

Larry also had this obsessively neurotic laundry list of preparations he'd go through before he went out on a date, like shaving. Then he had this thing about going to the bathroom—not the physical act of actually going, but being able to find one if nature called. So we'd get into conversations about it where he'd go, "When am I going to go to the bathroom? I've got to go to the bathroom before I go, because what happens if I get with her and I can't find a bathroom? What should I do? Should I bring her back here? And then what do I do if she likes me?"

We were both totally out of our element as far as members of the opposite sex were concerned. However, Larry did have this one girlfriend named Anna for a while and she was really pretty. So, when he did date, he went out with women that were hot, but they were few and far between.

BRUCE SMIRNOFF:

Larry David was an unfriendly kind of guy. I guess if you were his friend, he was the nicest guy in the world, but I was just this peon doorman who was also Budd's house emcee. I can't ever pinpoint a specific incident where Larry was mean to me, but he never went out of his way to be nice to me either.

Back when Larry was doing *Fridays* on ABC in the late seventies, he used to come into the Hollywood Improv dressed in a Chicago Blackhawks jacket. Then he'd go onstage, and God forbid, if somebody didn't laugh or they said something he didn't like, he'd literally start wishing cancer on them. Then he'd walk offstage and he could clear thirty or forty people out of the room in one fell swoop. He was exactly the way everyone says he was.

I remember one night we had a packed house. I don't know how they do it now, but when I was there, we did two shows on the weekends. The first one went from like eight o'clock to ten and the second one usually lasted from ten-thirty until two in the morning. Anyway, on this particular night, Richard Lewis, who was already a big star by then, was scheduled to go on during the peak spot at nine o'clock. By this time, there was almost nobody in the audience, because Larry had been there earlier and emptied out the room.

JUDY ORBACH:

Larry and I used to have these really long, drawn-out conversations about food. He'd come in and say to me, "What should I have for dinner tonight, sweetheart?"

"I don't know," I'd reply. "What did you have for lunch?"

And he'd say, "I had a hamburger."

"Well," I'd say, "maybe you should have a little pasta then."

So we would have these peculiar, neurotic conversations about food and what he should order from the menu—after which a bunch of us would often go to the Market Diner at four in the morning for breakfast when the Improv closed. Either we'd go there, or we would all go down to Sam Wo's in Chinatown.

In terms of performing, though, the other thing I remember about Larry is that he was absolutely horrified being up onstage. He would get up and if the audience wasn't paying attention for whatever reason—if they were chatty or they were heckling him—he'd drop the mic in the middle of a sentence and leave. He'd say, "I don't need this." He did this at the Improv and at Catch A Rising Star more times than I can count. He was always wearing an army jacket.

CHRIS ALBRECHT:

I remember that army jacket of Larry's extremely well. I think he wore it because he'd either been in the army reserves, or maybe he'd even been drafted in the army. In any case, he'd wear it whenever he came in and he'd hang out at the bar. He was always a bit of a dour character. Larry was never happy about anything.

BOB ZMUDA:

Larry was just so completely neurotic and unhinged. I remember one night when he was up onstage, Chris Albrecht and I were standing in the back of the room and we started laughing our asses off—which is what you're supposed to do at a fucking comedy club. Afterwards, Larry went ballistic. He came up to us and started screaming at the top of his lungs, "Why are you guys laughing at me?" He was one of the last guys you'd have ever predicted would make it big.

PAUL REISER:

Whenever I saw Larry doing a set at the Improv, it was usually combative. He'd dig a hole for himself with the audience and he'd relish being in that hole. It's like he thrived on that kind of adversity and he wasn't happy until he was unhappy.

JOHN DEBELLIS:

Another thing about Larry was that he was a textbook hypochondriac. He's mellowed with age, but back then, honest to God, anything he saw or heard about he thought he had. Sometime around 1982 while he was doing *Fridays* and he had a few bucks, he was living in Laurel Canyon when he got the idea that wearing gravity boots would help him live longer and prevent back problems. So he bought these humongous sci-fi-looking boots and he'd hang upside down in them.

One afternoon I was home when the phone rang and it was Larry. He said, "John, I can't get up. I'm stuck down here. Blood is racing to my head. What am I going to do?" He sounded more panicked than I had ever heard him, so I immediately got in my car and sped over there. When I finally arrived about twenty minutes later, I ran to the door as fast as I could, and just as I was about to go inside, I felt my shoe sink into this huge pyramid of dog shit. The stench was unbearable and the shit was all over my shoe. I was really worried that Larry might either be unconscious or dead by this point, too.

So I quickly scraped my shoe off on the pavement, which made an even bigger mess, and went inside. When I did, Larry—who would have thrown his shoe out if it had happened to him—was over in the corner. He was completely vertical, beet red, and hanging from his toes upside down. I had to push him up so he could pull himself enough to reach the pole that was attached to the boots and take them off.

I don't think he's ever worn gravity boots since then, but another time either before or after that, this famous cardiologist had just come out with a study about people with Type A and Type B risks for heart attacks. He'd also written a book, so another comedian named Lenny Maxwell and I decided to buy a copy, which we then autographed as if it had been signed by the author. We were very clever about it, too. We signed it with a black Sharpie and mailed it to Larry in a padded manila envelope.

Inside the front cover, the inscription we wrote was something to the effect of how we'd recently seen him onstage and thought he was a prime candidate for both Types A and B.

Well, needless to say, Larry fell for it hook, line, and sinker, because the next night he came running into the Improv out of breath and looking whiter than a sheet—at which point we realized we had to tell him. He was so worried we actually feared he might have a real heart attack right there.

TOM DREESEN:

I don't know who wrote it, but there's a great story in a book about Jerry Seinfeld about how I first met Larry David that I'll tell here. One night back in the midseventies, I went over to the Improv after Catch A Rising Star. Now mind you, I'd already done some *Tonight Show* appearances and I was getting some noise.

I'd gone over to the Improv where they all knew who I was, and this kid named Larry David went up and he was spectacular. He did about fifteen minutes and every line out of his mouth made me laugh. So I went over to him afterwards and said, "That was funny stuff. I really enjoyed it." Well, Larry could have cared less. He just stared at me for about a half a second and walked off.

The next night I was back at Catch A Rising Star and lo and behold, Larry was at Catch A Rising Star, where he did another fifteen minutes that was completely different. So I said to him again, "You're really funny. I saw you last night and tonight you did a totally different fifteen minutes." But again, Larry just looked at me, sighed, and walked away.

And then the very next day, honest to God, I was coming out of the Stage Door Deli over near the Improv when I ran smack dab into Larry—who I later found out had been on his way to see his shrink. Still not knowing quite what to say, but hoping the third time might be the charm, I decided to make one final attempt to ingratiate myself. I said, "I've got to tell you, I just thought you were fantastic the other night. I saw you two nights in a row and you had all this different material. I thought it was really good."

Yet again, Larry looked at me and sighed. Only instead of walking off this time, he said, "What's with all this nice guy shit?" And then he stormed off.

PAUL PROVENZA:

He did that a lot. Those stories are kind of legendary where he'd get up onstage, pick up the microphone, and cover his eyes just enough to where he could look out into the audience and go, "Nah, nah, nah, this isn't going to work for me"—and then turn around and leave. I always thought this was a great gag, although as a young comic just starting out, I also thought, "My God, I can't believe he would throw away an entire set just for that one laugh."

BILLY CRYSTAL:

In New York, I knew Larry a little bit from Catch A Rising Star, but not all that well. It wasn't until after we had moved to LA and I was doing *Soap* and he was doing *Fridays*, which both ran on ABC, that we became good friends.

It was sometime during this same period that we used to do this little improv routine together at the Hollywood Improv. The premise was that I played a radio therapist named Dr. Sydney Greene where we would take mock call-in questions from the audience as if it were a real show. We had a second microphone planted in the middle of the show room off to the side and I would say, "You're on the air with Dr. Sydney Greene."

At first, I would just pick somebody at random, but then later I started using a regular partner who eventually became Larry, whose part would be to keep calling and calling me incessantly throughout the entire bit. It was great fun and it became so popular that some of the other comics who happened to be at the club when we were doing it started joining in, too.

So one night, Larry and I were sitting at the bar waiting to go on when this woman came up to him and said hello. All of a sudden, Larry got this panicked look on his face. Then he turned to me and said, "Oh God, that's my cousin, Billy. I can't go on. She's my cousin and I can't stand her."

Well, right about then, Budd came up to him and said, "Larry, you're on." So Larry went on, but as soon as he picked up the mic, the first thing out of his mouth was, "I can't do this, Budd. Take me off." I swear, he was onstage for maybe thirty seconds and it was hilarious. He just didn't like this relative.

JUDY ORBACH:

You never quite knew what Larry was thinking or what his mood was going to be like on any given day, because he was always so into his own head. Now I'm no psychologist, but I do consider myself to be something of an expert on comedians. And you know something? I could say that about every single one of those comics who came through the Improv. None of them were all that gregarious. They all had this sort of quality where you'd see them onstage and you'd think it was their personality—when, in fact, they were struggling with life, or they were struggling with women, or whatever. However, they were usually nothing like they appeared to be onstage.

But then there were also those rare exceptions. For instance, I think Larry's good friend Richard Lewis is one of them because he's neurotic onstage as well as off. And to a certain extent, maybe Larry is, too. All I know is that he always had a lot of anger in him, although I don't know exactly why. Perhaps it was just his background and whatever was going on in his life at that particular moment.

Maybe he couldn't get laid. Richard always had a girl because he was gorgeous, whereas Larry was more out-there looking with his glasses and the frizzy hair. But he was also so fucking funny. I remember the first night he got up and looked at the audience. His first line was, "I know. I look like Howdy Doody." This would always get a crack-up whenever he said that.

PAUL PROVENZA:

Larry's neurosis about his hair and his resemblance to Howdy Doody were probably two of his most signature bits. He'd do this whole thing about going to the plastic surgeon and saying, "I want to look like Howdy Doody."

KEVIN NEALON:

Whenever there was a heckler in the audience in LA, he'd invariably get into an argument. From the stage, Larry couldn't tell if they were big or not—and a lot of times he couldn't even see them—but he'd say, "Come on, let's go. You, me, outside, right now . . . come on!"

GILBERT GOTTFRIED:

He was one of those people that there was no way to have predicted the success he's had. Back then, he looked like he could have just as easily wound up homeless, which he nearly was once.

Every time I saw him perform, he always seemed to hate it—and he hated the audience just as much—to the point where fights would often break out. Of course, this was the most fun part of watching. I think my hands-down favorite was the time this massive guy who must have weighed over three hundred pounds stood up. For a while, it even looked like they were going to go outside until Chris Albrecht or whoever was managing the club that night finally jumped in.

LARRY DAVID:

I never had any physical altercations with anybody, although I did have some fights and they were really more arguments. The way it usually went down was that if they gave me a hard time, I'd say something to them and then they'd say something back. I was never stupid about it, though. I always made sure I had the bouncers behind me anytime I ever said anything.

For his part, if Larry's antagonism often incited our audience's wrath—and as much as he enjoyed provoking it—he was also almost universally respected among his peers at the Improv.

LESLIE MOONVES:

I always loved Larry's humor, though he wasn't the greatest performer, so it didn't surprise me that he became a writer instead.

HOWARD KLEIN:

I'm not exaggerating when I say that Larry David was my hero at the Improv. Sometimes he would kill and some nights he would be completely silent, but he was always very pure. And you always knew how talented he was. This was the era when all those guys like Jerry Seinfeld and Paul Reiser were starting, and it was very hard to predict who was going to be a household name—especially since in stand-up you can get famous for your performing and not how great a writer you are. But Larry always knew what he wanted to do.

RICK OVERTON:

The thing about Larry was that he really knew his own style and he always had a great angle on what he was. I, on the other hand, didn't. I had no idea who I was in relationship to my style at the time. Back when Larry and I first knew one another at the New York Improv, and before I went out on my own, I'd been part of a two-man comedy team there called Overton & Sullivan. While I was doing it, there was the safety net of the team, so I could just be this or that until I figured it out. It wasn't until after we broke up that I got forced into figuring out who the hell I was in between jokes.

But Larry instantly was Larry. He used to do this routine about singles bars where he'd go, "My name is Al Banion and I need a companion." Then he did this bit about putting butter on a Samoan's face and eating it because he said they looked like pancakes.

PAUL PROVENZA:

It was this elaborate, hysterical, surreal piece where he'd say, "You put butter on their heads and it melts." Then he'd say, "All over Samoa, there are statues of their hero Aunt Jemima."

There was another one I loved about his mother buying fruit. He'd go, "My mother walks around the house muttering, 'I buy fruit and nobody eats it.' I think she's insane. That's all she's been doing for years—walking around the house muttering, 'I buy fruit and nobody eats it.'"

Say what you will about Larry, but he was always one of those guys who, whenever he'd come in, all of the comics would pile in back to see what he was going to do. He just had that effect on people. And despite all of his enormous accomplishments and success, the one thing I'm not sure a lot of people realize is what an outstanding stand-up comic he was.

MICHAEL RICHARDS:

The night Larry auditioned for *Fridays* in the late seventies, I had already been cast. The producers had seen me, Bruce Mahler—who later became known for his roles as Sergeant Fackler in the *Police Academy* films and as Rabbi Kirschbaum on *Seinfeld*—and a comedic actor named Mark Blankfield at the Improv. Anyway, for some reason, the producers had invited us to go see Larry's audition at The Comedy Store. At the time, I didn't even know who he was, but I remember thinking how funny looking he was from the moment he got up onstage. Then he started working, and I swear, within a minute or maybe a minute and a half, he just said, "Fuck you, people." And then he walked offstage. At first, I thought it was just part of his act, and I thought it was great, but when he didn't ever come back I just thought, "Jesus, this is the real thing."

GLENN HIRSCH, comedian and former New York Improv emcee:

For a period of about five years in the 1970s, Larry and I were at the New York Improv practically every night. I like Larry very much, but he's also an extremely shy guy. I think that the way his insecurity manifested itself onstage was that he could have an entire audience eating out of the palm of his hand, but then if one person didn't like him, he would belittle them to the point where it would eventually turn the entire audience off. In retrospect, though, I guess he knew what he was doing.

BOB SAGET:

I remember standing next to Larry once at the LA Improv right before he was about to go on. The comic before him was this prop act who was up there strumming a guitar. Right as he was doing it, Larry turned to me and said, "These people don't want jokes. They want guitar acts." And yet here I was, standing there also brandishing a guitar. But far as I know, Larry always liked me.

JUDD APPATOW:

One night in LA, I remember seeing Larry do this bit about how it was difficult to get the head of a South American country to wear a condom. I don't recall what the setup was, but it was hysterical. Very early on, the sense I got about Larry was that he had real integrity as both a performer and a writer. In other words, he wasn't trying to figure out what everybody else was doing so he could emulate it.

AL FRANKEN:

Larry is a really good friend of Alan Zweibel's who is a good friend of mine, so the three of us used to hang out when Alan and I were writing for *Saturday Night Live* and Larry was doing what he did. The first time I met him in Los Angeles was with Alan in the summer of 1977.

We were on hiatus from *Saturday Night Live*, and my comedy partner Tom Davis and I had rented a house out there because we were doing a show called *Kentucky Fried Theatre*. One afternoon Larry came by the house, and the entire time he was there I remember thinking to myself, "Okay, this guy's funny, but he's completely uncompromising and I wish him luck." Not that compromising was the key to anything mind you. It's just that Larry had this very, very specific point of view that hadn't clicked yet.

In due time, of course, it would click, in no small part thanks to his collaboration on a sitcom about nothing with another prodigious funnyman who began rising through the stand-up ranks not long after Larry did. From the beginning, Jerry Seinfeld was another comic we all knew was special.

JERRY SEINFELD:

Larry and I always loved to kibitz when we were at the clubs together and we would have these hilarious conversations at the bar. So when I got the NBC opportunity to do *Seinfeld*, I was immediately reminded of our camaraderie, thinking this is also how you wrote scripts.

The way the premise of *Seinfeld* unfolded was that I told Larry about it one night at Catch and then we met again a few nights later at the Improv. After that, we went over to the Westway Diner, which was right around the corner and still exists. After two cups of coffee, we essentially had the idea of what the show was going to be.

In the end, while the Improv can't entirely claim credit for *Seinfeld*'s gestation or Jerry's friendship with Larry—and a lion's share acknowledgment belongs to my friend Rick Newman who founded Catch A Rising Star—I'm proud to say that we had a hand in it. And when it comes to summing up what having Larry was really like at the Improv, you had to see for yourself to believe it, although these stories will hopefully give you some idea.

TWENTY-NINE
A Tsunami Named Robin

LESLIE MOONVES:

When I was the bartender at the Hollywood Improv in the late seventies, I usually worked weekends and Monday evenings. Budd was always fantastic to me, and I don't remember ever having a bad night the entire time I was there. But then, there was this one night in 1976 when a young comedian from San Francisco went on and did an entire hour that I'll especially never forget.

That comedian was Robin Williams, whose explosive arrival at Hollywood Improv in the spring of 1976 was the perfect storm. From the moment he walked in, it was obvious to me and everybody else that he was going to become a big star—perhaps even one of the biggest we'd ever seen, which, of course, turned out to be true beyond anything we could have ever imagined.

At the time, he had recently come back to the West Coast and relocated to LA after beginning his stand-up comedy career in San Francisco. The year before that, he had dropped out of the acting program at New York's famed Juilliard conservatory where he was considering returning to complete his degree. When Robin first told me this, I encouraged him because I thought that meant he could also perform on West 44th Street, which I still owned but was rapidly losing many of our best comics to our new club in LA.

Thus, I reasoned he could be our secret weapon. While Robin decided not to return to Juilliard, fortunately for us he soon chose to perform at both clubs. Again, it was the perfect storm of having our cake and getting to eat it, too—with sumptuous portions that were spectacularly satisfying for all of us.

JAY LENO:

The night he auditioned for Budd, he did this Russian accent that was so authentic I actually thought he was from Saint Petersburg. But then when I went up to introduce myself, he said hello to me in his normal voice.

HOWARD KLEIN:

Robin was one of those guys who got discovered in LA, got a television show, and became a household name right away. He was the first comedian who was like a big rock 'n' roll star. It was like having Paul McCartney or Mick Jagger onstage every time he came in.

LARRY MILLER, actor, writer, comedian, voice-over artist, and podcaster:

I'm not sure if I'd use the term "rock star," but Robin was definitely a megastar. When I met him, I remember being struck by the fact that I'd never seen anybody quite like him. He was already on *Mork and Mindy*, and the emcee would say, "We think you're going to like him. Welcome Robin Williams." And the audience just went nuts.

In New York, I shared a cab with him a few times from the Improv to Catch A Rising Star and the Comic Strip on the Upper East Side. One night in particular I remember doing this and thinking it was like sitting next to a beautiful woman and not having anything to say. It was a nice night, too—winter, but not too cold, nice to watch the city go by riding in a cab. But I really wasn't comfortable enough to foist myself on somebody of Robin's stature, so I thought of one or two things to say. We were both happy to leave it at that.

JERRY SEINFELD:

The first thing that comes to mind when I think of Robin was that he was the most generous comic I ever worked with on a stage. When I say generous, I mean he'd give everything up to you to the extent of knowing where you were coming from and knowing that there was a balance between two people on the stage.

JIMMY FALLON:

His love for comedians and his love for comedy were so contagious that it was almost like a fire you couldn't put out. He was one of those guys you could say, "Here's all the money in the world. You'll never have to do stand-up again." It wouldn't have fazed Robin. His attitude would be, "I don't care. It's part of me."

HOWIE MANDEL:

I'd never seen anything like him, and there was no other word to describe Robin but a phenomenon who could take an audience to a new level regardless of who else was there.

RITCH SHYDNER:

Robin was like a white shark when it came to laughs. Nobody wanted them more than he did. Once I saw him improvising with Billy Crystal at the Improv, and with every joke they did, Robin moved closer and closer to the edge of the stage. Finally, he went into the audience while Billy kind of threw his hands up in the air as if to say, "What are you going to do?"

JUDY ORBACH:

In New York, Robin used to come in and meow at me like a big cat. He'd met me a hundred times, but he could never remember my name so he'd just meow at me. He also had the hairiest body I've ever seen, which he loved to taunt me with. If I was sitting at the bar eating dinner or whatever, he would just sit there and stare at me to see if I would break. Finally, I would get so exasperated I'd say, "Get your fucking arms away from my soup with that hair."

MAX ALEXANDER:

Robin had hair on every part of his body and he could sweat like it was nobody's business. When he came offstage, he'd be dripping wet like he'd just come in out of the rain.

RICK OVERTON:

The first time Robin came to the Improv in New York, Elayne Boosler brought him in and we became great friends after that. One of the things that bonded us together was that we both had a mutual love for Jonathan Winters and so everything we did together was sort of honoring the spirit of play that Jonathan had.

Before that, I'd heard he'd come in for some shows that I wasn't there for, but we really clicked after 1977 or '78 and the stars just sort of aligned for us after that. It was like focused ball lightning where you could see the fierceness and preciousness of any timed talk—like you were being bombarded from every angle with a zero boundary line.

MIKE CARANO, longtime Hollywood Improv photographer:

I probably met Robin about eight times total and he always remembered my name. The first time this happened was backstage at *The Dennis Miller Show* when he came up to me and said, "Hi, Mike."

Then there was the time at Bobcat Goldthwait's house during a party where it was the end of the night and I found myself telling a story. It was some really juvenile thing about masturbation and actor Joel Murray, singer Tom Petty, and Eric Idle were all there. After I'd finished, Robin just looked at me and said, "Goodnight, Mike"—at which point Joel said to me, "That was pretty cool telling a story to Robin Williams."

All of the sudden, I was starstruck. I said, "Oh my God. You're right. That was weird."

KEVIN NEALON:

The Improv wasn't where I first met Robin. The first time was very early during my career at this little club in Newport Beach. I'll never forget it because he came in, walked through the crowd, and began rifling through women's purses. Then he put on this huge floppy hat and he began doing Shakespeare. I just remember thinking to myself, "What am I even doing here trying to do comedy?" Watching Robin was like seeing Mozart and then being the guy who always thought of himself as mediocre.

I started working at the Hollywood Improv right around the time Robin got really big on *Mork and Mindy*. When he used to come in from the studio unannounced to do a surprise set, he'd still have his suspenders on, and we used to have to sneak him back through the kitchen so he could get onstage without causing a scene.

JOE PISCOPO:

In New York, we had this steel door to the right of the stage that served as the fire exit. The running joke was that there'd sometimes be a knock at the door during the middle of the show. It was like *The Dean Martin Show*, but then whenever it happened, I'd open it and it would usually be Robin and I'd hand him the microphone. It wasn't always him, but most of the time it was.

JACK KNIGHT:

I'm not a comedian, so I never felt that sense of competition, but I remember seeing Robin perform and thinking he had a computer instead of a brain. I'd see him try stuff out, get a huge laugh, and then I'd never see it again until one night at the right time in the right place, he'd take it out from wherever it was stored and kill again.

PAULA POUNDSTONE:

The truth is that even before Robin got famous, he already had a reputation of being this kind of Tasmanian devil of stand-up comedy. I always tell people this because it's true. He didn't invent it by any means, but he certainly reinvigorated it because of the frenzied excitement he created by doing away with segues and grabbing things off the shelf willy-nilly.

Whenever Robin walked into the room, whoever was onstage at the time knew they might as well get off. However, he was never egotistical about it, and I don't think his attitude was ever, "Get off because I'm here." But even so, most of us had the good sense to say, "Robin's here, have a good time."

ADAM SANDLER:

I remember Robin coming in one night, killing, and then me following him. I did pretty well, which was something that I carried around for a while, and I still do.

GILBERT GOTTFRIED:

Robin would stop in everywhere. Once I was about to go on at the Improv in New York—literally down to the second they were getting ready to announce me—when in walked Robin. He was still doing *Mork and Mindy*, and like any other club, their attitude was, "Get Robin onstage!" But then he did the most incredible thing. He said, "I've got people coming to see me, but I want them to see Gilbert go on first."

DAVID STEINBERG, film producer and talent manager:

I managed Robin right up until his death, and our association dated all the way back to when he did the film *Popeye*. Back then, during the years when he was drinking heavily and doing drugs, he was out of his mind. When he came into the Improv, no one ever wanted to follow him and he never wanted to bump people off a show.

That's why he used to like to go on last, and because there was never any fifteen-minute rule for Robin, he would just go on and on and on without notes. Robin wrote while he was talking and it was always a stream of consciousness where he could thrive on somebody just saying something. Robin didn't give a shit if there were only ten people in the audience. He loved the danger of never knowing what he was going to be talking about.

While the other comedians almost all thrived on that adrenaline as well, there were also those occasions when Robin incited their wrath—especially if one of their jokes wound up in his act.

ROBERT WUHL:

There was always the argument that his mind worked so fast because he was absorbing everything. I used to say to him, "Do me a favor, Robin. Turn your mind absorption thing off while I'm onstage." It happened quite often with a lot of other comedians besides me. They would complain to me about it. Robin was indiscriminate and he was an equal opportunity joke stealer. That said, he was still an absolute force of nature.

RICHARD LEWIS:

Robin was the Muhammad Ali of comedians. No one was faster, and I knew him for over thirty-five years. I used to call him the pastor and he called me the rabbi. But again, the problem he always had that he admitted was that he was like a sponge. He could listen to a mediocre riff from a second-rate comedian and then turn it into gold without ever remembering where he first heard it.

It's very possible—I think—that with brain chemistry like his that he could have easily thought it was his. The heartbreak was when he did this with a young comic who was getting ready for his first shot on David Letterman or *The Tonight Show* and it's fair to say that some comics hated him for that.

But I wasn't one of them. I was never threatened by him at all and we were great friends. Once or twice, I told him not to come to my show. I said, "I know your problem, Robin, and I don't want to be part of it."

He was totally fine with that. He just said, "Okay."

Regularly continuing to flex his comic muscles at the Improv as he became one of the most beloved stars on the planet over the next three and a half decades, Robin's life would, of course, come to a heartbreaking end on August 11, 2014, when he committed suicide by hanging himself in his home at the age of sixty-three.

Obviously, you're never prepared for something like this when it happens—and despite his well-publicized bouts with substance abuse and depression—we were all overcome with tremendous grief. It was also, sadly, a road that by now we'd traveled down several times before, beginning with another brilliant comic who was already at the apex of his fame just as Robin's star was rising. What none of us knew at the time was that both their lives would end by different means, yet ultimately in the same way. We will never get over our grief.

THIRTY
Comedy's Tragic Prinze

The name of this other comedian is Freddie Prinze, and of all the chapters in this book, this is probably one of the most bittersweet and important for me to write. The biggest reason for this is that younger people today are likely more familiar with his son, actor Freddie Prinze Jr. Though he's a tremendous talent in his own right, in the mid-1970s, his dad, Freddie Sr., was arguably the biggest overnight sensation in America. My hope in sharing my own memories, the good and the bad—along with the ones of those who knew Freddie best—is that it will shed new light on both his prodigious gifts as a comedian as well as his demons.

The year I opened the Hollywood Improv in 1975, he was starring in the title role of one of the decade's most popular sitcoms, *Chico and the Man*, which ran for four seasons on NBC from 1974 until 1978. Freddie played Francisco "Chico" Rodriguez, a wisecracking Chicano auto mechanic working for "the Man"—Ed Brown (portrayed by veteran actor Jack Albertson)—the verbally abusive, hard-drinking owner of a run-down East Los Angeles garage. While the premise was basically a Hispanic variation of Fred Sanford, the cantankerous African American junk dealer played by Redd Foxx on *Sanford and Son*, which it followed on Friday nights, viewers old enough to remember still regard *Chico and the Man* as one of the funniest TV comedies of all time, even though it's rarely shown in reruns.

To say that America had an instant love affair with Freddie, who went on to become a popular guest host on *The Tonight Show* in addition to headlining at Caesars Palace in Las Vegas and entertaining at Jimmy

Carter's 1977 presidential inaugural gala, isn't an overstatement. My personal association with Freddie, like Jay Leno, who also auditioned for me in New York on the same night, had a storybook beginning and I immediately made him a regular. Born Frederick Karl Pruetzel and raised in the Washington Heights neighborhood of Manhattan, he was just seventeen when I first met him.

At the time, he was a senior on the verge of dropping out of the Fiorello LaGuardia High School of Performing Arts, which he soon did. Though his early material, where he introduced himself to audiences as "Hungarican" (part Hungarian and part Puerto Rican), wasn't terribly remarkable, his stage presence, delivery, and sense of timing were incredible, and he absolutely blew me away with his catchphrases "Lookin good!" and "Ees not my job!" Freddie knew it, too, because not long after I met him, he decided that since comedian Alan King already had a lock on the "King of Comedy" sobriquet, he could be the "prince"—hence the name change. I always used to say that Freddie was seventeen going on forty. I had never seen that much raw talent and charisma in somebody so young and he could also be incredibly sweet.

ROBERT KLEIN:

I got a phone call from Budd telling me to come down and see this new kid named Freddie Prinze soon after he auditioned at the Improv. It was the only time I saw him perform live, and he was basically imitating Lenny Bruce—and doing it very well, I might add.

The thing I remember most is being struck by the fact that I'd never seen anyone who was as good at that age. He was just a force of nature. The other thing I remember was taking issue with some of the self-deprecating Puerto Rican material he was doing. Part of that had to do with my own personal tastes coming into play—like when I used to see a black comic using the word *shvartza* in front of a Jewish audience up in the Catskills to get a laugh. I just didn't like it and I told Freddie that. But in terms of comedic ability and timing, he was absolutely brilliant.

RICHARD LEWIS:

I can't say we were thick as thieves, but yeah, Freddie and I were friends, and I'll echo Robert's sentiments by saying that

Freddie had maybe the strongest presence of anyone that age I had ever seen.

PAUL RODRIGUEZ, comedian and actor:

Freddie Prinze was one of my first points of reference. Later on, when I was stationed in Iceland while serving in the Air Force, I had top-secret clearance for encryptions. That meant I had special access to Armed Forces Radio, and I used to order tapes of *Chico and the Man* and copies of Freddie's comedy albums. Even though I never met him, he had a huge influence on me. He was in the moment, he was fast, and he was smart. I knew his routines by heart.

LIZ TORRES:

Freddie was a lot younger than me, but we had a natural bond because we're both Hispanic and I always thought he was incredibly talented. At one point, though, I was away from New York for about a year living in Los Angeles and no longer working at the Improv. And I'd heard rumors from a number of reliable sources that Freddie had supposedly been stealing my material.

So one night sometime in early or mid 1973, I was back at the club, and Freddie was there with David Brenner, who was Budd's nemesis. But David and Freddie were great friends, and David asked me if I wanted to meet him. When I said yes and David introduced us, I said, "How do you do? I hear you're stealing my act, how are you doing with it?"

"I'm killing," Freddie said.

"Good," I said, "because if you were bombing I'd hate you and I'd have to kick your ass."

I don't know if he really was or wasn't stealing anything, but he acted very nervous about it.

ALAN ZWEIBEL:

I don't know if the rumors about Freddie stealing other people's material were true or not, but I did write some jokes he never paid me for, so I still considered them mine. In fact, one of them, which I later heard he put on an album, was also the first joke I'd ever had on "Weekend Update" on *Saturday Night Live* when George Carlin hosted. The joke was, "The post office is about to issue a stamp commemorating prostitution.

It's a ten-cent stamp, but if you want to lick it, it's a quarter."
The joke doesn't work as well today because people rarely lick
stamps because of the adhesive on the backs of them.

DAVID STEINBERG, comedian, director, actor, writer, and talk-show host:

Freddie's first manager, David Jonas, was a friend of mine, so
I used to go see him a lot. He was a terrific comic who could
do just about anything. Then when he became an actor, he
was terrific at that, too. It's like he came from out of nowhere,
which he basically did.

MARVIN BRAVERMAN:

His talent notwithstanding, the thing I remember most about
Freddie is that he made you want to take him under your wing,
especially since most of us were a lot older than he was. He
kind of became our surrogate son.

TOM DREESEN:

While Tim Reid and I had our comedy team, we eventually
began working the Playboy Club circuit. This is how we got
really good because in most of the clubs you had to do four
to six shows a night. When we worked the New York Playboy
Club, this was how I first met Freddie Prinze when he was
seventeen. They had a playroom and a penthouse. When one
room filled up, you had to wait in the other one until it was
time for you to go on.

So one night, Tim and I were up in the penthouse when
the drummer came up to me and said, "There's a comedian
downstairs and he's really, really funny." I went downstairs
and saw him, and he was incredible on top of being this really
good-looking kid. The other thing about Freddie was that he
was relatively clean, because believe it or not, they didn't want
your material to be too dirty at the Playboy Club—although
later on he did this routine about how every guy wanted to
suck his own dick where he started talking about how he
pulled his leg up over the bedpost.

We became fast friends and we used to hang out at both the
New York and LA Improv a lot. Also, not long after we first met,
Freddie was opening for a jazz musician named Jonah Jones at
the Playboy Club in Chicago where I was still living. Nobody in

Chicago really knew who Freddie was at that point, so I tried to get him on a local TV show. I couldn't get him on, but I got him on a radio show hosted by a guy named Eddie Schwartz. After that, whenever he was in town, Freddie did his show.

I think Freddie realized he was going to become famous long before he was. He just had that self-confidence and he knew it. The thing that made me realize this was the time we were sitting in a bar on Rush Street in Chicago called Jay's and some music trio was playing on the television in the background. That's when Freddie turned to me and said, "I'm going to be a big star, Tommy—a BIG star."

BILLY CRYSTAL:

I didn't know Freddie exceptionally well, but I do know Eddie Murphy, and I remember thinking of Freddie in a similar way as I later came to regard Eddie, which is that they both always had this superstar quality about them. They were very parallel in that they had that little something extra.

BYRON ALLEN:

Freddie's wife, Kathy, was pregnant with their son when I sold him a joke. At the time, I recall thinking to myself, "Wow, Freddie's wife is so beautiful; he's so young and he has everything." But as much as I looked up to him, I also wanted to beat him when it came to doing *The Tonight Show* for the first time. And I did. He was nineteen and I was eighteen.

GLENN HIRSCH:

With Freddie, there was definitely an arrogance about him, but not in a bad way because he had this rare ability to own the room when he was onstage. He talked from his point of view. In other words, he was telling his story and not simply mother-in-law jokes.

PAUL REISER:

I was still in college when he became a star, but Freddie definitely had a major impact on me. His trajectory was one you sort of just watched in amazement, because you realized that the Improv really was a breeding ground for most of the major comics you'd see on television. I remember watching him just get bigger and bigger and bigger.

JIMMIE WALKER:

Freddie was probably the most confident comic I've ever seen in my life. He was the first guy out of all of us to say, "I'm the best, I'm the handsomest, I'm the funniest—I'm *the* guy." If you didn't laugh at the way he delivered it, you'd think, "Gee, there must be something wrong with *me*."

CRAIG TENNIS:

I'm pretty sure that when I started seeing Freddie perform at the New York Improv, he was the closer. Aside from the fact that he was always very personable and engaging, the thing I remember most about him initially was that when he didn't get a laugh, he'd go right for the throat. It's like he became Andrew Dice Clay and every other word out of his mouth would be shit, fuck, bitch—language that you wouldn't think anything about now that was still very out there at the time.

Then suddenly Freddie's act started to become polished, although even after I finally got him booked for his first appearance on *The Tonight Show*, I still felt like I was taking a huge gamble. The night he went on in 1973, he arrived at the studio dressed in a dark-green velvet suit, looking like a million dollars. Everything seemed fine until the producer, Freddie DeCordova, came rushing up to me about ten minutes before air in a state of panic. He said, "Freddie Prinze. Everyone's going to hate it. I hate it. He's not getting on. He's never getting on."

But this was DeCordova's attitude when it came to new guests practically all the time and I was used to it. We also had no one else to fill the spot, so I immediately tried to reassure him and we put him on anyway. As Freddie's good luck would have it, Sammy Davis Jr. was also on that night, and when he sat down next to Johnny, he had absolutely nothing to say. Now we were in this huge predicament, so when we brought Freddie out, he just absolutely blew the roof off to the point where both Sammy and Johnny were laughing so hard they were literally falling off the couch.

JAY LENO:

What's interesting about Freddie's Carson debut was that he had done Merv Griffin the day before and he was just okay. But then when he did *The Tonight Show*, Sammy Davis Jr. was doing that applause thing where you slap your knee and that's when everything took off.

CRAIG TENNIS:

Between Freddie, Sammy Davis Jr., and Carson laughing, the audience basically followed their lead and fell in love with Freddie. Though it seemed inconceivable at the time, Freddie got *Chico and the Man* almost immediately after, and Sammy eventually took him on the road. It was a virtual disaster turned into instant success by sheer luck.

In the end, however, few entertainers fell more swiftly or tragically than Freddie, who died at the age of twenty-two on January 29, 1977, two days after he shot himself with a .32 caliber pistol. Freddie's sudden death came as a traumatic shock on so many different levels.

For the comedy community in particular, memories of where people were that day remain as forever seared as September 11th, the Space Shuttle *Challenger* explosion, and the assassinations of John F. Kennedy and Martin Luther King Jr. It was the first time we had lost one of our own. Life as we knew it, even for those who didn't know Freddie personally, would never be the same again.

PAUL RODRIGUEZ:

Although I realize now that Freddie had been unhappy and was deeply troubled, I had no idea at the time. Back then, he was just a comic role model for me. When I first heard he'd shot himself I was in the Air Force stationed in Iceland, and when the news came over the teletype, I just lost it. I cried like a baby. I remember my senior sergeant coming up to me and saying, "Why the fuck are you crying?" He didn't understand why I was so upset when I'd never even met Freddie. I just couldn't believe it, and it hit me like a ton of bricks. Had Freddie lived, he would have been the elder statesman of Latino comics and we would have hung out together at the Improv, giving Budd shit about his monocle.

One of the first professional jobs I got was because I had a moustache, and the producers told me I looked like Freddie Prinze. This was also one of the reasons I wanted to perform at the Improv, because Freddie had gotten his start there. When I did, I used to sit there for hours grilling Budd about Freddie. He knew it all and he told me everything.

He also told me I had to find my own voice and that I couldn't compete with a dead guy. I give Budd total credit for that. He was the one who told me that if he saw me come in the next week with a moustache, he wasn't going to put me on. It was very hard for me to do, because it was very easy for me to get girls with one—kind of like catching fish in a barrel—but I did what Budd told me to and I shaved it off.

January 28, 1977, was a Friday. As usual, I was at the Hollywood Improv, where we were either preparing to begin or already in the middle of our first show of the night. I don't recall who we had performing, or how we first received the news that Freddie had shot himself early that morning, but we were all stunned.

Though the details were still very sketchy, it would quickly emerge that he had been despondent after being slapped with a restraining order from his estranged wife two days earlier, and that he'd apparently phoned her and his parents before pulling the trigger. That morning, around 4 AM, he'd been in his room at the Beverly Hills Plaza Hotel with his business manager, Marvin "Dusty" Snyder, who told police that Freddie had suddenly pulled out a .32 Magnum revolver from under a pillow on his sofa and shot himself before he could stop him.

At the time, however, the only news we had was that Freddie remained in a coma in UCLA Medical Center's intensive care unit following emergency surgery. Hospital authorities issued this bulletin: "He tolerated operative treatment well. However, because the brain tissue was badly injured, it is premature at this time to offer a prediction as to whether he will survive or what disability (brain damage) will be sustained."

When a shock hits your system this hard, you feel like you can't breathe, and that was how I felt then. Luckily, I wasn't alone. I was surrounded by comedians, many of whom knew Freddie and looked at me as a surrogate father figure, so I tried to remain stoic even as a whirlwind of feelings and thoughts came flooding in a rush.

The first one was why Freddie would do this, although it still hadn't been confirmed if it had been an accident. My second thought was whether or not I could have done something to prevent it. After hearing rumors about his ever-increasing appetite for quaaludes and cocaine, I'd seen it up close just a few months before, when I'd gone with Jay Leno to see him open for Shirley MacLaine at Caesars Palace in Las Vegas.

Freddie was so strung out that when we went backstage to his dressing room afterwards, he just sat there with his dinner tray, barely aware of who we were, and struggling to lift his fork. However, I didn't think anything of it at the time.

Jokingly, I'd even turned to Jay and said, "This guy's boring. Let's go say hello to Shirley." Not only did we leave with me mainly chalking Freddie's strange behavior up to fatigue, I also didn't know what a quaalude was. I had honestly never heard of the stuff.

I was also aware of his mounting legal troubles, with an impending divorce from his wife, Kathy; a custody battle over their infant son, Freddie Jr.; and a breach-of-contract lawsuit with his first manager, David Jonas, which I'd felt had been a bad match from the beginning.

There were also the growing tensions between Freddie and *Chico and the Man* creator Jimmy Komack, which had become tabloid fodder. Still, he had just performed at Jimmy Carter's presidential inaugural in Washington, DC, two weeks earlier, and the last time I talked to Freddie a couple of days before, he seemed upbeat about the future.

Now he was probably near death, but as the gravity of the moment set in, there was no time to process any of it, as reporters from every major news outlet in the country were already trying to get a hold of me. But I was in no mood to talk to them, and knowing that they would probably soon start descending upon the Improv, I immediately got into my car and drove over to Canter's Deli, a popular after-hours hangout for comedians then as now, to see if I could get any more information.

JAY LENO:

I'm sure I was either at the Improv or The Comedy Store, which was the other big showcase club in LA, when everyone first got word Freddie had shot himself, although by this point he had already begun to drift away from his old friends. Some of this might have been conjecture on our part, but he was a huge star and none of us were, so when he came into the Improv, he'd be with whoever was famous and he didn't sit with us.

I think there are some people who might tell you this happens to everyone, in the sense that there are people you thought you were closer to than you actually were, so that when they make it big, you feel betrayed. But Freddie and I didn't have a lot in common. He liked drugs and alcohol and

I never had an interest in those things, so we didn't have a connection there.

Really, our only connection was the fact that we were both comics, like Seinfeld and me. Whenever Jerry and I get on the phone, we always end up talking to each other for an hour because each conversation invariably begins with something funny and we make each other laugh.

When Freddie and I were just starting out, we had that same kind of a thing where one of us would come up with a bit and the other one would come up with the punch line. And because most comics write by talking and getting a reaction, you'd be like, "This guy's good for me and I can write with him," although with Freddie and me it didn't really go beyond that.

But his death was still very rough, especially when you were twenty-four or twenty-five like most of us were and you'd never had much experience with this kind of thing before. It just seemed so odd, although I'd been to his apartment enough times to know he liked to show off with guns, particularly when there were women present.

He'd do things like go in the bedroom and fire his gun into the air. Then the woman would come running in, and Freddie would be lying on the bed pretending he shot himself. As soon as Freddie heard her scream, he'd go, "Ha, ha."

RICHARD LEWIS:

I was at the Improv when his friend Alan Bursky came in and said these exact words: "Freddie shot himself." I became so enraged when he said it that I grabbed him by the collar and threw him up against the wall. I said, "This better not be a fucking joke." I mean, I wanted it to be a joke, and yet because I thought he was making a joke, I went ballistic because I was so angry if he was.

It turned out to be true, of course. The drugs and his fascination with guns were what did him in. But it was mainly the drugs and the stardom. What else is new?

BYRON ALLEN:

My mother worked in the publicity department for NBC and she was the publicist for *Sanford and Son* and *Chico and the Man*. And when you're the publicist on a show, who gets the first call? I remember the phone ringing at three o'clock in the morning and the person on the other end was Paul Hall, who was a news producer at KNBC.

There weren't any answering machines back then, so I picked up the phone, and Paul said, "Byron, it's Paul. I need to speak to your mother." I asked him why and that was when he told me Freddie had shot himself. When I handed the phone to my mom, she was hysterical, but she still gave him the phone numbers of everyone connected with the show so he could tell them before the news broke.

KITTY BRUCE:

There are four dates that I remember like they were yesterday—my father's death, Freddie's, and the assassinations of John Lennon and John F. Kennedy. It took me a long time to get over Freddie's death and I used to have such resentment against California because nearly everybody I ever loved died there. As soon as I heard the news, I remember thinking to myself, "Fucking Hollywood. It took another one."

PAUL REISER:

I never met Freddie because I was still in college when he was starting out, but he was very impactful. His trajectory was one you watched, and he just got bigger and bigger and bigger. I was glued to the television after he shot himself because he didn't die right away.

It was just so sad and it left this taste in my mouth that this was the bad side of comedy—and that you didn't want to make it too big too quickly. Not that I ever thought I would. And I would amend that because what made it especially sad was Freddie was so funny.

KEVIN NEALON:

Before I began performing stand-up, I would watch every comic appearing on TV to the point where I knew all their acts by heart. I knew people loved to laugh and they loved stand-ups, but it didn't really hit me how important stand-up was until Freddie Prinze died.

The day he shot himself, I was raking leaves in my parents' yard in Connecticut when I heard the news on the radio. The country was devastated by it and there were massive amounts of media coverage. I remember thinking to myself, "Wow, a comic really makes a big impact on the world." I think that was my impetus for moving to California to become a comedian. In a sick way, I thought, "A spot has become available."

DANNY AIELLO:

I don't know if I should say this, but after Freddie died people used to say things like, "Hollywood killed Freddie Prinze." The pressures he was under may have contributed to it, but I can tell you that oftentimes when he was performing at the club in New York he appeared stoned. I never actually witnessed him taking anything, but I did see some of the behavior onstage. He was always brilliant comedically, but I always felt he was on something.

SHELLEY ACKERMAN:

The last time I saw him was in New York about five or six months before he died and I remember being frightened. I just had this sense that he was going down the tubes as if a piece of his soul had shifted. On the day he died, I remember standing in the kitchen of my friend's Manhattan apartment where I was staying when the news came over the radio. As soon as I heard it, I was doubled over choking and crying.

No one was with me that day, but not long before—maybe even the last time I saw him—Freddie borrowed a record album from me that he never returned. It was the soundtrack from the movie *Car Wash* and it had a song called "I'm Going Down." Before he borrowed it, Freddie played it over and over that day. When he died, I truly think he hypnotized himself into a drug-induced state, took a gun, and didn't know what he was doing.

JIMMIE WALKER:

I was on my way to Philadelphia when I heard the news he shot himself. I was literally frozen because in the beginning, they said he was wounded and he might make it. And this is exactly what I said to myself. I said, "It's just like fucking Freddie to wound himself so everybody has to go to the hospital and say, 'Freddie, what's the problem?'"

MARTY NADLER:

I knew Freddie both when he was just starting out and after he made it big. The best analogy I can use was that this was a guy who went from the A train in New York to a red Corvette at NBC.

I witnessed a lot of that firsthand because I was a writer on *Chico and the Man* during its second season. By that time, the people who ran the show and managed him were controlling him to a point that I think he kind of knew this was the beginning of the end for him.

About a year before he died, we were working on a script one afternoon at my house for an episode called "Chico Runs Away." I remember that we were right in the middle of writing it when Freddie suddenly reached into his man purse and pulled out a gun. I had no idea he was going to do this and I was terrified that it might go off, so I said, "Look, Freddie, you put any joke you want into the script and it's fine with me."

So he put the gun away and we continued writing. But if I'd had any idea what was going to happen, I'm sure I would have given him more shit about the gun.

ALAN BURSKY:

Freddie was one of my best friends and I loved him, but he was sort of a psychic vampire. We lived together for a while after he first moved to Hollywood to do *Chico and the Man*. We were both about the same age and we went on *The Tonight Show* around the same time. I'd done it several months before him and he was still in New York, but Freddie used to call me in the middle of the night and we would bullshit. Then we met at Catch A Rising Star and we became fast friends. When he came out a few weeks later to do *Chico and the Man*, I told him he could stay with me.

Anyway, the first time we met, I was expecting to see some kid, but then this guy who was about six two comes in. He had the mustache and broads on his arm. I was flabbergasted. The night he flew out to do *Chico*, I picked him up at the airport and he was wearing a blue wool peacoat. It was pouring rain out; we were both drenched and the coat reeked.

By the time we got to my apartment, it smelled so bad that I was like, "Give me your coat and I'll hang it in the shower." I've told this story a million times, but when I said this, he asked me for a mirror and a blade, which I took to mean that he wanted to shave. So I handed him my electric razor and he said, "No, it's for this."

That was when he pulled out this thing of cellophane from his wet coat and there was wax paper inside. In the wax paper was tinfoil, and in the tinfoil was more wax paper, which he finally opened up and there were pieces of what looked like crushed sugar cubes in the middle.

I was like, "What's that?"

"Cocaine," Freddie said.

When I told him I'd never seen coke before, he told me he needed a mirror and a razor so he could chop it up. Instead of a mirror and a razor, I took my autographed picture of Woody Allen down from the wall and gave him an X-ACTO knife.

Looking back, people don't realize what happened to him—and to me years later. Cocaine psychosis set in. You'd hallucinate and then there'd be paranoia, but nobody knew what that was back then.

Now this is where it got strange—and again, I didn't know what cocaine psychosis was—but Freddie put the bullet in his head early on the morning of January 28th, then lasted thirty-three hours on life support, and died the following afternoon. Several months before, say around October of 1976, any time that I was hanging out with him, he was so paranoid he made me flush anything I touched down the toilet. Anything I couldn't flush, I had to wipe my fingerprints off of, including doorknobs, which he made me wipe with a napkin. Then I had to take the napkin with me.

Even after Freddie's death had been ruled an accidental shooting, everybody still speculated because he always talked about suicide. He would say, "Can you see the headlines— FREDDIE PRINZE DEAD."

Once I remember him saying this to me and I said, "You better hope there's not an earthquake that day." Eerily enough, the day Freddie died there was a huge snowstorm in New York and the headline in all the papers was "SNOW STUNS CITY." And then underneath in a little box, there was: "Freddie Prinze Succumbs to Self-Inflicted Gunshot Wound."

LIZ TORRES:

I was at home in Los Angeles watching television when I found out. It was the day after and he was on life support. I don't remember what it was about, but we'd recently had a knockdown, drag-out fight, and we were on the outs.

As soon as I heard the news, I got right in my car and drove over to UCLA Medical Center. They weren't letting anyone in, although Tony Orlando was also there and he went straight up to his room. He and Freddie had also recently had a fight and Freddie flung the Rolex watch Tony had given him up against the wall.

My heart absolutely went through the floor, although I continued to believe that Freddie would make it as long as he was alive. When Freddie's mother got there, I wrote a note to her in English and Spanish for one of the nurses to give her. When

> I found out he had died, I got in the car and drove home, but I
> had to keep pulling over. When I finally got home, I went on a
> three-day bender after that. It was just awful. I still can't think
> about it without crying.

As we continued to get periodic reports from the hospital that there
had been no change in his condition, I decided to keep the Improv
open and go on with the show. I like to think Freddie would have
wanted it that way.

The official time of Freddie's death was Saturday, January 29, at
1 PM Pacific Standard after his mother, Maria Pruetzel, who hadn't left
his side, decided to take him off life support. The reactions over the next
forty-eight hours and during the weeks after were a surreal blend of
sadness, what-ifs, and whys. The funeral was that Monday at the Old
North Church Forest Lawn in the Hollywood Hills.

Many of his old comedy friends were also conspicuously absent
from the service's invitation-only VIP list in favor of stars like Lucille
Ball, Tony Orlando, Sammy Davis Jr., and his *Chico and the Man* co-star
Jack Albertson. Composer Paul Williams was one of the pallbearers. For
Freddie's old friends, being shunned only added insult to their injury.
But even so, several of them, including Jay Leno and Richard Lewis,
decided to attend anyway.

JAY LENO:

> We were sort of hysterical because here we were, all of the
> guys who'd started out with him in New York seated in the
> back row, and Freddie's "close friends" like Lucille Ball and
> Tony Orlando were up front. We were all like, "How do they
> even know who he is?"

I knew Freddie well, of course, and we both considered each other
friends, which is why I chose to stay away. Knowing the three-ring
celebrity circus it would be, and how fame itself had largely propelled his
demise, I just couldn't stand to witness the spectacle. I had a quiet lunch
alone at Schwab's drugstore instead. I also needed to mourn Freddie on
my own terms. In many ways, I've never stopped.

THIRTY-ONE
A Troubling Nemesis Named Mitzi Shore

Especially in the beginning at the Hollywood Improv, having Freddie Prinze and Robin Williams alongside our constantly growing roster of celebrity customers like Redd Foxx—who was then starring on the NBC mega-hit *Sanford and Son* and came in one night and bought champagne for everyone not long after we opened—certainly convinced me that the West Coast comedy gold rush, created in large part because of Johnny Carson's arrival, was far more potent than I'd ever imagined.

Every week, it seemed like one of our comedians was either appearing on *The Tonight Show* or well on their way towards landing a sitcom because of it. There were also hundreds of former class clowns and assorted office watercooler cutups migrating to Los Angeles like Pied Pipers from all across the country, hoping to join the fray. Some even called it Comedy Camelot.

The New York club was also thriving thanks to a bumper crop of young acts, who were all either just starting to come into their own or simply trying to find their footing on West 44th Street.

STEVE MITTLEMAN:

During the summer of 1976—my third or fourth time ever at the Improv—Diana Ross was in the audience and I freaked out. I literally smacked myself on the forehead like they used to do in those V8 tomato juice commercials and said, "Holy shit!"

I'm not sure if Diana heard me or not, but I quickly regained my composure because I knew I had to and I did just fine. Back then, I had this routine where I did a fairly decent imitation of Richard Nixon. I also had a bit about bakeries that were located in New York subway stations where they used to have these signs that said, "We do wedding cakes."

I'd go, "Who would buy their wedding cake in a subway bake shop?" Then I'd pretend to be a customer and say, "Hello, subway bake shop. Do you do wedding cakes? Can you make mine in the shape of the M train?" Then I'd make these gestures where on top of the cake the bride and groom would be holding onto a strap.

It got big laughs and whenever the emcee would introduce me they'd say, "Ladies and gentlemen, this guy's got hormones in all the right places. Ladies, sit back on your hands. Gentlemen, hold on to your dates." That was all it took for them to start laughing before I even said a word. Sometimes this would go on for thirty seconds or more.

PAUL PROVENZA:

I was a kid obsessed with comedians, and whenever you'd see them on one of the talk shows, they'd all say the same thing: "I started at the Improv." I remember literally going through the Yellow Pages when it was still listed as the Improvisation and calling the club to find out how you became a comedian.

I'd been going there once a month for about two years before I finally started auditioning in 1975. The hot young act was a comedy team called Overton & Sullivan. Rick Overton really took me under his wing and championed me along with another comic named Glenn Hirsch. Glenn was the house emcee and he was really electrifying because he was so unpredictable.

Budd had already gone to LA by this point, but he'd still come back a few times a year and whenever he did, it was very clear that he was *the* authority. The sentiment among the younger comics was that Budd was the grandfather and Chris Albrecht was the avuncular father figure, which he was to me in a lot of ways because my own father died when I was seventeen.

More than comedy lessons, Chris would give me life lessons. He'd say things to me like, "You know what, cool your jets. You're probably not going to get on for a while until you can demonstrate that you understand what the other comics are trying to do here and that it's about more than you just trying to get stage time."

JOE PISCOPO:

Chris's nickname was The General. We called him that because he was our boss. Then when the grand, exalted mystic ruler Budd Friedman walked in, it was like, "Whoa!" I did a lot of observational humor back then—"Hey, how about this?" or, "Did you ever do that?"—and then one night I was seated back near the kitchen, which was where all the comics who wanted to become regulars sat, and Chris gestured to me with his index finger and told me I was going to be one of them.

It was just like being knighted, and then not long after that, he made me one of the emcees. One of the first lessons I learned was that if I saw something, I wasn't going to say anything. As a matter of fact, there used to be a slogan in the midseventies: "If you see something, *don't* say something."

So I tried to follow that mantra until one night in 1976, this guy walked into the club stoned out of his mind singing Paul McCartney's song "Let 'Em In"—you know, "Somebody's knocking at the door, someone's ringing the bell . . ." Then he sat down and took his shoes off.

First, he removed one sneaker, then the other, and when he did this, they both hit the floor with a loud thud. However, I didn't say anything, and then the next thing I knew he took off his shirt and threw it in the middle of the floor. But I still didn't say anything—and neither did anybody else—until he took his pants off, sans underwear, and suddenly he was standing there completely stark-ass naked in the middle of the Improv.

Well, as soon as Chris saw this, he said, "What the fuck are you doing?" Next, he gingerly grabbed him by the back of the arms and with Glenn Hirsch, who was working the door, they pushed him out onto the street and into the snow where he was still singing "Somebody's knocking at the door" stark naked.

But then the strangest thing happened, because Judy Orbach, who was the assistant manager and was there with her boyfriend that night, started to take pity on the guy. So they grabbed his pants and started to run after him, getting mugged in the process. What saved them was giving the mugger this guy's wallet, which I never questioned. I just figured this was the new world I was in.

With the continued rise of our good fortunes, there was also the groundswell of publicity that the Hollywood Improv was receiving thanks to *On Location: Freddie Prinze and Friends*, which would be the very first of HBO's stand-up specials featuring Freddie, Jay, Andy, Elayne, and other then unknowns like Tim Thomerson, Gary Mule Deer, and Bob Shaw.

There were also no signs that the frenzied excitement and frenetic activity on both coasts were going to be letting up anytime soon either. In 1977, the *LA Times* even began devoting an entire beat to stand-up comedy.

WILLIAM KNOEDELSEDER:

They'd recently hired a guy named Irv Letofsky to take over the Calendar section, which was pretty much a sales tool for the entertainment industry back then. Irv came from Minneapolis and he wanted to make the section grittier and more on the inside as opposed to just reporting on the new movies that were premiering that week. Irv had a different take on things, and I guess he'd been to some comedy clubs and the acts weren't like the comics he'd seen before. When I walked into his office one day looking for work, he said, "There's something going on here. It feels like Greenwich Village in the 1960s." Then he asked me if I wanted to cover it, and it became my beat. Mostly I was writing profiles, and the comics were all twenty-six or twenty-seven like me. We'd all come from someplace else recently, so it was easy to understand them. They were the class clowns and I'd been the class clown even though I never wanted to do it professionally. However, the idea of covering comedy and learning about these people who were my age turned out to be the best job I ever had.

At the same time all of this was happening, however, I continued to square off with an increasingly antagonistic adversary. You know that old saying—one bad apple spoils the whole bunch? Well, in my case the proverbial worm came in the form of a frizzy-haired fellow club owner named Mitzi Shore, who owned the nearby Comedy Store less than a mile from the Hollywood Improv.

Some history: Several weeks before Johnny Carson moved *The Tonight Show* to LA in the spring of 1972, an old-school comic and old acquaintance of mine named Sammy Shore and his writing partner Rudy DeLuca decided to open a small comedy club at 8433 Sunset Boulevard in the heart of the Sunset Strip. Formerly the home of the famed celebrity nightclub Ciro's—and once frequented by virtually every A-list Hollywood celebrity of the 1940s and '50s from Ronald Reagan, Clark Gable, and Humphrey Bogart to Betty Grable, Ava Gardner, and

Lana Turner—the building's lineage was the stuff show-business legends are made of.

Though he was never a household name, Sammy, too, had had a formidable career as an opening act for Sammy Davis Jr., Ann-Margret, Tony Bennett, and most recently on tour and in Las Vegas for Elvis Presley. At the time, Sammy and Rudy, who had recently joined the writing staff of *The Carol Burnett Show*, had been coming in to the New York club off and on for several years.

I wouldn't say the three of us were close necessarily, but I certainly liked and respected them. Moreover, when they were first considering opening The Comedy Store, which my pal Jack Knight also helped them to build, one of the first people they consulted was me. Basically their idea had been to create a smaller-scale version of the Improv, a place for them to hang out with their other comedian friends and try out new material when they weren't on the road. Plus, they'd gotten a rent-free deal from the owner on top of a handshake agreement to split whatever was left over on drinks and cover charges minus expenses.

RUDY DELUCA, screenwriter, actor, and co-founder of The Comedy Store:

I don't recall a lot of specific evenings, and I didn't know Budd terribly well in those days, but Sammy and I used to drop in to the New York Improv on a fairly regular basis to hear comics and singers. By the time I'd moved to California to write comedy when I was working with Sammy, we'd been tossing around the idea of opening a place of our own where comics could go and try out new material. I was also having trouble finding other work and I was looking for something to do.

One day not long after this, we were driving past Ciro's, which had recently closed, and Sammy said to me, "Gee, I'd like to get this place, rent it out, and just call it the Sammy Shore Room." But knowing this could never work, I said, "Sammy, how many people are going to come see you at the Sammy Shore Room? Your family and three others. Let's make it an Improv like Budd Friedman has in New York."

That's exactly how it happened. Not too long after that, I talked to Budd and he said, "Go ahead. Open it up." I asked him for permission in a way, although I didn't need it. It was just opening up another kind of club. We didn't even have a name for it, nor did we know exactly what it was going to be.

With my decision to open a second club in LA still at least another two years away, I gave Rudy and Sammy my blessing without hesitation. Naturally, I had no idea that when Sammy and his wife, Mitzi, split up soon after this, she would be taking over The Comedy Store—which she'd named and later repainted and remodeled—as part of the divorce settlement.

As a result, not only had the Store become hugely successful by the time I arrived on the scene, Mitzi also had a monopoly—attributable in no small part to the fact that she was now using many of my best former New York comics, including Freddie Prinze, Steve Landesberg, Jay Leno, and Jimmie Walker.

JAY LENO:

You had to live on your wits as a comedian, and that's how I decided I was going to live when I left Boston and moved to LA in 1972. In Boston, I had acquired a few things and I was in my apartment one afternoon when I thought to myself, "If I stay here, I'm going to buy more stuff. Then I'm going to have to get a job to pay for this stuff."

I basically told my neighbors they could take anything they wanted and I left. I booked a red-eye to LA and when I got off the plane, I went straight to The Comedy Store and slept on the stairs for the next week.

Mitzi was fine at the time. She had just gotten the club in the divorce from Sammy. Like the Improv in New York, it was a great place because you finally got to meet people who did the same thing as you. She was wonderful to me in the beginning. She ran the Store like a housemother.

In truth, Mitzi really saw her role more as being LA's self-appointed queen bee of comedy, although at the time of my arrival, I still had no indication that I was walking into a hornet's nest.

The main reason I didn't know it was because I barely knew Mitzi at all. I'd actually only met her once about a year earlier, when I was in town with a comedian and impressionist I managed named Maureen Murphy who was scheduled to appear on *The Merv Griffin Show*. The night before, Maureen and I hitchhiked over to the Store from the nearby motel we were staying in, and Mitzi couldn't have been nicer or more gracious. She even gave us free drinks and invited Maureen to perform.

But when I moved there in 1975, all niceties were off from day one. First, she laid down the law to the comics that they could only work at her place and not the Improv, literally forcing their hands and pitting them against me, which made absolutely no sense, especially since comics needed practice on more than one stage to get better.

She also began attacking me in the press, and in an attempt to rewrite history and kill my baby in the cradle, she even told any reporter who would listen that I had stolen her idea.

Fortunately, many of the comedians refused to cave in. Most vocally, Jay Leno, who was already a huge draw even though it would be another seventeen years before he took over as host of *The Tonight Show*, was the first one to call her bluff. After telling her that I had been his first manager and that he would only work for me if he had to choose, she immediately backed down. While a then unknown David Letterman stayed almost exclusively with The Comedy Store, Freddie Prinze, who was one of my first investors, worked at both clubs.

So did Elayne Boosler and her then boyfriend Andy Kaufman, both of whom I'd personally brought out separately to headline for a month when I first opened—and where I also introduced Andy to his future manager, George Shapiro, on the same day that George's uncle, Carl Reiner, had told him about Andy.

GEORGE SHAPIRO:

My connection with Budd runs very deep and goes back more than fifty years. I first met him because I used to go to the New York Improv a lot even though I was already living out in California when he opened. We weren't close, close friends, but we had enough of a rapport for him to tell me about Andy the same day Carl Reiner did.

This is what happened. Uncle Carl has total recall and he had just gotten back from New York where he'd seen Andy perform at Catch A Rising Star. On this particular day, I was having lunch with him and Dick Van Dyke in the NBC commissary, when Uncle Carl did Andy's entire act for me verbatim with the intonations and impersonating Jimmy Carter in the Foreign Man accent exactly the way Andy did. He said, "He's so unique. You have to fly to New York and see him because he's so special."

CARL REINER:

My wife Estelle and I were in New York and we'd gone to Catch A Rising Star one night where Andy happened to be perform- ing. We were sitting about twenty feet away, and when he got onstage, he started to do things that were so crazy and so bad. Every impression sounded exactly the same and at first I thought he was an idiot.

But then he did a spot-on impression of Elvis Presley. And then, I don't know if it was before or after, he sat on a stool and started reading *The Great Gatsby*. I went backstage after- wards and asked him where the hell he'd been. He told me this was his first paying job and that he was getting paid fifteen dollars. So I told him to look me up if he ever came out to the West Coast, and I immediately told George about him as soon as I got back to LA.

As luck would have it, I was gearing up to do a Dick Van Dyke special, and he and I were having lunch with George at the NBC commissary a few days later. At first, George was resistant to the idea of managing Andy. But then when I started impersonating his entire act in his Foreign Man voice, Dick said, "That's hysterical. Let's have him on." And then George called him and he became his manager.

GEORGE SHAPIRO:

I've known Uncle Carl ever since I was twelve when he mar- ried my Aunt Estelle, and I'd never seen him this excited about anything. His enthusiasm about Andy was absolutely infec- tious, but my plate was already full with other clients. Then, about four or five o'clock that same afternoon, I was back in my office when I got a call from Budd.

He said, "I'm flying this kid Andy Kaufman out from New York and I'd like for you to take a look at his act for management."

I said, "I can't believe this. Carl Reiner just did his act for me and he loves him. I'll definitely come to see him."

From the moment I did, Andy captured my heart, particu- larly Foreign Man, which I thought was such a funny, wonder- ful thing. I also thought he was amazing musically—playing the conga drums, singing, and dancing. I absolutely loved what he did because it was so bizarre. My immediate reaction was that I wanted to work with him and here's why.

> For a personal manager working in comedy, if you like a comedian and you laugh in your soul, it's like falling in love. However, I also had a fear of him being insane. At first, I didn't know if he was on drugs or just absolutely crazy. But then after meeting with him and discovering he wasn't insane—just partially insane—Andy won me over.

Unfortunately, bringing Andy out to the West Coast did little to quell my escalating troubles with Mitzi even after he began performing at The Comedy Store also. Happily, by the same token, Mitzi's constant bullying and threats for the most part fell on deaf ears when it came to many of the more established comedians. In fact, the only out-and-out holdouts were Jimmie Walker and Steve Landesberg, who each had hit TV shows.

While I never complained or tried to stop them, I was particularly disappointed when it came to Steve, who had been one of my first comics in New York and was by then starring as the erudite New York City police detective Arthur P. Dietrich on ABC's *Barney Miller*. However, he was also now Mitzi's live-in boyfriend and so his reasons were at least understandable.

Even if he hadn't been involved with her, I can't say I was terribly surprised by Mitzi's behavior either, especially since this kind of one-upmanship happens regularly in almost every business. Plus, she had just opened a second club in Westwood. So in one sense I could relate to her fears, and I had even experienced similar suspicions myself with Rick Newman back in New York after he opened Catch A Rising Star in 1972. But Rick and I had since become good friends, which we've remained. Our clubs also ultimately benefited from one another on nights when we didn't have enough comics. For months, I held out hope that I might be able to have a similar arrangement with Mitzi, or that at the very least, we could be cordial even if we never became friends.

However, this was simply not to be, and as her unfounded accusations and vicious retaliation against me grew worse, I literally felt like I was being stung. What angered me even more was that Jimmie Walker refused to perform at the Hollywood Improv. Jimmie had been one of my first investors in LA and had gotten his big break on the Norman

Lear sitcom *Good Times* as a direct result of Allan Manings, one of Lear's producers, seeing him in the New York club and recommending him to Norman for the breakout role of J. J. "Dynomite!" Evans.

His reasons for not doing so—because he claimed we had too many people from the industry and that it hampered his ability to experiment— were also completely without merit. In the first place, Mitzi had a much bigger show-business crowd simply by virtue of the fact the Store had been there longer. Regardless, I felt Jimmie owed me. From my vantage point, it was the ultimate slap in the face and more than forty years later, he remains the single most ungrateful comic I have ever known.

JIMMIE WALKER:

Mitzi was always going ballistic, so you couldn't say, "I'm more aware of this ballistic outbreak than that outbreak." It was kind of like saying, "Donald Trump said something crazy today."

Mitzi was always going crazy about something. It could have been about anything, so you basically took it with a grain of salt. When Budd opened out here, her reaction seemed like no big deal, and I was so busy with *Good Times* that I'm not sure if I was even paying attention.

However, the real reason why I chose to remain exclusively with The Comedy Store was because by that point I'd already been in LA for a few years and I was established there. I was also happy to invest in Budd's club, and I give the New York Improv credit for what I became. But by this time, I'd already moved on to another stage, which happened to be The Comedy Store's, so I just said, "In order to keep peace in the family, I'll just stay where I am." It was nothing against Budd at all— absolutely nothing.

THIRTY-TWO
Going Up in Flames

E ven as my ongoing battles with Mitzi continued on top of the Improv's lingering grief over the sudden death of Freddie Prinze in January 1977, that following year—1978—also turned out to be one of the most successful, if not seminal, years in the history of American comedy.

Starting with Woody Allen's unprecedented four-win Oscar sweep for *Annie Hall*, including Best Picture, Best Original Screenplay, and Best Director, in April, Tinsel Town suddenly had more comedy films than you could count. Fortified with optimism by *Annie Hall*'s triumph—and in an effort to trump it—virtually all the major studios had multipicture deals with everyone from Steve Martin, Chevy Chase, and Cheech and Chong to Improv alums Richard Pryor, Lily Tomlin, and David Steinberg. That fall, National Lampoon's *Animal House* starring John Belushi became the highest grossing comedy film of all time.

As a result, the pot got even sweeter as many stars like Steve Martin received what was becoming known as "the Woody Allen deal." It netted him half a million dollars to write and star in his first movie, *The Jerk*, plus 50 percent of the profits and the option to direct it, along with the last word on both the film's final cut and marketing campaign.

On the TV sitcom front, even though the decade's biggest trailblazer Norman Lear had decided to call it quits to devote more time to political activism, most of his shows like *All in the Family*, *One Day at a Time*, and *The Jeffersons* remained in the top ten. You also had Improv regulars like Robin Williams and Andy Kaufman, whose new shows *Mork and Mindy* and *Taxi* had taken the country by storm almost overnight.

And with stand-up comedy albums also now going multi-platinum and selling off the charts, this put me and Mitzi Shore in the catbird seat as armies of talent managers, agents, studio heads, and network executives swarmed both our clubs nightly in search of new, young blood to feed the public's increasingly voracious appetite for humor.

At first, it seemed like I stood the most to gain, especially after Mitzi lost the lease on her Sunset Boulevard club within days of Freddie's death because of a grandfathered tenant from the previous owner who still held the rights to the show room even though the building was legally hers. In effect, she was a squatter in her own domain, which forced her to move the entire base of operations to the Store's smaller satellite club in Westwood.

But unfortunately, I wasn't able to benefit because I was saddled with my own real estate nightmare following an ill-timed attempt to start another Improv in Las Vegas. In doing so, I temporarily left Chris Albrecht in charge of Melrose Avenue, which thrived in my absence. However, my first foray into Vegas turned out to be a disaster thanks to a leaky roof that caved in one night, along with my balance sheet, following a bad thunderstorm.

CHRIS ALBRECHT:

When Budd left me in charge of the New York Improv, he pretty much let me do whatever I wanted as long as we made money, which we did. So when he called to tell me he was opening a club in Las Vegas, the first thing I told him was that he needed to leave somebody he could trust in charge in LA, not knowing I was the person he had in mind.

But then the very next day, he called me again and said, "I've been thinking about what you told me and I have just one question for you—How soon can you start?"

I think this was maybe in September of '78. I don't remember when the Las Vegas club officially started, but I do remember flying out there to see it and thinking that its location in a strip mall made absolutely no sense.

I also had my doubts about my ability to run the LA club, which was in shambles when I got there. The kitchen was a mess and there were roaches everywhere. Plus, the ceiling was too high, and I didn't think it was a great room for comedy acoustically. So I ended up hiring a scene designer who built a backdrop that was draped, which made the sound better. I also changed exterminators, or maybe I even hired one. All I know is that it became like a self-fulfilling prophecy and the people came because I made it more fun.

The Improv was always fun and I kind of resent Chris saying that, although I'll grant you that the improvements he made were needed ones that I probably overlooked because I'd been there every day and I was too busy to notice.

On top of my first Vegas club going under and my ongoing travails with Mitzi Shore, I was also having problems in my personal life. My already-troubled marriage to Silver had gotten much worse since we moved to California and we'd recently begun divorce proceedings.

Not that I was complaining. We were both miserable and I felt like a caged animal. I also wanted the divorce to be as easy as possible, and with Silver planning to move back East with our two daughters anyway, I said, "You take the New York club," not realizing it would eventually edge Chris out and have far-reaching consequences down the road.

RITA RUDNER, comedian, writer, and actor:

When I started doing stand-up in 1980, I was in *Annie* on Broadway where the theater was right around the corner from the New York Improv. Chris took a liking to me instantly and put me right on, but when Silver came back, I didn't start going on until well after midnight, by which point I was exhausted after having just done a full performance of *Annie*.

Her reason was because she said my voice was too quiet, and she told me I had to take voice lessons even though people were laughing. I never understood that—especially since the fact that I have a softer voice usually means that I don't command an audience as well if they aren't entirely sober, which most of them usually weren't at that hour. I never got what her beef was, and so finally I decided to start going to Catch A Rising Star where they immediately began giving me earlier spots.

CHRIS ALBRECHT:

Silver saw plots everywhere and when she came back to New York, the whole spirit of the club changed. I remember we had this chef named George who made decent food, but Silver decided to fire him. When she did, she also withheld his paycheck and George went into the kitchen, got a butcher knife, and came back out threatening to kill himself. He literally said, "I'm going to get my money or I'm going to die tonight."

Silver and I got along okay personally, although I eventually became an agent for International Creative Management (ICM) and sold her my share in the club for $100,000. But she was also suspicious of everyone from the beginning, including me, and I think she was angry about what had happened between her and Budd. They were already separated by the time I came out to run the LA club in 1978.

RITCH SHYDNER:

I was there during all this and my take, for what it's worth, is that when Silver came back, she wanted to establish that she was running the club. In doing so, she decided to pick the comics she was going to champion, plus Chris took a lot of guys to LA with him when he joined ICM. This opened the door for a lot of newer guys to say, "Here's my opportunity to get to know Silver," although her temperament wasn't the same as Chris's.

So between that and having different comedic tastes, there were definitely some conflicts there. I will say, however, that Silver was one of my biggest champions when it came to recommending me to Budd for *An Evening at the Improv*. She basically told him he had to use me and he did.

Because the New York Improv was easily worth five times what the LA club was at the time, Silver had to pay me $400 a month in alimony, plus travel expenses to New York so I could visit our two daughters four times a year.

In the meantime, I lost 80 percent of my net worth, which complicated matters even further with Mitzi, who'd gotten her lease back on Sunset Boulevard. As a result, she now owned two clubs, which were both booming, and I was again the underdog.

What I did have, however, was a bar and a restaurant with a full menu. The Comedy Store had neither, meaning that the only way you could order drinks was at your table and the only food items she offered were snacks.

And meaning also that the comics preferred to hang out at the Improv even if they weren't performing. Some of them even met their future spouses as I eventually did. It was incredible and I was thrilled, especially since they weren't all comedians either. Not unlike my New York club, we had practically every A-lister in Hollywood coming in at the time. Jessica Lange, Sam Shepard, Faye Dunaway, John Travolta, a young and still unknown Bruce Willis, and O. J. Simpson—the list goes on and on. Nobody ever bothered them and they were there practically every single night.

As all this star mixing was taking place, Mitzi's manipulative, domineering ways were about to come back and bite her. Though she'd long had that reputation, she'd managed to prevail, largely because she owned two clubs, and many comedians, especially the less-established ones, still feared her wrath—provided they could even get on.

KEVIN NEALON:

My dream, by the way, was to get my name on The Comedy Store alongside all the other "professional comics" working there. Unfortunately, it didn't happen until recently. Even though I would kill and get standing ovations on open mic nights there, Mitzi told me to go work someplace else because she knew I was Budd's bartender. She also used the excuse that she already had a tall comic working there by the name of Tom Wilson. The great thing was that I eventually got my name on a huge billboard across the street from the Store when I did *Weeds* on Showtime. I felt it was my redemption.

Well, before that, Mitzi's fiefdom would nearly collapse—and deservedly so—with the first chinks in her armor already starting to appear not long after she aggressively began expanding her empire in 1978. First, she spent $50,000 overhauling the Sunset Strip club, upgrading it into a 450-seat show room called "the Main Room," alongside a second one off to the side for women comics, which she christened "the Belly Room," in addition to maintaining what had been the club's smaller first space, now called "the Original Room."

With most of her labor force composed of willing young male comedians, she next opened a Comedy Store outpost in the Pacific Beach section of San Diego. She also launched a national college concert tour branded "A Night at The Comedy Store."

Meanwhile, the shit had already started to hit the fan when Mitzi began giving headliners whatever she made on the cover charge to perform in the Main Room on Sunset Boulevard, but refused to give the showcase comics who were her bread and butter anything.

On the other hand, as much grief as she'd caused me, I could also understand her position, particularly since I wasn't paying the comics either, and it was a policy I'd actually started when I first opened in New York. But I also hadn't just undergone a major expansion. And even if I had, and I couldn't pay them—which I was now in no position to anyway—I was still sympathetic to their plight, especially since many of them were so broke they couldn't afford basic necessities like food and gas.

My own uncertain financial situation at the time aside, though, it's important to note that one of the reasons I didn't pay comics in the beginning, and still wasn't at that time, was that the thought never really occurred to me. For one thing, the New York Improv didn't become profitable until our second decade. The second thing is that we were strictly a singer-oriented club at first and the whole idea was to create a comfortable place where they could eat, drink, unwind, and perform if they wanted to. But there was never any pressure, nor was it ever a requirement. It was the same thing with the comics, even after they began to dominate and we became a comedy club as a result. Not only that, we gave them a stage and a live audience where they could experiment and work out—essentially a gym or an incubator—where in exchange they got the opportunity to get seen by the right people who could jump-start their careers virtually overnight.

Ditto when it came to the already-established comics whom we never paid either because they weren't being billed as headliners when they came to give what was basically an impromptu dress rehearsal for an upcoming appearance on *The Tonight Show*.

Compared to what Mitzi was doing, it was an apples-to-oranges scenario that had worked in our favor. The comedians got what they needed, oftentimes more, and nobody ever complained, especially since I never told them they couldn't work anywhere else.

All of this said, though, by the late seventies, times were changing. And fortuitously around the same period, many of Mitzi's comics were so fed up with her that they'd already slowly begun coming over to my side. Consequently, when a group of them, including Jay Leno, David Letterman, George Miller, Elayne Boosler, Dottie Archibald, Tom Dreesen, JoAnne Astrow, and Marsha Warfield decided to organize a talent strike against her, there was every indication to suggest that I'd have the upper hand.

I'm not exactly sure how soon the dice begun to be cast after her expansion, but one of the most telling signs that something was amiss purportedly occurred in the early hours of New Year's Day morning 1979. That's when several from this group gathered at Canter's Deli to blow off steam and get something to eat after having just come down off the high of their New Year's Eve performances at the Store. Both the Sunset Strip and Westwood clubs had been filled to the rafters, and after one of the comics—Michael Rapaport—finished raving about his killer set, he leaned over to Tom Dreesen and asked in a whisper if he could borrow five dollars for breakfast.

Without saying a word, Dreesen reached into his wallet and gave him the money. Then, after performing at the Sunset Strip Store about two weeks later, Dreesen and another group of comics, including Jay Leno, were back at Canters, when Jay said this, according to author Bill Knoedelseder's 2009 book, *I'm Dying Up Here*: "Does anyone think this system is fair anymore? I mean, that place was fuckin' packed tonight. It took five of us to do it, but it was still packed, at fifteen dollars a head with a two-drink minimum. Shouldn't we get something for that? When Rodney [Dangerfield] and Richard [Pryor] play the room, Mitzi gives them the door. Shouldn't we get, like, I don't know, half the door?"

TOM DREESEN:

I think it was mid-January or early February that we first started talking about it. The night the first discussion happened was the same night I went to The Comedy Store thinking that I was going to be in the Original Room and they put me in the Main Room. But it definitely wasn't New Year's Eve because I worked different places in those days and I wasn't at the Store that night.

The story I've always told was that when I later went to Mitzi, I said, "I was just at Canter's where one of the comics informed me that when he worked for you on New Year's Eve, you had a full house in Westwood and on Sunset. He said, 'I just worked in front of a packed house. It was wonderful. I'd never worked in front of that many people and I killed them. Tommy, can I borrow five dollars from you? I want to get something to eat.'"

When I recounted this to Mitzi, her response was, "Well, he should get a goddamn job."

"Mitzi," I said, "he has a job. He works for you."

That's where the story came from, but it started after that, the night the five of us—me, David Letterman, Elayne Boosler, Jay Leno, and Robin Williams—had all just worked the Main Room at the Store and we went to Canter's afterwards. That's when Jay said, "This is fucking bullshit that she pays the other comics like Shecky Greene and Jackie Mason, but we pack the room, too."

Within days, they had formed a group led by Dreesen called Comedians for Compensation. However, even after attending the first meeting, some people still thought it might be part of an elaborate joke.

WILLIAM KNOEDELSEDER:

I knew that the comics weren't getting paid, but that never struck me as weird because this was Hollywood and I figured this was how the system worked. So I never questioned it, and none of the other comics ever complained in front of me and said, "This is fucked."

Looking back, I think a lot of that had to do with the fact that I was a representative of the *Los Angeles Times* and nobody wanted to open up to me because they were afraid it might hurt their careers. So when I went to the first Comedians for Compensation meeting at The Comedy Store, I was surprised to see all of this anger they hadn't hinted to me before.

It even seemed kind of funny. When I met Tom Dreesen there for the first time, I'll never forget that he had a green-plaid three-piece suit on and the comics were standing in this big picket line. From my vantage point, it was actually a lot of fun. My first article wound up being about having fun with the idea of stand-up comics being on strike and how funny it was.

But of course, it wasn't, and as the days wore on, it became increasingly apparent that a *Norma Rae*–sized labor movement was rapidly gaining a full head of steam.

WILLIAM KNOEDELSEDER:

It was comedian Elayne Boosler who first made me aware of how serious they were. The way she did it was just as serious because she already had an ax to grind stemming from an article I'd written about a year or so before about four comics who were about to break and she didn't like the way she came off.

The four that I chose—and I'm very proud of it to this day—were David Letterman, Jay Leno, Richard Lewis, and Elayne. But of those four, Elayne wasn't breaking quite as fast probably because she was a woman at a time when comedy was still very much a boys' club, which I didn't mention because I hadn't looked into it at that point. It hadn't even occurred to me, honestly.

Elayne was still pissed at me about that. And when she read my first story making light of the strike, she literally poked me in the chest during the second meeting and said, "You should be ashamed of yourself. You shouldn't be making fun of these people." Then she said something to the effect of, "This is a really serious issue and you ought to look into it." When I did, it was actually a big turn in my career in terms of how I started looking at things.

My perspective quickly began evolving, too. While ostensibly I couldn't afford to pay them either, I knew that I couldn't withstand the bad publicity if they went on strike against the Improv and so I decided to negotiate. In good faith, I told them I would match any agreement they made with Mitzi, if they were able to, which they weren't. But once the dust finally settled and I was able to, I began paying five dollars per set during the week and ten dollars on the weekends to the regular comics, with the headliners getting twenty-five to fifty dollars a show, and sometimes more depending on who they were.

Before any of this transpired, however, Mitzi basically told them all to go fuck themselves. Meanwhile, reinforcement for the comedians' cause became almost unanimous as Connie Chung began covering it, Bob Hope wrote a letter of support, Johnny Carson's attorney got involved, and established comedians like Jay Leno, Robin Williams, Richard Pryor, and Richard Lewis all agreed not to cross the picket line if it came to that, which it did, beginning in mid-March for eight weeks.

JAY LENO:

I was paying attention to it in the sense that I had a foot in both camps. It wasn't something that had to happen if Mitzi had only been willing to negotiate and pay the comics something, which she was in a much stronger position to do than Budd was then. But she was so adamant about controlling them, it got to a point where she was trying to tell people how they should dress and do their acts.

DOTTIE ARCHIBALD, television producer, former comedian, and longtime Hollywood Improv stockholder:

I was one of the lucky ones who worked at both clubs. I didn't really have a sense of how bad things were with Mitzi until after the strike started and Budd immediately began to pay, although it really didn't make much difference to me financially because I was married and I wasn't in dire straits the way that a lot of the other comics were.

So I really didn't think about it a lot in the beginning, although once I realized how much money Mitzi was making, I immediately became involved as I had been in the Civil Rights Movement because I knew they were right.

TOM DREESEN:

At the very core of things, it brought together a group of comics who weren't getting paid, which Mitzi didn't deem necessary because she was giving them stage time and a chance to be discovered by the industry. Meanwhile, she was making a fortune off their talent and she was paying everyone else at The Comedy Store from the waitresses and bartenders on down to the parking lot attendant and the guy who cleaned the toilets. Unless you were directly involved, you'll never understand the ramifications of that strike because it forced every comedy club in the world to start paying their acts. I'm still very proud of what we did to this day even though many never got on at The Comedy Store again.

The one who most catastrophically didn't get on was an insecure and emotionally fragile comedian few people remember named Steve Lubetkin, whom I never particularly cared for the handful of times he performed at the Improv in New York. Maybe I might have been overlooking something and he would have eventually gotten better, but back then I just didn't think he was very funny.

Nor had he improved that much during the two or three times after that when he performed on Melrose Avenue. As a result, he never became a regular. When Mitzi permanently banned him for crossing the picket line and begrudgingly agreed to a sliding-scale compensation arrangement that May, Lubetkin committed suicide in the most heinous, if not appallingly symbolic, way a month later.

On June 1, 1979, at around 6:40 PM, he jumped off the roof of the Continental Hyatt House hotel across the street from The Comedy Store, plunging approximately 105 feet and landing directly in front of it. Finding him with a gaping forehead wound and blood flowing from his ears and nose, police investigators later pulled a handwritten note from the stained left hip pocket of his blue jeans. It said: "My name is Steve Lubetkin. I used to work at The Comedy Store. Maybe this will help bring about fairness."

Although I didn't know it yet, the Improv was also about to receive a major blow that would be no less near catastrophic—albeit in a much different way—when the club went up in flames several nights later.

Despite all my recent troubles, I had been feeling on top of the world until the fire that evening. I had even taken a rare night off and gone on a double date with my friends Dottie and Tom Archibald to hear cabaret singer Bobby Short perform in Century City. The plan was to be back at the Improv by midnight so I could close up.

DOTTIE ARCHIBALD:

Tom and I picked Budd and his date up at the club around seven-thirty. I had a new Chrysler convertible that I was showing off, which he loved, and he was in a great mood that night.

Bobby Short was always the consummate showman and tonight was no exception. Back at the Improv meanwhile, a young singer named Barbara McGraw was onstage, bantering with the midweek audience and about to go into her next song, when Cliff Grisham, the piano player, whispered to her that he smelled smoke.

BARBARA MCGRAW:

It was like the third or fourth song when Cliff said, "I think I smell smoke."

I stopped for a second and said, "What?"

"I think I'm smelling smoke," he repeated. "We'd better move people out of here."

We stopped the song and I said, "We are smelling smoke here. Everyone should leave the room in an orderly fashion." But as we said this, we got the impression that none of the customers smelled anything yet because they seemed surprised. So we said, "Really, we're serious. You need to leave the room right away. Don't run. Just move out right away." It took them a second, but then they started to leave very quickly.

KEVIN NEALON:

I was working the bar that night and so I was up front when another comic named Jack Graiman came running out of the show room. He said, "Kevin, I'm not kidding around. There's a fire back there. We've got to call the fire department." I'm not sure if there was even 911 then. I may have just called them directly.

MICHAEL RICHARDS:

I was either in the bar, the show room, or somewhere in the vicinity when Jack Graiman yelled out, "FIRE!" at the top of his lungs. I hadn't smelled smoke yet, so I started pretending I was a fireman. I told the audience they couldn't leave the room. I said something to the effect that the doors had to remain locked because of a fire code and that we were most likely all going to go up in flames.

I was making up all this crazy improv shit, just basically saying whatever came to mind, until Jack said, "There really is a fucking fire." Then I walked outside and saw flames up near the top of the roof. At first, it didn't look too bad, but then it started to spread fast and we all thought it was going to be the end of the Improv. The whole place looked like it was going to burn down.

BARBARA MCGRAW:

I know that Cliff and I were the last ones out. Budd had just spent a bunch of money on new sound equipment. It may have been the second or third night it was used and we were all happy to have it. As we were leaving, I remember thinking to myself, "I wish we could grab it before we go." But the smoke was so bad by this point that I decided it was better not to stop. Then, as we all moved outside, it got worse and it took the fire department forever to show up. When they finally did, they had everybody move away from the building, although we were still standing pretty close as we watched it go up in flames.

One person, however, has a slightly different version of these events.

JACK KNIGHT:

Barbara wasn't even onstage when the fire happened. I was performing with the Improv's resident improv troupe and actress Betty Thomas, who would later go on to star in *Hill Street Blues*, was also with us.

We were all onstage when the assistant manager of the club came across the show room floor and got my attention. He said, "There's a fire out back."

Barbara may have performed that evening, but it wasn't during the time of the fire starting and I have no recollection of that at all. I don't think I'd even know her if I bumped into her today. Anyway, the assistant manager got my attention when he said there was a fire. He told me to empty the room, which I did, after which I went to the back of the stage where there was a door facing on to the alley where the fire started. When I saw how bad it was, I tried to get the garden hose that was outside to work, but I wasn't having much luck, and it took quite some time after that for the fire department to get there.

As either of these scenarios was unfolding, my date and I were sitting in the backseat of Dottie and Tom Archibald's car on our way back to the Improv as it inched along in unusually heavy traffic, when out of nowhere, I began smelling smoke, too. I remember saying out loud, "What the hell is this?" as the acrid smell grew thicker. Then my heart began pounding against my chest as I suddenly realized it was coming from the Improv.

DOTTIE ARCHIBALD:

One of the firemen stopped us about a block away before we even got to the Improv. That's when Budd hurled himself out

of the car and began running. He was out of the car before he
even realized that the club was on fire.

The first thing I encountered as I stood outside the entrance a few minutes later was a group of performers and customers huddled together in
disbelief. As the firefighters struggled to put out the blaze, a number of
the comics were crying.

BARBARA MCGRAW:

When the word got out, it seemed like everybody was showing up even if they hadn't been there when the fire started.

Perhaps most random was the appearance of Robert Schimmel, a stereo salesman suddenly turned comic from Scottsdale, Arizona, who had
performed at the Improv for the first time in his life on an open mic
night two weeks earlier on a dare from his sister. It had been completely
unplanned, but he was so good that I told him afterwards he could come
back anytime he wanted to.

What I didn't know at the time, though, was that he immediately
took my invitation to mean that he should quit his job, sell his house,
and move to Los Angeles with his wife. That same night when Robert pulled off the freeway, he drove straight to the club to show her a
glimpse of their new future when he noticed the fire.

But instead of turning back, he parked their car a few blocks away
and came straight to the scene where he found me pacing back and
forth out in front. He said, "Jesus, Budd. I can't believe this."

I was dumbfounded—not so much by the words, but by the super-
ficially insensitive way they seemed to come out—so I just looked at him
blankly and said, "Who are you?"

Then I just completely lost it and began sobbing uncontrollably. But
what good would that do, I quickly reasoned. I also suddenly realized
that since I couldn't do anything, the best thing was to try to remain
calm even though I was in a state of sheer panic as the firefighters
refused to let me inside.

That was when I suddenly had another impulse that may seem odd.
In an effort to lift our collective spirits, I invited everybody who was

still there over to the French restaurant Moustache across the street and ordered champagne as if it were a wake. Whether or not any of us really believed it or not, we all still tried to hold on to some glimmer of hope as we got shitfaced for the next three hours.

Though it didn't take nearly that long to put the fire out, it wasn't until around 1 AM that we were allowed back inside, at which point the tingly buzz I was feeling from the booze quickly turned to despair as I walked through the badly charred show room. The only way I can describe how I felt is to say that it was a picture of black despair made even worse by my dark mood.

The first thing that occurred to me was that I was out of business. Without insurance, which I didn't have and couldn't afford, I knew there was no way I'd ever be able to rebuild, and so in another strange attempt to console myself, I invited everyone who was still there into the front bar, which hadn't been touched, and we continued to drink until we'd depleted my champagne supply.

I returned to my home in the Hollywood Hills at about 4 AM. I was now living alone. I can't remember what I did first, but I was angry, hurt, scared, sad, and disgruntled. Worst of all, my most overriding emotion was a niggling suspicion I had that Mitzi might have somehow been involved, especially since one of my waitresses had secretly been at a Comedy Store staff meeting several days earlier when she overheard someone say, "What if there were no Improv?"

But I was exhausted and I tried to repress it as I got undressed, climbed into bed, and drifted off into a restless, uneasy sleep. When I arrived back at the club several hours later, news about the fire had already ricocheted across the comedy community even though it hadn't made any of the local newspapers yet. Whirling around, too, were the growing rumors that Mitzi had started the blaze, which I was becoming increasingly convinced of after several people had already told me she'd been ecstatic when she first heard the news, presuming that, with me now out of business, she'd have a monopoly again to do whatever she pleased.

However, even after the fire marshal ruled later that day that the cause had been arson—and that the blaze had originated in the rear of the building, where our alley's easy access and quick escape was practically an open invitation for anyone to strike a match—none of us, the more we all thought about it, believed that Mitzi could be that vindictive when it came right down to it.

We were a lot less confident when it came to two wannabe comics who were among her biggest supporters, Biff Maynard and Ollie Joe Prater, each of whom had well-known substance abuse problems and were just unstable and impressionable enough to maybe do it. We wouldn't know for certain until 2014, nearly thirty years after the incident, when Ollie Joe confessed to setting the fire on his deathbed in a Los Angeles hospital.

But, of course, nobody could prove anything definitively at the time. And more pressing during the aftermath of the fire was how I was going to rebuild the club.

By that afternoon, however, things were beginning to slowly look up as I realized that even with my show room in ruins, the restaurant, bar, and the bathrooms were all fine. And so in the grand spirit of Improv tradition—doing something I first did on West 44th Street in 1963 and again when we'd opened on Melrose Avenue four years earlier—I decided to get my friends, staff, and a few of the comics to help me, most of whom volunteered.

Tom Archibald, an amateur electrician, patched a makeshift line from the alley to restore electricity, which his wife Dottie lent me the money for. Cliff Grisham, the piano player, was a fairly decent carpenter, and while the rest were pretty unskilled, we managed to wall off the scorched back room with sheets of plywood and build a makeshift stage in the front.

In some ways, it even felt like the old days when I was first getting ready to open in New York, especially since the new, temporary configuration sat seventy-four people, which was the exact number we originally had on West 44th Street.

Forty-eight hours after the fire, the Hollywood Improv was halfway back in business. And with comedy's newest powerbroker Tom Dreesen convincing the comedians to work for free until we were fully operational again, we also managed to finagle a few of them to do benefits hosted by Robin Williams and Andy Kaufman that we appropriately called "Up from the Ashes."

Collectively and individually, it was an amazing achievement that I'm extremely proud of, and the benefits Andy and Robin hosted certainly lived up to their name.

However, it would still take nearly another year before everything could be fully restored. Things were considerably more complicated now than they had been since the days I'd started out as an ambitious young dreamer on West 44th Street sixteen years earlier. Both personally and professionally, the stakes had become much higher. With my divorce from Silver almost final, and my forty-sixth birthday fast approaching, I seriously began to consider getting out of the comedy business.

THIRTY-THREE
Old Enemies and New Beginnings

BRUCE SMIRNOFF:

I moved to Hollywood to become a comic three weeks after *Mork and Mindy* premiered in September 1978. Unequivocally, it was absolutely one hundred thousand percent the worst thing I could have done at the time because I wasn't ready and I wasn't that good. When you get pronounced bad, it's very hard to get out of.

The comedy scene had exploded by this point: Robin Williams was everywhere; and The Comedy Store, which had three rooms, was the place to be. Mitzi Shore was also the queen, and I remember our first encounter like it was yesterday. I was having coffee one afternoon at the Continental Hyatt House hotel next door with another comic Mitzi knew. She was seated a couple of tables away and when she came over to say hello to him, she took one look at me and said, "Who are you?"

When I told her my name, she said, "That's one of the best faces I've ever seen for comedy. I'll see you Monday night at my club." Of course, I was flattered, although knowing I still needed more time to develop, I politely tried to decline and asked her if I could wait. However, Mitzi wouldn't hear of it. She said, "Never mind. You don't have to be ready. I know talent."

I decided to give it a try anyway against my better judgment. So when I nervously showed up at the Store the following Monday night, it was predictably with the results I feared—after which I tried to thank her for giving me the opportunity and she just stared at me and said, "You stink. You have no talent. Don't ever think about becoming a comedian."

Suffice it to say, I was crushed by her rejection, but not completely deterred because I also went to the Improv on a Monday night not long after that. Mondays were their audition night where they drew everybody's name out of a hat during a time when comedy was so hot that if you didn't give up, you'd eventually go on, which I ultimately did.

I used to come in dressed in a jacket and tie, and I carried an attaché case. I took myself so seriously that I looked like an accountant, but I was definitely a cut above everyone else who basically came in looking like slobs. Because I did this on a regular basis, and I had a decent stage presence even if my material wasn't great, Budd gradually let me emcee during the late show on Sunday nights.

I also became the doorman, where I took on more and more responsibilities, although right around the time I first got to the Improv, which was the year between Freddie Prinze's death and the strike and the fire, the club wasn't doing well. I really think it was Freddie who kept the place floating when Budd first opened in LA, but after he committed suicide it went downhill pretty quickly.

As the doorman, I would usually get to the club early in the afternoon, and one of the things I remember about this period was the guy who delivered the liquor coming in and shoving a pink slip under my nose, demanding to be paid. That's how bad things had gotten and everything was falling apart. Plus, people were stealing from him—not the comics who wanted to go on, but the waiters—because Budd was so mean to everybody. He just didn't give a shit and people were robbing him blind.

Though we'd survived and were back in business in less than two days, in the immediate weeks and months after the fire, I felt like a piece of my soul had also been singed. Not only that, a part of me felt like a failure even though Robin Williams and Andy Kaufman who'd held fundraisers for me were two of the hottest comics in the country at the time.

Still, I just couldn't shake the feeling that the fire had somehow indirectly been my fault; that even though it had been ruled arson, I could have done something to prevent it if I'd only been smarter or at the very least been there that night. Nor did I feel any more comforted by the fact that because of Mitzi's behavior during the strike and Steve Lubetkin's subsequent suicide, she had essentially been declawed; or that Richard Lewis, Jay Leno, and Tom Dreesen never worked at The Comedy Store again.

Things might have been easier all the way around, of course, had one of us attempted to extend an olive branch and tried to reach some sort of truce. But considering all of the constant problems she'd caused me from the moment I came to Los Angeles, I wasn't about to swallow my pride and make the first move, and neither did Mitzi.

Thus continued the turf war between the Hollywood Improv and The Comedy Store that for all intents and purposes still lingers to this day, even though Mitzi now suffers from Parkinson's disease and is no longer at the helm. Though it was never as overt again after the strike and the fire, to say that the damage had already been done and the battle lines were drawn is putting it mildly. And while there were obvious exceptions, even if Mitzi hadn't forced them to choose, there ultimately came a time when many comics only performed at the Improv.

DREW CAREY:

I had been to The Comedy Store to audition once when I was doing *Star Search*, which is why I came to LA to begin with. In between the time I won and lost, I went back to the Store to audition for Mitzi. The tryouts were held in a little room, and she had this thing where you could only do two or three minutes. I just remember feeling weird about the whole thing and I didn't really like it there. The next time I came back to town after being on the road, I went to the Improv exclusively.

HOWIE MANDEL:

I was friends with another comedian named Mike Binder and it was through him that I got on at The Comedy Store. My fiancée and I were out in LA on vacation, and I'd auditioned on a dare, although I'd done stand-up in Canada before. So I went on at the Store and there was a producer in the audience named George Foster, who had a game show called *Make Me Laugh*, which he immediately hired me to do for five episodes.

After that, I started getting calls from *The Merv Griffin Show* and *The Mike Douglas Show*, and so I briefly commuted back and forth from Canada before moving to LA in June 1979. As soon as I got to town, Mitzi invited me to come back to the Store. But within the first week of my being there, Steve Lubetkin committed suicide and people were still picketing.

I think that because I went on at The Comedy Store, I got caught up in all of this, although I had no idea at the time. The thought really never occurred to me that I was a Comedy Store guy and not an Improv guy. I was a comedy guy and so I used to hang out at the Improv anyway. The first time I went was right after the fire, and the first person I saw was Michael Richards.

It was in the bar area and he was literally leaning against the wall on the makeshift stage they had with his pants down around his ankles and drool coming out of his mouth, screaming "What the hell are you looking at?" to the audience. This went on for a good twenty minutes and it was the funniest thing I had ever seen in comedy. I wanted to be part of it because it was so bizarre, although I had already cemented my ownership to The Comedy Store.

BILL MAHER:

Would I have liked to work at the Store? Yeah, but they just never seemed to have any use for me. At the time, it was a different kind of place and I always felt the Improv was more pure for me at that point in my career because it was steadier. It was a place where you could go and see good comics—and where Budd, unlike Mitzi, nurtured real monologists.

JIMMY FALLON:

I worked the Store a couple of times back in the early nineties, but it was never my home. Even then, it's like there were two separate families—The Comedy Store or the Improv. I was always an Improv guy.

BYRON ALLEN:

Mitzi favored the ones who only worked for her. For some reason, though, I was able to escape that, largely I think, because of my age, and Budd immediately became like a second father to me. So I was able to go back and forth, but I know Mitzi wasn't happy about it.

STEVE MITTLEMAN:

Somehow—and I don't exactly know how—I managed to work at both clubs. But it was definitely a delicate balance and Budd was much more easygoing about it than Mitzi was.

KEVIN NEALON:

Obviously, this wasn't how it really was, but I'll tell you that at first—and even though Mitzi never made me a regular because I worked for Budd—my initial impression was that they respected each other because they both owned comedy clubs even though they didn't communicate much.

To tell you the truth, I never found that odd either, because they both had different styles of running their businesses. I had the impression that Mitzi was more reclusive, whereas Budd was more of a people person who enjoyed mingling with his customers and introducing the acts in the show room as the owner of the Improv. He enjoyed the attention and recognition, but I don't think Mitzi did.

JERRY SEINFELD:

The Comedy Store was where my manager, George Shapiro, first saw me in the early eighties, but I was never comfortable there, so the Improv was always my home club in LA, and I'll tell you why. I'm a very independent person and I didn't think I needed anybody's help, which in my opinion and from my observation was the antithesis of what Mitzi liked. She was looking for the wounded birds that would flock around her for help. People would do anything to get on at The Comedy Store. I just wasn't that kind of guy, so I never tried to get on there at all.

BILLY CRYSTAL:

In New York, Catch A Rising Star was my main club and I worked at the Store a few times when I first moved to LA in 1976. But I knew Budd from New York, and when he opened on the West Coast I started going to Melrose. I liked the stage better, plus it felt a little less desperate than the Store, which was always more touristy. Budd was always very grateful to me for that.

RITCH SHYDNER:

Thanks to a few people who championed me, I got to play both clubs, although I sometimes used to think that the people who did the bookings at the Store checked the Improv's schedule and vice versa. Before they gave you a spot, it wasn't uncommon for them to arrange to put you on at the exact same times just to throw the other one off.

I remember once going to the Store and this guy blocking me in the entranceway and telling me that I was an Improv act. I was like, "I'm an anywhere-I-want-to-get-on act, you better move out of my way." I always found the politics of the Store to be strange. Mitzi also had this weird thing she used to do with crystals where she'd sit you down at a table to see how your aura fit in.

CATHY LADMAN:

From a pure fun standpoint, the Improv had it hands down over The Comedy Store, which was a dark and kind of creepy place. Some people even said it was haunted, which I don't doubt, and it wasn't wholesome at all whereas the Improv had a much lighter vibe to it.

One thing I'll say about Mitzi, though, is that she was much more nurturing to female comics than Budd was. I never experienced any overt male chauvinism on Budd's part, but Mitzi was definitely more welcoming and I'll give you an example. Not long after I moved to LA in the mideighties, George Schlatter, who created *Laugh-In*, was producing a new series for NBC called *The Shape of Things*.

It turned out to be a flop, but it had a unique premise about funny things that happen in everyday life, and one of the segments was about the women from The Comedy Store. At first, Mitzi wasn't going to use me because I was new, but she wound up putting me on at the last minute, and it was during those rehearsals that she also arranged for *The Tonight Show*'s talent coordinator Jim McCawley to come see Roseanne Barr, which led to her first appearance on Johnny Carson.

DAVID SPADE:

I never even met Mitzi, but comedian Louie Anderson, who was a friend of a friend of mine, said he could get me an audition, which he did. Afterwards, I waited out front while he went to talk to her and he came back a few minutes later and said, "Sorry, she didn't like it."

My response at the time was, "What's not to like?" although I didn't have a great set, in all honesty. What happened was that right before, I had a drink at the bar and I took an aspirin that got stuck in my throat, which threw me off. I should have been able to overcome that, but regardless, she just didn't like my style or she felt I wasn't ready. And I get that—especially since I thought it was a long shot to begin with.

Budd was a lot easier on me. He liked the fact that I looked fifteen because he had no one like me.

MAX ALEXANDER:

I moved to LA from New York in the winter of 1984 to do a TV pilot. They put me up in the Continental Hyatt House hotel next door to The Comedy Store, and Paul Provenza, George Wallace, and a comedy manager named Rick Messina arranged for me to audition for Mitzi on the night I arrived. I was exhausted from my trip, but I decided to do it anyway because I was scheduled to go on at eight o'clock, which never happened. Instead, she kept me waiting for two hours, and I was starting to get pissed because in the meantime she put this young comic from San Francisco on who was being billed as the next Robin Williams.

He wasn't, but that was beside the point. The point was that she'd made me wait and when I finally did go on at ten o'clock, I had a good set. It wasn't great, but it wasn't mediocre either, and what I mean by that is that all my jokes worked and people laughed even though I didn't bring the house down. I was feeling pretty confident when I got offstage, but when I went up to Mitzi afterwards and asked if she was going to make me a regular, she just looked at me and said, "All we need is another fat Jew in the business."

That was when I absolutely lost it and called her a cunt right to her face before storming out of the club. When I arrived back at my hotel room about ten minutes later, I flopped down on the bed without turning on the lights or removing my suitcase, which was lying unopened on top. But then, right as the seriousness of what I'd just said to Mitzi was hitting me like a ton of bricks, the phone rang. It was Rick Messina calling to tell me he'd arranged an audition with Budd for me for the following night. Before we hung up, the last thing he said to me was, "Do me a favor. Don't call Budd Friedman a cunt."

I went to the Improv the next night, and in those days I was a heavyset guy. A good part of my act was about my weight, and I used to wear these colorful boxer shorts with the top hanging out. And for some reason, I either wasn't wearing a belt or it wasn't tight enough because I was so nervous and it doesn't take a genius to figure out what happened next.

As the emcee announced me while I walked towards the stage, my pants dropped down to my ankles and I was standing there in nothing but my shirt and boxer shorts, which either had polka dots or giant hearts on them. It wasn't pretty, and when I made it to the stage I was so flummoxed that I forgot my entire routine. All I could think of to say was, "That's all I've got," and I left.

Just as I did, I noticed Budd standing in the back, doubled over. When he finally stopped laughing, he said, "Don't drop your pants onstage anymore."

Between 1979 and 1982, one unspoken partiality followed another. The tension got so bad that the Sunday *LA Times* Calendar section even ran a cover story called "Did You Hear the One about Budd and Mitzi?— Their Feud Isn't Funny to Hollywood's Young Comics," which ran on Halloween 1982 no less.

But as all my well-documented troubles with Mitzi were being rehashed in the pages of the *LA Times*, in the grand scheme of things, I didn't really care, especially since my personal life had also recently taken a positive turn in the form of a new marriage following my divorce from Silver, which had become official in the summer of 1979. Though I had been relieved that our troubled marriage was finally over, I paid an emotional price that was far more heartbreaking than relinquishing my New York club when our daughters, Zoe and Beth, who were then nine and ten, went back East to live with her.

Even when ending a marriage is for the best, you're never fully prepared for the finality of it—especially when young children are involved and you suddenly begin to realize all the things you'll be missing that you once took for granted, like having breakfast together, testing the kids on spelling words, going to the zoo, etc. It isn't so much the activities themselves as it is the fact you won't physically be present to do them—plus you also become aware of the things in the future that you won't be there for, like first dates and learning to drive.

Not that I was always as much of a hands-on parent as I would have liked to have been because I was so busy running the club, which now only seemed to magnify the pain. On top of that, I had also lost a parent myself—albeit in a much different and permanent way—and I knew all too well the void it leaves, which was the last thing I wanted for my girls.

Though I was still a neophyte at being a single father, I did everything I could to make the best of a difficult situation by trying to visit them as often as I could in New York and making their trips to Los

Angeles memorable. In between, I tried to ease my emptiness by reliving my youth in what basically amounted to a midlife crisis.

Perhaps "crisis" is too strong a word, and the truth is that it was far from that, although suffice it to say I had plenty of wild oats to sow, which I did at every opportunity. After selling my house in Nichols Canyon in the Hollywood Hills, which I had planned to build onto and add a swimming pool, I temporarily moved into a residential hotel off of Sunset Boulevard. Actually, it was more of a mid-level apartment building for people in transition, as I certainly was. While it was by no means luxurious, it wasn't a dump either, and it turned out to be just what I needed at the time.

As a result of living there, I also became friendly with Mickey Ross, a prominent television writer, who was one-third of the production team Nicholl Ross West, whose credits included producing and writing for *All in the Family* and *The Jeffersons*, as well as creating and producing *Three's Company*.

Mickey and his wife lived down the hall from me, and we became especially close years later after we became involved with the LA Free Clinic, which provides pro bono health care services to unwed mothers—and which roasted me in 1988 at their annual fund-raiser.

It's a charity with which I'm still actively involved, and that roast turned out to be one of the greatest nights of my life because I got television producer Garry Marshall to be the emcee, although in an amusing aside, right after Garry agreed, I ran into Brandon Tartikoff, then the head of NBC, who begged me to let him do it instead.

However, I wasn't about to bump Garry, so I happily agreed to let Brandon be on the dais where we also had comedians Paul Rodriguez and Pat McCormick alongside Bette Midler, who sang four songs, three of which were parodies about me. To top it off, we even raised $50,000 more than the year before when they honored Hollywood super-agent Bernie Brillstein.

But getting back to the days of sowing my wild oats when I was single again, I also bought a Porsche 914, which I immediately affixed with a personalized license plate that had the moniker "Improv One." I felt like the cat's meow when I drove it, although when my car-aficionado pal Jay Leno found out about it, he was aghast. His response was, "You're not a car person, Budd. You have to take care of a Porsche." When I tried to explain that it had an automatic transmission, he just turned and walked away.

And when it came to the women I was dating, the people closest to me thought my choices were no less ridiculous. Naturally, I tended to go much younger, and one of my girlfriends during this period was a twenty-three-year-old singer I met at the Improv who was twenty-four years my junior. Then there was the time that I got invited to an orgy, where members of the opposite sex were screwing everywhere you turned, although I declined to participate.

There was never any shortage of beautiful women at my beck and call, especially at the Improv bar where I smoked cigars and routinely invited them to join me for champagne at my VIP table. Some even accused me of running a casting couch operation and giving stage time to the women I favored, although that was never the case. And at any rate, despite outward appearances, business overall was sluggish even after the show room had been fully rebuilt and we still occasionally had nights when comedians showed up unexpectedly, like the time film-maker Albert Brooks called us out of the blue in 1980 and performed stand-up for the first time in nearly four years.

BRUCE SMIRNOFF:

It was on a Monday night around eleven-thirty, and I was sitting on my stool by the door. There were seven guys at the bar, a couple of women in the restaurant area, and maybe about ten people in the show room when the pay phone rang. I picked it up and said, "Improv."

The guy on the other end said, "Hi, this is Albert. Who's this?"

When I told him my name, he said, "Listen, I want to come down and do a little comedy," although he still hadn't told me his last name, so I asked him. He said, "It's Albert Brooks. Is there anybody there?" When I told him we had about twelve people and asked him when he wanted to come in, he said around midnight.

So I told him I would take care of it. This was in 1980, when the cost of a pay phone call was still a dime, so I hung up, went to the cash register, and took out a handful of dimes. I think we had two pay phones at the time and I scattered the dimes

They weren't dating anymore and they hadn't seen each other in a while, and it was never a serious romance. I was also dating several other men at the time, one of whom was a film producer at MGM. However, I promised to ask my friend and I told Budd I would get back to him the next day.

All I could think was, "I hope she means it and I better think of something clever to say now to seal the deal." And, of course, I was as nervous as a schoolboy while I waited for Alix to call.

ALIX FRIEDMAN:

When I asked my friend, she had no qualms about it whatsoever, so Budd and I made a lunch date for the very next day, which was quickly followed by Budd sending me roses and taking me out for champagne on my birthday the night after. At first, he asked me if he could join me and my sons for dinner, which didn't seem appropriate, and I said no, but I agreed to let him pick me up afterwards around ten o'clock. When we got back from the restaurant, Budd was there waiting for me and that was the beginning of our romance.

As much as I may have been head over heels, I knew that I had to play it cool. Though our conversations early on were mainly of the innocuous getting-to-know-each-other kind, we quickly realized we had a lot in common.

What's more, I immediately began to feel my anxieties over the Improv's uncertain future melting away. It was as if my world was suddenly becoming a better place because Alix was part of it. Not only that, but when I told her I was considering selling the Improv and going into real estate, she immediately said I was making a huge mistake.

As for the depression I was feeling over being separated from my kids and my lingering animosity towards Mitzi, this, too, began melting away. Along with it was the end of an era that some comics used to call "BA"—before Alix—where I used to walk into the club and shove the tables and chairs around just to make my presence known. With Alix now having a tangible impact on my business, largely because she wasn't officially in it, people soon began to take notice. She also proved to be an invaluable asset when it came to spotting and valuing talent that I had somehow managed to overlook. Over the years, some of the best examples were Adam Sandler, Rita Rudner, Arsenio Hall, and Sandra Bernhard, although there are many more.

People even started saying, "If Budd Friedman can meet a woman like that at the Improv, it must be the place to go."

ROSS MARK, radio executive, former comedy producer, and Budd's stepson:

It was a fascinating transformation to watch. Before Budd met my mom, he used to wear these hideous-looking vests and he had a goatee. He was also driving around in a Porsche with personalized license plates, but he had no style, which drove my mother crazy. She quickly took care of that.

BILL MAHER:

I'm not sure if I knew Budd and Alix at all at this point, but I remember sitting behind them once in the audience at David Letterman's old morning talk show in New York and they were like a couple of teenagers. They couldn't take their hands off of each other.

JAY LENO:

Everybody liked Alix and they still do. Budd suddenly became much calmer and it was as if everything didn't take on the weight of the world as it once had.

EDDIE BERKE:

I'll just give you an idea of what Budd was like before he met Alix. For Christmas one year, a female comedian I won't name gave him a framed picture of herself holding a bunch of kittens. On the inscription, she wrote: "Dear Budd, this is as close to my pussy as you will ever get."

Deservedly or not, that was his reputation, but when Alix came along, that was it. He was a changed man. It was like he had found his soul mate.

I also loved that Alix had no real connection to the comedy business, although one night after seeing Robin Williams perform at the club not long after we met, she casually remarked that she might want to try doing stand-up because he made it seem so easy.

Of course, it wasn't, but Robin always had that effect on people. At first I couldn't tell if Alix was pulling my leg or not. But after seeing Robin perform several more times with completely different material each time, she did an about-face. She also quickly got a crash course when it came to the eccentric ways of comedians.

Most memorably was the time we had dinner at the Palm steakhouse in Beverly Hills with Professor Irwin Corey, the wild-haired, gibberish-talking monologist who recently died at the age of 102. Billed as the "World's Foremost Authority," Irwin had been a popular nightclub fixture since the 1940s and used to perform at the New York Improv, which is how I knew him.

On this particular night Alix and I were with him, it was during the Jewish holidays and he was in Los Angeles alone, so we invited him to join us for dinner. As it was, Irwin was a slovenly dresser who could have easily been mistaken for a homeless person. To Alix's dismay, when we got to the restaurant, he proceeded to chew with his mouth open throughout the entire meal and he used the tablecloth for a napkin. Not only that, but while we were eating, he informed the waiter he was cold. Then he asked the waiter to bring him another tablecloth, which he did, and Irwin wrapped it around himself like a blanket. It was vintage Irwin and I would have given anything to have had a camera with me that night to capture the look on Alix's face.

After a yearlong courtship, Alix and I tied the knot on May 14, 1981. Though it was the second marriage for both of us, I spared no expense. Among the guests were Milton Berle, Harvey Korman, and Richard Lewis. Following a traditional Jewish ceremony and a lavish reception on the rooftop of a luxury condominium in West Hollywood that a friend of mine owned, we took a five-week cruise around Europe on the *Queen Mary*. When we returned to Los Angeles in mid-June, we discovered an unexpected wedding gift that would change our lives forever.

PART FOUR

THIRTY-FOUR
An Evening at the Improv

M y marriage to Alix was a fresh start for me, one made all the more blissful after returning from our honeymoon and receiving the news that there was interest in developing a syndicated weekly television series that would be called *An Evening at the Improv*, which soon began filming on Melrose Avenue and eventually at our club in Santa Monica, which opened in 1987.

Of course, comedians had been a popular staple on television well before I entered the picture, all the way back to its earliest days with Arthur Godfrey, Ed Sullivan, Steve Allen, and Jack Paar. And the still-embryonic concept of pre-taped stand-up comedy specials, like *Richard Pyror: Live & Smokin'*, which was filmed at the New York club in 1971, and *On Location: Freddie Prinze and Friends*, which had been HBO's first-ever stand-up show filmed on Melrose Avenue beginning in 1976, had also given us a major shot in the arm.

However, a regular weekly show devoted entirely to stand-up hadn't been done before, nor had anyone ever come up with the financing, despite the fact that I'd long been intrigued by the idea and had had a number of suitors. But the outcome had always been the same: no money, no show.

This time the scenario was different, thanks to my longtime attorney Stan Handman introducing me to a former television commercial producer named Lawrence O'Daly, who already had a formidable track record hawking children's toys like Duncan yo-yos and Silly Putty. An army veteran like me, he had also developed and promoted G.I. Joe action figures in the 1960s.

BARBARA O'DALY, co-producer of *An Evening at the Improv* and Lawrence O'Daly's widow:

Larry was very ambitious and he was an idea guy who'd moved over to the TV syndication side from advertising where he'd had some success. I forget how they first met, but Budd's attorney Stan Handman, who had a fairly large stable of celebrity clients, said, "I'd like you to meet Budd because we've been kicking around the idea of trying to tie the Improv in with some sort of television show." That was how that happened. I loved the idea, and when Larry told me about it, I told him that I knew Budd in passing from when I used to go to the New York club in the late sixties and early seventies.

I vaguely remember meeting Barbara back then, but when Stan told me about Larry's pedigree, it certainly got my attention. I'll say, though, that from my own jaded personal experience, I wasn't particularly keen on people who came out of advertising, whom I often compared to snake-oil salesmen.

My suspicions would later prove correct—most pointedly in the form of a lawsuit over rerun syndication rights that took nearly two decades to resolve, which we won in 2015. Nevertheless, the offer Larry made me was too good to refuse, especially when I discovered it included both capital and huge tax breaks.

We officially made the deal in the fall of 1981. Initially, the arrangement was to use a Canadian producer, a Canadian director, and as many Canadian comics as we could find since the Screen Actors Guild prohibited us from using anyone in the United States for logistical reasons. The only problem was that the Canadian comedy scene wasn't nearly as fertile as America's and the number of even halfway-decent comics we had to choose from was few and far between. As a result, we ended up with fewer than twenty comedians whom we flew to Los Angeles, put onstage, and edited out before the show ever got on the air.

Just as disastrous was the decision to broadcast the show in different time slots on various independent stations across the country, including KNBC in Los Angeles, WOR in New York, and WGN in Chicago. Even though I knew almost nothing about the television syndication business back then, the slipshod move dismayed me. I quickly realized that with the show airing at different times in different places, it would be next to impossible to promote it properly to find an audience, which ultimately proved to be true.

In spite of these challenges, however—and with me hosting it and comics like Howie Mandel and Jim Carrey, who were two of the three Canadian comics we didn't eliminate, along with Richard Lewis, Robin Williams, and Andy Kaufman—we still managed to get fifty-two episodes in the can, all of which had decent ratings right out of the gate when we began airing on February 2, 1982. This continued for about a year as business at both the New York and LA clubs grew rapidly as a result. In the meantime, the show had a recurring cast and scored a major coup when we decided to use a different celebrity guest host each week.

Virtually any Hollywood actor from any decade was a prime candidate to host, with almost everyone we asked happy to oblige. Some of the bold-faced and no-longer-were names included Morgan Fairchild, William Shatner, Estelle Getty, Mr. T, Phyllis Diller, Phil Silvers, Vincent Price, Sherman Hemsley, Monty Hall, Doc Severinsen, Janet Leigh, Mort Sahl, Pee-wee Herman, Victoria Principal, Madeline Kahn, Milton Berle, Phil Foster, Patrick Macnee, Tom Bosley, Vicki Lawrence, Louis Gossett Jr., Kim Fields, Patrick Duffy, Alan Thicke, Flip Wilson, and Gary Coleman. We also had musical guests like Cyndi Lauper, Weird Al Yankovic, the band Kansas, and MTV VJ Martha Quinn.

On the comedy side, we had Billy Crystal, Elayne Boosler, Bob Saget, Jeff Altman, Larry Miller, Paula Poundstone, Paul Reiser, Janeane Garofalo, Phil Hartman, Dana Carvey, David Spade, Dennis Miller, Adam Sandler, Dave Chappelle, Bobcat Goldthwait, Dennis Wolfberg, Jerry Seinfeld, Tim Allen, Ellen DeGeneres, Greg Giraldo, Jay Mohr, Chris Rock, Kevin Pollak, D.L. Hughley, Arsenio Hall, Steven Wright, Dave Attell, and Sarah Silverman, many of whom had never appeared on television before.

Then there were the wannabes, like diver Greg Louganis, who flew in from Korea to perform the night before the closing ceremonies of the 1988 Summer Olympics, and O. J. Simpson's girlfriend, who was onstage while Simpson and his wife Nicole watched from the audience.

However, just as it seemed as if we were unstoppable, it all came to a screeching halt because of a change in Canadian law that caused us to lose our financing and tax breaks, which forced us to shut down production for nearly two years. Needless to say, I wasn't a happy camper, not only because of what happened but also with myself for not having a better handle on things. Happily, though, we managed to license the existing fifty-two episodes to cable's Arts & Entertainment Network, which launched on February 1, 1982, and reran them constantly. After that, thirteen new episodes were commissioned, followed by thirteen more, then twenty-six, and finally fifty-two a year that ran until 1996, culminating into a library of about 400 hours, some of which are now available on DVD.

NICKOLAS DAVATZES, CEO emeritus and founder of the Arts & Entertainment Network:

I think the first agreement we made was in 1985. We already had a lot of British comedy and we wanted some American comedy that would attract a younger demographic, which it did, and it was mutually beneficial for both of us.

I don't think it's a stretch at all to say that we made A&E because in those days most of their other programming was either reruns or documentaries of Winston Churchill and Teddy Roosevelt.

Because of this, our show—rebranded as *A&E's An Evening at the Improv*—permanently put us on the map, and I quickly became as well known around the country as many of the people we had on—plus I got a free wardrobe. All of the sudden, people were stopping me in the street and in airports asking for autographs, which I loved, not to mention the fact that the Improv became the Kentucky Fried Chicken of stand-up comedy. I was now Colonel Sanders.

JIMMY FALLON:

An Evening at the Improv was where you'd go, "That's the brick wall." No pun intended, but this cemented in my mind what stand-up comedy is—you stand in front of a brick wall with a microphone and that's it. When you'd watch it at home, you'd be like, "How can you go up and just make people laugh like this?"

Besides being a comedy fan as a kid and wanting to be a comic, I was a video-game freak, which I still am. When the show was on, A&E put out this video game that was like Atari. But instead of playing an actual game, you'd go through this simulated Improv that was on the screen and click on the headshots of the various comics to listen to their acts, which I did constantly.

JEFF FOXWORTHY:

The first time I was on the show, I was headlining at a club in Charlotte, North Carolina, called the Punchline. This was on a Wednesday night, and when I got the call they told me they wanted me for the next night; I left the following morning. I did the show and then I flew back to Charlotte to finish my gig on Friday.

When I got to the Improv to tape it, the crowd wasn't very good, so Budd said, "Don't worry, we're going to sweeten it and it'll look great on TV."

Picture it: I'm this rube from Georgia who had never, ever done television before and when I delivered my first joke, there was dead silence. Immediately, I started to panic and I began thinking to myself, "Okay, if I'm going to die, Budd said they're going to sweeten it so I'd better look like I'm killing." That was my thought process and if a joke didn't get a laugh, what I did was nod and grin as if it had. Then I did the same thing with the Punchline.

About six months later, I was in New York when another southern comic named Vic Henley came up to me and said, "I thought you told me you died on *An Evening at the Improv*."

"Oh my God, I did," I said. "It was terrible. There were thirty people and nobody was laughing at anything."

"Dude, I saw it and you killed," said Vic.

"Well," I said, "it *looked* that way because my pauses were so long that they had to put giggle laughs in between to cover them up."

So that experience was me learning how to do TV, and what Budd did was very instructive, because even though I didn't do that well, I still had a credit. When I went back out on the road to perform, people were like, "He must be pretty good. He did *An Evening at the Improv*."

LARRY THE CABLE GUY, comedian and actor:

This had to be around 1987 or '88. The very first time I ever went to LA, I'd gone out there to help a friend of mine move, and as soon as we got to town, the first place we went was the Improv. It was the middle of the afternoon, the club was open, and I happened to be wearing a pair of shorts and a black *An Evening at the Improv* T-shirt. I got so caught up in the moment that I got up onstage and my friend took four or five pictures of me. Before we finished, I said, "I'm going to be working here someday."

When I finally did, it was one of the biggest stepping-stones of my career because performing on Budd Friedman's stage meant that you weren't just another comedian anymore.

BYRON ALLEN:

A lot of stand-up "purists" kind of put [the show] down, but to me it was a really cool thing to do because it was easy. You went on and you did your set, and it was a great advertisement for the club and you'd see all these young acts that were so eager and passionate.

GREG BEHRENDT, comedian and writer:

If you did the show, you could headline. There was a point where the goal was obviously Johnny Carson or David Letterman, but right underneath that was *An Evening at the Improv*.

DREW CAREY:

There was kind of a running joke among comics back then that if you couldn't do *An Evening at the Improv* then you should get out of the business. It was such an easy show to do comparatively and every comic did it.

PAUL REISER:

In retrospect, they were pretty cookie-cutter episodes, but it was still a huge step because you had a much better chance of getting one step closer to what you really wanted to do. Your whole attitude after that was, "Now I have a tape. I can be seen."

JUDY GOLD, comedian, actor, writer, and producer:

At first, it was whether you did *An Evening at the Improv* and then it became how many times you did it.

DAVID SPADE:

All I remember is wearing Bugs Bunny blue jeans on one of them. After a while, it kind of became like doing jury duty because there was Budd's show and so many others like them. It got to a point that it was difficult to keep coming up with new material. It's like you'd start to burn out your whole act. This wasn't good if you weren't a headliner because you didn't have enough material to blow.

PAUL RODRIGUEZ:

Maybe because I'm a minority it was just me, but doing that show brought to the surface the fact that everything that was getting me attention was starting to bother me. I was the Mexican guy, and because I had no one to measure myself against, I began to wonder if I should change. It didn't last long, though, because then I realized that this was my hook and I had something to say. My attitude sort of became, "I made my bed and I'm comfortable sleeping in it, to hell with everyone else."

LEWIS BLACK:

As long as I've been doing this, which is a long time now, I get anxious before a show. This was especially true back then, because the mentality was that you could eat tomorrow depending on how well you did or didn't do. So doing *An Evening at the Improv* that first time nearly put me over the top, a lot of which had to do with the name, because right before I went on, I literally felt like I was high on cocaine.

Of course, anxiety can work really well for you if you channel it right, and I did fine, but it was hands-down the strangest performing experience I've ever had in my life.

KEVIN NEALON:

The night I did it, Harvey Korman, who was one of Budd's partners, hosted and the air conditioner conked out. It was hot as hell and they had to take a break right before I went to fix it. The audience wound up having to sit in the sweltering show room for forty minutes before it was finally fixed and the show resumed with Harvey introducing me. It was not a good night for me.

ADAM SANDLER:

Budd was the one who urged me to come out to LA to begin with, and for me doing that show was like a huge rite of passage because you were also on with guys you loved who were already famous. I just remember saying to myself, "Holy shit, I'm on this show with *that* person," and being really excited about it. It was my first taste of having the pressure of—this is being recorded and there's no turning back.

PAULA POUNDSTONE:

Besides giving young comics exposure and having celebrity guest emcees, one of the great things they did was have other celebrities and semi-celebrities planted in the audience. Budd prearranged this, of course, but it was still great because it reflected a typical night at the Improv where they had a lot of famous people there to begin with.

One night, they had Ted Bessell, who played Marlo Thomas's boyfriend Donald Hollinger on the 1960s sitcom *That Girl*, which I loved as a kid. If you remember, he'd say "Who is *that* girl?" at the beginning of each episode, and when I came offstage, he said this to me. True story.

Another night, Jim Backus, the actor who played Mr. Magoo and Thurston Howell III on *Gilligan's Island*, was there. The whole time I was on he had his hands folded, which isn't exactly the most supportive thing to see when you're onstage. He wasn't doing it intentionally, I don't think, but afterwards I kind of made a promise to myself. I said, "You know what? If *Gilligan's Island* ever does a reunion, I'm coming to the set just so I can fold my hands."

My all-time favorite memory was the night Bea Arthur was hosting. I wasn't scheduled to go on, but when Budd invited me to do another show that same season, I said, "Yeah, but can I pick who my host is?"

I told him I wanted Bea, and he specifically got her for me. I was thrilled. On the night of the show, they'd partitioned off a section backstage for a makeshift dressing room for the host. Anyway, I was standing there pestering one of the stagehands to tell me when Bea got there so I could say hello, which I did. I said, "It's so nice to meet you. I asked Budd to put me on the same night as you and he did."

I also told her what a huge fan I was, not realizing how nervous she was, because stand-up was foreign territory to her even though she was a comedic actress. But I had no idea *how* nervous, especially since she'd played these ballsy characters on *The Golden Girls* and *Maude*.

The more we talked, the more nervous she got, so I tried to make her feel at ease by saying, "Bea, if there's anything at all I can do for you, just name it."

She just looked at me and said, "Just get me the fuck out of here." She wound up doing a fine job and I think she was kidding when she said it, but I also think she was genuinely scared.

DOTTIE ARCHIBALD:

Before A&E picked it up, I did the show a number of times where I was part of the recurring cast that used to play the Improv employees. I was the cashier and they'd have me seated outside the club on a stool during the opening, which was great fun because there'd be all these unscripted jokes going back and forth and I got to riff with all these celebrities as they went by me.

The one I remember the most is Flip Wilson, whose variety show had been off the air for a number of years and he'd gained a ton of weight. In the same episode, there was another overweight comic who's now dead named Mark Goldstein. Budd loved him, but he never went anywhere and when Budd brought him out, the first words out of Mark's mouth were, "Can you believe there's anyone fatter than Flip Wilson?" He didn't get one laugh.

Just as I was savoring the success of what I'd always wanted during the first incarnation of *An Evening at the Improv*, in October 1983, Showtime feted us with an hour-long special commemorating the club's twentieth anniversary called *20 Years of Laughter at the Improv*, which I dedicated to Alix and which later won a CableACE Award. Hosted by Robert Klein, it was a night filled with joy and nostalgia as many of our biggest stars like Robin Williams, Billy Crystal, Andy Kaufman, Joe Piscopo, Byron Allen, and newcomer Dana Carvey took to the stage alongside such guests as Bea Arthur, Lainie Kazan, Mamie Van Doren, and *The Love Boat*'s Ted Lange, who all came out to pay tribute on Melrose Avenue.

Bette Midler sent videotaped remarks from New York, while a subdued Richard Pryor, four years into recovery from his near-fatal freebasing incident in 1979, called me his mentor during a segment we prerecorded weeks earlier at his Hollywood home. As the special concluded, I thanked everyone for making the Improv what it had become.

Sadly, the special also marked what would be one of the last performances of Andy Kaufman, who died at Cedars-Sinai Medical Center on May 16, 1984, following a courageous six-month battle with lung cancer at the age of thirty-five. Despite his over-the-top, often bizarre behavior onstage and off, his sudden illness came as a complete shock because Andy had always been a health nut, who in his latter years practiced transcendental meditation and never smoked, drank, or used drugs. Two months before his death—which for many years later those who knew him best hoped and still believed had been a hoax—Andy held a screening for his final film, *My Breakfast with Blassie*, at a small theater on Santa Monica Boulevard that his longtime manager George Shapiro rented.

Andy was emaciated and appeared onstage with his head completely shaven except for a Mohawk down the middle. Afterwards, I asked George if he thought Andy might like to invite his friends over to the Improv to have an ice cream sundae party. George said, "I'm sure he'd love it," and the next day he called me and said, "This is the best thing that happened to him in the last two years."

For me, though, having Andy's memorial service at the Improv eight weeks later—attended by George; Robin Williams; Andy's recent and former girlfriends Lynne Margulies, Little Wendy, and Elayne Boosler; longtime writing partner Bob Zmuda; and *Taxi* co-stars Judd Hirsch, Danny DeVito, Marilu Henner, Tony Danza, and Jeff Conaway—turned out to be one of the worst days of my entire life. When I got up onstage to deliver one of the eulogies, I was so overcome with emotion I couldn't get the words out for all the tears. Yes, Andy drove me crazy at times as he did everyone that knew him, but I loved him.

I'm not sure I fully ever came to terms with how much either, until fifteen years later when I played myself in Jim Carrey's 1999 biopic, *Man on the Moon*. I broke down again while we were shooting the scene about Andy's audition for me at the New York Improv. Indeed, he remains one of the most extraordinarily gifted and special comics that I have ever known. Perhaps Robert Klein summed it up best when he was introducing Andy during our twentieth anniversary special, comparing him to a Jackson Pollock painting—"That is, everybody interprets it differently." There will never be another Andy.

THIRTY-FIVE

The Improv Explodes . . . and the Stakes Get Even Higher

What a decade! Though the stand-up comedy community had been growing steadily since the 1970s, nothing could have completely prepared me for the dizzying array of established and new talent that the enormous popularity of *An Evening at the Improv* would bring to Melrose Avenue and West 44th Street throughout the mid to late eighties.

In LA, the slogan "Over One Billion Jokes Told" was painted underneath the Improv sign on our brick wall. And yet even with all this success, I still had no idea just how fast we were becoming one of the biggest conduits for America's comedy boom, a barometer by which every future generation would be celebrated for and measured against—if also to avoid the same mistakes.

BILL MAHER:

Monologists hated magicians or anybody who did gimmicky things back then. We worked hard to craft jokes and we thought of ourselves as much cleverer. We were trying to do something with language, and we thought these prop comics, who went to a novelty shop and bought a fucking magic trick, were cheap ways to get laughs.

DAVID SPADE:

I had a Playskool xylophone I used for my killer *Jeopardy!* bit I did—you know, the one where Alex Trebek says, "Ask a question." And then they go, "bing, bing, bing . . ." At the end, I'd say, "Okay, pencils down."

I also had a spatula because I did a bit about how expensive everything on *Wheel of Fortune* was, where I'd say, "I'll take the spatula for $600." I can't even remember what else, but I thought they were effective and then Dennis Miller actually talked me out of them.

"Your jokes are very solid," he said, "but you don't want to drag these props around like an asshole for the rest of your life."

BOB SAGET:

I had a lot of weird riffs. I would say, "My mother is Gumby, my father is Pokey, and I'm Mr. Potato Head. I have the brain of a German shepherd and the body of a sixteen-year-old boy—and they're both in my car." That's not a nightclub joke. That's a pedophile murder joke. I was about eighteen when I wrote that. When I first started, I was purely an attitude comedian, non sequiturs and strange lines—all the stuff you do when you're a personality-driven comedian. I think I did my first six minutes for ten years.

BRUCE SMIRNOFF:

We've already talked about how Budd is with celebrities—it's like he could be talking to you and if somebody famous came in, he'd just stop the conversation in midsentence and walk away. To Budd, celebrities were like big, shiny objects and to a certain extent they probably still are. One of my most unforgettable memories during this period was the time that David Letterman was scheduled to do an unannounced set at the Hollywood Improv that nobody was supposed to know about, and Budd spilled the beans because he couldn't keep his mouth shut. It was around 1980 or '81, shortly after Dave's daytime talk show on NBC was cancelled and about a year before he started doing *Late Night with David Letterman*. It was also after the fire at the LA club and before Budd got *An Evening at the Improv*. Business and morale were just awful, and we didn't know if we'd survive from one day to the next.

Because Dave had a holding deal with NBC where he couldn't work because he was under contract, he was doing a lot of stand-up to pass the time. He was also still on the outs with Mitzi Shore at The Comedy Store because of the strike. Offstage, Dave always dressed like a slob kind of the way he does now in the pictures that have surfaced since his retirement. Back then, he also drove this beat-up red pickup truck and he couldn't have cared less about his appearance. It was as if nothing mattered to him.

So one afternoon during this period, I was working at the club to earn some extra money, when Dave walked in. His hair was messy, he had on an old T-shirt, and he was unshaven. Immediately, Budd stopped whatever we were doing and said, "Hey, David."

Without returning the greeting, Dave said, "You know, Budd. I'm back now and I think I'd like to come in tomorrow night."

Of course, Budd was just over the moon about this and said, "We'd love to have you."

This was on a Thursday and they arranged for him to come in at nine-thirty the following night. However, Dave expressly told Budd that he didn't want anyone to know about it. He said, "You can't tell anybody. I don't want this to be a media event."

Budd gave his word that he wouldn't. He said, "I promise, David. I would never do that."

No sooner than Dave got back in his truck and drove away, Budd ran over to the phone and started calling people. And he didn't just run. It was more like he levitated. The next night, the line was so long that it literally stretched all the way to Crescent Heights. Needless to say, when Dave pulled up in front of the club, he was pissed. He wasn't nasty or anything, but when he walked inside and saw all these people sitting in the show room, he kind of got this perturbed look on his face. He said, "Budd went and told everyone, didn't he?"

And I said, "Uh-huh."

This was all it took, and Dave just walked out of the club, got back in his truck, and drove away.

As the 1980s wore on, not only were we attracting the biggest names in stand-up as comics, it was their loutish behavior offstage that sometimes drew the most attention.

LEWIS BLACK:

I never will forget the night Roseanne Barr and Tom Arnold got into a fight while I was onstage. I don't recall who started it or what was said, but they started screaming at each other right in the middle of my set and then they stormed out. I was like, "Really? Here I am on the first two rungs of the ladder and she's at the top, but she doesn't have the courtesy to control herself."

Then there was the evening in 1983 when the King of Late-Night Television himself showed up unannounced on Melrose Avenue.

BRUCE SMIRNOFF:

The night Johnny Carson came in unannounced in 1983, people gave him a standing ovation. People who were already standing started to clap. The ones who were sitting at the bar stood. This was when he was still anointing stars on a regular basis and everybody knew what a huge deal it was to have Johnny Carson coming into a comedy club.

Budd was beside himself. He was three feet off the ground and he was running up to anybody he could find to tell them about it. Carson was completely oblivious because he was already shitfaced. He just walked right up to the bar past the commotion and ordered three shots of Jack Daniels.

A few minutes later, he turned around and walked down the hall into the show room. From my vantage point, I was like, "Whoever's onstage now is going to be seen by Johnny Carson. Who's going to be so lucky?"

No sooner than I opened my mouth, Budd walked up to me and said, "Brucie, two guys just called and cancelled. You're on next." I don't remember who else was performing that night, but because it was prime time, they were all big names. Anyway, I went onstage, Carson knew I was there, and I can still relive it. I did my first joke, the audience laughed, and I was like, "They're going to help Johnny Carson discover me."

It was just like something out of a storybook. I did my second joke and they laughed again. I was like, "Oh my God, this is happening to me." Then I did my third joke and a fourth joke. Each one was better than the last and I was on a build. And then suddenly, from out of nowhere, somebody yelled out, "Stolen! You're doing somebody else's material."

I looked out and saw it was my agent's son. He had four empty beer bottles in front of him and he was smoking a cigarette, slurring his words, and going, "I don't know why my dad handles you. You're a fucking thief. You suck."

All within a matter of seconds, I'd gone from being in my dream to being in the middle of a nightmare. I felt like I was Linda Blair in *The Exorcist* and I absolutely flipped out. I said, "Adam, we've got some big people here tonight."

But he started up again. He said, "I don't know why my father even handles you."

By this point, I couldn't even talk. Luckily, someone got Budd, who quickly got me offstage, and then the bouncer literally threw this kid out onto the sidewalk because he was being so belligerent.

About five minutes later, I went outside. I stood right in front of his Jeep and confronted him. I said, "Why did you do this to me, Adam?" And he told me to go fuck myself, shifted into high gear, and drove off, literally missing my foot by inches.

But the story gets even better because as soon as I walked back into the club, Bud Robinson, who was the manager of *Tonight Show*'s bandleader, Doc Severinsen, came up to me and said, "Bruce, Johnny's too drunk to drive home. You're the only responsible person we know here. You're going to have to do it."

So they got Carson out of the club and into his Mercedes. He's with this young girl he'd just met who was in town from Chicago and couldn't have been more than eighteen. I saw them in the backseat making out, but before we left, I went back into the club to tell this guy Sandy Shire, a musical conductor, to follow us back to Carson's place in Bel Air.

By the time I got back to the car, Johnny was doing a full-court press with this girl and we drove off. Every so often, they stopped kissing and she looked up at me in the rearview mirror. Then she looked back at Johnny and said, "You should really put him on your show."

As I was about to find out, however, his reputation for not being a nice guy was true, because that was when he said, "What are you talking about, him?" Then after a couple of seconds, he said to me, "What's your name, kid?"

"I'm Bruce Smirnoff," I said.

"Let me tell you something, Smirnoff," Johnny said. "You don't know what you're doing. You've got no structure. You stink."

By the time we got to his house, I still couldn't believe what was happening. There was an armed guard with a shotgun sitting at the gate who saw me in Johnny's car and gave me a thumbs-up. So we drove up, I got out of the car and opened the passenger side—where Johnny was on top of this girl in the backseat and he wouldn't let her out. He also couldn't see what I saw, which was the guy I told to follow me from the Improv leading a parade of about six cars full of people he'd invited to a party over at Johnny Carson's house.

Finally, Johnny got out and he looked up at me and said, "What the fuck are all these people doing here?" He threatened to call the police if we didn't leave. Then on Monday, my agent dropped me as a client because of what his son had done. He couldn't face me.

There were plenty more stories like this to come as the growing swells of celebrity customers on Melrose Avenue continued to multiply by the night, along with the collective intake of alcohol and drugs on both coasts among Improv performers, patrons, and staff, although I was never a participant. I always had a zero-tolerance policy, as did Silver when she ran the New York club. However, it was a policy that was oftentimes overlooked, especially when we weren't around.

JUDY ORBACH:

There was a guy named Angel Rodriguez who was really close friends with Chris Albrecht. He and his brother had a beauty salon around the corner from the New York Improv, and Angel was a coke dealer. We were all very much into cocaine in the eighties, and Angel would take a bunch of air conditioners down to Puerto Rico and come back with blow. We would snort the blow off of the tables in the Improv show room. He'd take it out, line it up, and we'd all sit around.

I remember doing cocaine behind the bar where there was a little liquor storage room that if two people were in it, it was crowded. I don't know where we got it from, but we kept a tiny piece of marble back there and one of the male bartenders would open the service gate for the waitresses who wanted to take a coke break. Everybody got drunk and high and it was just accepted, although most of us weren't addicts. We were just users.

EDDIE BERKE:

I can't speak for New York, but it's hard to say how rampant cocaine use was on Melrose, although it was definitely there and everybody and their mother was doing it. I know that when Budd found out about it, particularly if people were selling it, he kicked them out immediately.

I also know that the stall door in the men's restroom went from a foot from the ceiling to the bottom of the floor. I remember Budd walked in there one day and found three guys snorting coke. He went ballistic and the next day he had the door cut down.

As these chemically induced incidents continued, so, too, did the surge of high-wattage celebrities we had on Melrose during much of the eighties, including John Belushi, who came in the night before his death of a drug overdose on March 5, 1982. Belushi's tragic demise, like so many others, would cause many in the Hollywood community to take pause—and to try and find relief and refuge at the Improv during times of grief, although it was usually simply to unwind or be adulated. For a while, there was a time when just about anybody you could name was here for one reason or another, even if they hadn't come to watch comedy.

LARRY MILLER:

One night, O. J. Simpson was in the audience. He was very happy to be there and he enjoyed the adulation of being well known. I'm a big sports fan, but not to the extent where I would say, "Look who's in the audience," so I just kind of smiled and waved.

Another night Mike Tyson was there, and when you see somebody like that who's in such incredible physical shape, you can't help but think to yourself, "Wow, this is pretty cool."

ROSS MARK:

Before I started helping Budd book the comics, I used to do a lot of odd jobs at the Hollywood Improv during high school— busing tables, answering the phone, working the door. I did everything and it was great because I got to see everybody. Christopher Lloyd from *Taxi* would come in, and for some reason, he used to give me twenty dollars every time he went to the men's room.

The Improv was also where Mike Tyson brought Robin Givens on their first date. He asked me for the best seat in the house and gave me a hundred-dollar bill. When he left, he gave me another hundred.

In addition to names like Barbra Streisand, Michael J. Fox, Denzel Washington, Brad Pitt, and Arnold Schwarzenegger, two of our most regular regulars were John Goodman, who usually drove to the Improv in his Volkswagen Beetle, and Bruce Willis. Both were at the height of their fame on *Roseanne* and *Moonlighting*. Together, they came in almost nightly to sing and play the harmonica accompanied by the jukebox, although at times, the resultant media attention this attracted was not of the kind any of us liked.

EDDIE BERKE:

Back then, I used to get offered money all the time from the tabloids to talk about this one or that one, but I never did it because as far I was concerned—and not to sound cliché—I, being the bartender, thought of myself as their shrink. Celebrities came in to let loose and unwind, which is what we wanted.

So I was always very careful about what I said, and there was never enough money for me to answer their questions, and I didn't. But one time Bruce Willis came in after having a little too much to drink and the first words out of his mouth without even saying hello were, "I'm pissed at you."

"Why?" I said.

"Because you talked to the *National Enquirer* about me."

I was floored, so I said, "I didn't talk to anybody."

Before I even had a chance to defend myself, he shot back, "Yeah, you did. The reporter told me you told him I come in every night and play my harmonica at the end of the bar." Which turned out to be true in the context of what was written, because the very next day, I went out to buy the paper and that was exactly what it claimed I said—"Bruce Willis comes in every night and sits at the end of the bar at the Hollywood Improv playing his harmonica."

Only I never said it, and then that same night Bruce came in and he ordered a beer. When he asked me for it, I said, "Bruce, I don't even think I want to serve you." But he had no idea what I was talking about. It was as if his accusation the night before had never occurred, so I said, "You were on my case all last night about the bartender at the Improv."

But as upset as I was, I tried to keep my composure when he said, "I don't remember that." And he didn't. I later found out his reasoning was because at the time I was the only male bartender at the Improv. All the others were women. The article said bartender—not bartendress—so that was his whole beef. I can't remember if we immediately made up, but I became even more careful about what I said after that.

By the mid-1980s, stand-up comedy had become what rock 'n' roll was in the 1960s, and the residual press coverage we were receiving was almost always positive. A prime example of this was an April 1986 article by legendary *Variety* columnist Army Archerd, who wrote: "What a night at the Improv! First Eddie Murphy came onstage, then Byron Allen followed with Murphy remaining onstage. Next Bruce Willis jumped up, followed by Whoopi Goldberg, and to cap the evening: Robin Williams and Rick Overton came up for a finale."

But for us, this was now considered just another typical evening at the Improv.

Two years earlier, *The Cosby Show* had premiered on NBC and was instantly the biggest hit of the decade that would also be credited for saving the sitcom genre itself. Though comics had always flourished on sitcoms, largely because of the characters they played, none of the shows had ever been built on their act. That would forever change after producers Marcy Carsey and Tom Werner saw the 1983 concert film *Bill Cosby: Himself* and decided to develop a sitcom about an upwardly mobile African American family that was essentially Cosby's act. For me, it also represented another jewel in the Improv crown, where suddenly the autobiographical, observational style of comedy that for so many years had been a mainstay on our stage would reach unimagined new heights.

As a result, virtually any comic with a unique personal point of view and the goods to deliver it—young married life and the adult perils of living too close to your family (*Mad About You* and *Everybody Loves Raymond*), postmodern cynicism (*Seinfeld*), blue-collar motherhood (*Roseanne*)—suddenly held the keys to the kingdom with performers flocking into the Improv and producers, agents, and talent bookers flocking after them faster than you could say "laugh track."

Though Johnny Carson's presumptive heir apparent David Letterman would be responsible for giving many of the decade's hottest young acts their first national television exposure—and even with *The Tonight Show* now only airing new shows three nights a week, one of them sans Carson—make no mistake about it: It was still the place that virtually every comedian wanted to be. It also put the fear of God into them whenever the late Jim McCawley, Carson's talent coordinator and surrogate comedic filter, came into the Improv—even if they had already been guests on the show.

BILL MAHER:

I really don't have anything bad to say about McCawley, although he always gave the impression that he was kind of a troubled guy and it was nerve-wracking to get a call from him because it meant I had to run my set by him. If you did it over the phone, it was tough because that's not how comedy is meant to be done. If you did it at a club where there was a bad crowd, he might say, "Well, you can't do this joke on the show," even if it had nothing to do with your material.

RITCH SHYDNER:

The funny thing about Jim McCawley is that I would audition for him and he'd go, "I don't think you're Johnny's kind of comedian." But then I'd do all these little clubs and they'd say, "Have you done Carson? You're Johnny's kind of comedian." So I persisted and when I finally got it, Jim introduced me to Johnny after the show and he said, "You are my kind of comedian."

Something else happened in 1985, when Ellen DeGeneres became the first female comedian ever to be invited to join Johnny Carson on the couch following her debut appearance on *The Tonight Show*, ushering in an even bigger sea change. Suddenly you had more female comedians (Susie Essman, Joy Behar, Rosie O'Donnell, Rita Rudner, Kathy Griffin, and Paula Poundstone), African American comedians (Eddie Murphy, Arsenio Hall, D.L. Hughley, Martin Lawrence, and the Wayans Brothers—the oldest, Keenen Ivory Wayans, had even started out as a doorman when he was first performing on the New York Improv's stage), novelty and oddball acts (Emo Philips, Judy Tenuta, and Carrot Top), and triple-X macho acts (Andrew Dice Clay).

With more performers than we knew what to do with, and *An Evening at the Improv* going gangbusters, the next logical step, even though it wasn't originally my idea, was to start a franchise. The person who first approached me about it was a comedian named Mark Anderson, who was also a Princeton graduate, a psychologist, and an Olympic diver, in addition to being an eccentric alcoholic turned Born Again Christian who was later found dead in an Oklahoma hotel room in 2012.

One day in the winter of 1985, Mark came to me out of the blue and said, "I want to open an Improv in San Diego." Since the thought had never really occurred to me before, even though we already had two thriving clubs in New York and LA, I said, "Do you mean a franchise?"

This was basically all it took and we made a handshake agreement right there. Over the next few months, we went down, scouted locations, and he put up most of the capital for the club, which Alix helped decorate. To make the events leading up to it as festive as possible, we rented a Pullman car that we attached to an Amtrak train where the guests, including Bea Arthur, Wil Shriner, and Bill Maher, met at Los Angeles's Union Station. On the trip down, we set up a champagne bar and Bill went into the bathroom and came back out wearing a red smoking jacket.

Even more unforgettable, however, was our grand opening, when I invited Robin Williams to perform, and Mark Anderson then called up Robin's idol Jonathan Winters and said, "Robin Williams is going to be here and he'd love for you to come down." So we had Robin and Jonathan performing together for the first time ever.

With the help of my old friend Lou Alexander the year after that, we opened an Improv at the Riviera Hotel in Las Vegas, followed by locations in Atlantic City, Reno, and Lake Tahoe. Then came more, including locations in London, San Francisco, Chicago, Atlanta, Cleveland, Houston, Kansas City, Orlando, Denver, and Pittsburgh, with a current total of twenty-two independent franchises nationwide, and with the Improv licensing the name in exchange for a fee and a percentage of the weekly gross under the governance of our holding company, Improv West Associates.

And, of course, by the late eighties, lots of fresh talent like Ray Romano, Mario Cantone, Colin Quinn, and Dave Attell were still coming out of the New York Improv, with my former manager and partner Chris Albrecht also now being one of comedy's biggest power brokers. Chris left the Improv in 1980 to become an agent for International Creative Management and built up one of the best stables of talent in the comedy business, including Whoopi Goldberg, Billy Crystal, Joe Piscopo, and Keenen Ivory Wayans, many of whom were plucked right from our stage when they were virtual unknowns. In June 1985, he joined HBO as senior vice president of original programming before eventually becoming chairman in 2002.

There's nothing more exciting than watching a person you helped nurture succeed beyond your biggest expectations, and Chris has deservedly done so beyond anything I could have ever imagined. During a spectacular twenty-two-year run at HBO and a list of accomplish-ments longer than you can count, he drove up the number of stand-up specials and original programming, including *Comic Relief*, *The Larry Sanders Show*, *Curb Your Enthusiasm*, and *Sex and the City*, not to men-tion award-winning dramas like *Oz*, *The Wire*, *Band of Brothers*, and *The Sopranos*.

With one of our own feeding the cable TV pipeline—not to men-tion being the chief purveyor of talent—we were now, it seemed, even more unstoppable. The late eighties also saw the arrival of young acts like Drew Carey, Janeane Garofalo, Jon Stewart, David Spade, Rob Schneider, Bill Hicks, Denis Leary, and Judd Apatow and his roommate Adam Sandler on Melrose Avenue.

ADAM SANDLER:

It was unbelievable. Just total fear and the most insane thing was that my first Improv spot was on a Saturday night at 9:20, which was a really crushing spot, but I did well. I didn't kill, but I did okay. I'm not sure if Budd was even there that night, but in any case he started giving me two or three spots a week after that. Either I was on or I was hanging out there, having the best time of my life and hoping that somebody would dis-cover me.

JUDD APATOW:

Adam moved to LA because Budd told him if he did, he'd take care of him, which was how I met Adam. I'd go to the club to see him and he was getting good spots because he was really funny. I remember the entire time I was doing this, I kept trying to figure out how I was going to get strong enough to audition for Budd. You knew if you weren't ready he wasn't going to let you do it again for a long time.

Anyway, I finally worked up the nerve, and when I did, Budd very quickly asked me to be the emcee. I was sometimes on four or five nights a week on Melrose and in Santa Monica.

DAVID SPADE:

The night I found out Budd liked me, I was in shock because you sort of wait. Budd had a big circular table in the bar where he held court and if you were one of the bigger-name comics you got to sit there regardless of whether he was there or not.

Anyway, the night I auditioned, I was there with an improv troupe called The Funny Boys who I first met when I did an open mic night at the Improv down in San Diego.

On the night I found out I'd passed my audition on Melrose, we were sitting at Budd's table when Bruce Willis came over and offered to buy a round of shots to celebrate, which they carded me for. It was horribly embarrassing and they wouldn't serve me because I was under twenty-one, but I love Bruce Willis. Then Budd started putting me in Vegas where I drove down the next day and did twenty-one shows over the next week. I made $500.

DREW CAREY:

I made my first *Tonight Show* appearance in November 1991, and it was always a big tradition to go to the Improv after the taping. What they'd do is play your set on the TV in the bar so that everybody could watch. So I did my first set on *The Tonight Show* and I couldn't believe how well it went. Then I went straight from NBC to the Improv.

I remember that when I walked in, Budd had a great table waiting for me and my friends. And when *The Tonight Show* came on, they turned off the jukebox and turned up the TV—at which point the whole place just busted out with applause with all these other comics patting me on the back and shaking my hand. Budd sent over a bottle of champagne and I was like a made man from then on.

Thanks to the constant flow of talent we had in addition to the endless stream of agents, managers, and producers, we also became a scouting mecca for the comedy festivals, including Just for Laughs in Montreal, which remains by far the biggest. And besides briefly launching our own comedy festival, in 1987 I co-founded the American Comedy Awards with Eddie Kritzer. During our first year alone, two Improv alums, Lily Tomlin and Robin Williams, won female and male stand-ups respectively, while Bette Midler and Woody Allen won for their performances in *Ruthless People* and *Hannah and Her Sisters*.

To top it off, *Saturday Night Live* was also resurgent thanks in no small part to Improv comics like Kevin Nealon and Dana Carvey who were now cast members. Plus, we saw the debuts of *The Arsenio Hall Show* and Keenen Ivory Wayans's *In Living Color*—two FOX shows with two other Improv guys that broke new barriers in race and comedy on television.

Then there was the debut of The Comedy Channel, later rebranded Comedy Central, the first basic cable network exclusively devoted to stand-up, on November 15, 1989, followed by the short-lived Ha! network six months later on April 1, 1990.

Before that, with the comedy boom at its zenith and the Improv franchising machine moving up to thirteen clubs nationwide, there were talks of a possible over-the-counter IPO that, had it gone through, would have made us a publicly traded company. It didn't, but that same year, in 1987, I also decided to take on a business partner, Mark Lonow, a former comedian turned actor who first joined the Improv in 1981. Though it hasn't always been a perfect match, and he declined to be interviewed for this book due to an ongoing personal matter, I do give him credit for helping me to keep a better eye on the Improv's bottom line.

Still, no matter how rocky things have been between me and Mark over the years, nothing can compare to the potentially near-fatal partnership I had with a comedian and his girlfriend who briefly ran the restaurant on Melrose in the mideighties.

I should preface this by saying that even though the bar had always done well, even during times when the rest of the club wasn't, the one thing we'd never managed to get a handle on was the restaurant. We were and still are first and foremost a comedy club, which is why people came, and I never aspired to be Spago or Chasen's. Nevertheless, it became such a point of frustration that I was willing to try anything.

So when this comic and his girlfriend, neither of whom I'll name, approached me about running the restaurant, I said yes without hesitation because not only was he in the middle of a major career resurgence at the time, he was selling out shows nightly during an extended multi-weekend engagement on Melrose.

Here was the problem I didn't discover until it was too late: They were both control freaks, they had no restaurant experience, and we butted heads from day one. Besides completely redoing the menu and eliminating some of our most popular dishes, they alienated our staff. And that wasn't the only thing. Without consulting me, they did away with our policy of giving free meals to the comics, and even banished the ones who were performing from being in the restaurant before their sets—many of whom couldn't afford to buy anything because they raised the prices so much.

Okay, nobody forced me to go into business with them and I was so caught up in how well this comic's shows were going that I didn't think things through. I also bit my tongue, believing almost to the end that if I did, things would gradually work themselves out.

But they didn't. In fact, they rapidly went from bad to worse, and we were losing money and customers left and right. So I decided to end our arrangement and that was how things nearly turned lethal because when I told them, they demanded that I give them money as a payoff, which I didn't have and wouldn't have given them even if I did. And when they persisted, I said, "I'll see you in court," and I called my attorney to begin legal proceedings.

A couple of days later, I received a menacing phone call at the club from a guy named Ralph, demanding that I immediately fly to New York to meet with him in person. Obviously, I was shaken, but after getting in touch with my attorney, he advised me not to do anything, assuring me it was probably just a scare tactic that would blow over—which wasn't the case, as the phone calls continued.

That following Sunday night, Alix and I arrived at the Hollywood Improv around nine o'clock. As we walked in, the first thing we noticed were four men seated at the bar dressed in dark suits whom I immediately knew were Mafia guys. I also suspected that there might be problems if I tried to talk to them, and so in an attempt to diffuse the situation and knowing they probably wouldn't cause a scene with a woman, I asked Alix to find out what they wanted. When she tried to talk to them, she noticed a gun strapped to one of the men's ankles, and he informed her in no uncertain terms that he wanted to talk to me instead.

After that, we went upstairs to my office to talk in private, where they proceeded to ask me for money again as I continued to refuse to cave in to their demands—which aside from going into business with this comedian and his girlfriend, turned out to be mistakes two, three, four, and five. Though I didn't know it yet, they were about to begin terrorizing me and my family in a nightmare battle of cat and mouse that would last for the next eight weeks, including following our sons, Ross and Dax, to school and making more menacing phone calls.

Things finally got so bad that we were temporarily forced go to a hotel in Santa Monica for several days on the advice of my attorney. Thankfully, my daughters, Zoe and Beth, were in New York with their mother and we sent our sons to stay with friends.

I also stayed away from the club on the advice of my attorney who had warned me that it would be the first place they'd go when they discovered I wasn't at home. Still, I feared for the comics and my staff, so I hired private security guards for the club in addition to installing a burglar alarm in my home.

Making things even worse was that when we called the FBI, no one would return our phone calls, nor did we get anywhere when we consulted with several actor friends who had connections to the Mafia. Meanwhile, the threats continued to escalate until finally one of the guys from the Mafia ordered me to fly to New York and meet with them in a restaurant near the Garment Center, which I did.

The meeting subsequently lasted five hours while Alix nervously waited back at our hotel. I begrudgingly agreed to give this guy Ralph, who'd first tried to put the arm on me, six postdated checks for $10,000 apiece. And then that was that. I lost a ton of money, but at least we were all safe, and as I flew back to Los Angeles, I was greatly relieved.

About three weeks later, three guys from the FBI came into the Improv one night finally offering to help, although by this point I didn't need it. And in a sudden reversal of fortune, the club had also been doing so well in the weeks since I'd gone to New York that I could have afforded to give the Mafia $60,000 all at once, although I opted not to do that either.

THIRTY-SIX

The Comedy Boom Busts
and Finding Fallon

GREG BEHRENDT:

I always did well at the Improv and other clubs, but there became a period after a while when you didn't want to be seen as a "club comic" and it kind of became my secret shame.

JUDD APATOW:

By the time I started in the late eighties, you'd see big names come in to watch shows with Budd, so it didn't feel as cutting-edge after a while, although there were also those moments when it still felt like you were trying to become the next Jerry Seinfeld or Tim Allen, and that this was the place where you could get mainstream success, so it crackled with tension.

BILL MAHER:

I remember there was this one guy who was a dentist by day, and sitting around with the younger comics, I'd say, "For a dentist he's very funny, but for a comic he's a fucking dentist." What used to bug me the most is that I thought what terrible luck it was that I came along just when every other idiot was trying to do it and it clogged the way.

As much as Alix and I loved our home in Beverly Hills, we never again felt completely safe after our extortion ordeal. In 1996, we decided to move to a twenty-four-hour-doorman building in Westwood where we still live. For better or worse, it turned out to be the right decision, though, because just as we were starting to feel safe, the comedy business was tanking, which Bill Maher would later chronicle in his 1994 auto-biographical novel, *True Story*:

> The showcase clubs had ceased to exist for some years as great venues of experimentation. There were no poetic types hoping to be challenged by Lenny Bruce. It had lots of tourists and bache-lor parties from New Jersey hoping to hear dick jokes. The more non-cognoscenti took over the club scene, the more comedians tailored their acts along crowd-pleasing lines to survive. And the more the comedians did that, the more people in berets stayed away.

Of course, the nineties would also make Bill into a one-man cul-tural and commercial force as the outspoken host of *Politically Incorrect*, although the hard truth was that right as he was coming into his own, stand-up had become so overexposed it could no longer sustain itself, even as sitcoms like *Seinfeld, Roseanne, Home Improvement, Grace Under Fire, All-American Girl, Ellen, Martin*, and *Hangin' with Mr. Cooper* ruled the airwaves well into the decade.

Consequently, comedy clubs took a massive hit, including the orig-inal New York Improv, which closed in December 1992, becoming one of the first casualties along with Catch A Rising Star two years later. Though I hadn't been involved at all in the New York club for more than seventeen years and I don't completely fault Silver, who unsuccess-fully tried to keep it afloat in several other locations, having it fold was very traumatic—kind of like having your childhood home hit with the wrecking ball even though you aren't there to witness it.

What happened? My own personal issues with my ex-wife notwithstanding, the short answer—even though this may be an overgeneralization—is that club owners, myself included, had become victims of our own success. Quite possibly without even realizing it, the showcase-style business model we invented had also accidentally created a monster as countless others tried to imitate both us and our show.

Maybe the Improv could have avoided this if we had just stuck to the more inventive and original Robert Klein-Jay Leno-Andy Kaufman type acts that had first made us who we were. It's not something I'm particularly proud of, although I can live with it because in between the would-be and never-really-would-be comics who occasionally performed at the Improv, the comedy boom also saw the rise of some of the greatest comedians of all time, many of whom were vetted and streamlined on our stage. Unfortunately, the problem still was that with comedy fans now also flocking to second-rate chains and jerry-rigged stages in bowling alleys and hotel bars, it eventually became so difficult to tell the good from the bad that many stopped trying—and in the process, not only did the New York Improv close along with our other club in Santa Monica, business on Melrose also began to suffer, although this dip was happily short-lived.

No matter how oversaturated stand-up comedy became towards the late eighties and into the early nineties, I've always firmly believed that cream not only rises to the top, but that a new generation of even better comics comes along every five to seven years. For me, unquestionably the biggest and most-satisfying affirmation of this was when the all-time top of the Improv's crop, Jay Leno, became the host of *The Tonight Show* in June 1992, following his very public feud with David Letterman.

Though some accused Jay of forgetting about his friends and not championing comedians enough, it was a charge that I found completely without merit. Regardless—and thanks in no small part to a grassroots comedy scene in cities like San Francisco and Boston, not unlike the Greenwich Village coffeehouses of the early 1960s—many of the best young comics who would emerge in the mid to late nineties like Bill Hicks, Andy Kindler, Marc Maron, Dave Attell, Janeane Garofalo, and Margaret Cho would all eventually find their way to Melrose Avenue. Ditto when it came to drawing from the ranks of improv troupes, both new and old like Upright Citizens Brigade in New York, Second City in Chicago, and The Groundlings in Los Angeles, which is where another future *Tonight Show* host named Jimmy Fallon was performing in 1996 when he first came to my attention via my stepson Ross.

ROSS MARK:

After working in television for several years after college, I decided I didn't want to do it anymore and so Budd hired me to help him book the comics. One of the first showcases I did was for Lorne Michaels, who was in LA scouting potential hosts for what would become *Late Night with Conan O'Brien*. We had about ten comics on that night, including Conan and Jon Stewart.

About six months, maybe a year, after that, a woman at Brillstein-Grey named Randi Siegel sent me a tape from this kid from New York named Jimmy Fallon. So I put it in the VCR and it was hilarious—he played the guitar, his impressions were incredible, and he had this thing he did with a troll doll. And I was like, "Oh my God. This kid is going to be a huge star."

And so I called his manager up to tell her this, and when I did, I asked him not to work at other clubs, which he did anyway. But I didn't care and I immediately put him on during prime time on Friday and Saturday nights. And I told Budd the same thing. I said, "This kid's going to be a huge star. Trust me. Book him whenever he wants."

JIMMY FALLON:

You don't forget it. You walk down Melrose Avenue, you see the lights, and it feels like showbiz. As soon as I walked in, I saw Budd sitting at his table with his monocle dangling by his lapel. He's a very sharp dresser—fashion forward and he sticks out, because you can just tell he's a classy, cool guy. And I thought to myself, "I can't believe that's Budd, that's BUDD FRIEDMAN."

My first time at the Improv instantly reminded me of that scene from *Goodfellas* where you walk in and you know every-body. And they were all there that night—Richard Lewis, Dom Irrera, Margaret Cho, Janeane Garofalo, John Mendoza, Ray Romano—just talking and hanging out. It was insane because it was like going to a party of comedians I never knew existed. I was freaking out, because I knew everybody's act by heart and I could do everybody's act, when all of the sudden my manager, Randi Siegel, took me over to meet Budd.

He's one of the few guys I don't impersonate, but when I spoke to him he was like, "Right, right. Good to meet you." I don't really remember much else because I was so nervous and intimidated to meet him. Then I went into the show room just to see what it was like. I went in through the swinging doors, past the bathroom area, and the first thing I saw was the brick wall, the mic stand, and the light. People could still smoke back then, so there was this kind of cool haze, almost like stage smoke like you'd see at a rock concert.

And it's a decent-sized room and all you hear are the people laughing, so immediately I got nervous even though I wasn't going on. I was soaking it in like, "This is the Improv." Then this guy Brett, who was the sound engineer, came up to me. He said, "You can stand over there." That was when I was shown the back corner of the room where the comedians sat to watch each other's acts. So I did, too—boom, boom, boom—the people that I love.

The very next day I came back to talk to Budd's stepson Ross whom he'd told me to come see, and we arranged a time for me to do an audition but during the daytime. When that day came, the vibe at the Improv was entirely different because nobody was there and the whole room reeked of stale cigarette smoke and beer. So I got up onstage with my troll doll and my guitar. And I started doing my act and Ross started laughing. He said, "This is good. You should come on. I'll give you a spot Wednesday night."

So I came back and I did my usual act—Seinfeld, Travolta. Sometimes I would close with Pee-wee Herman because that was a big scandal at the time. I said something like, "This doll is cool, but I'd rather play with myself." My other closer was George Michael. I would play the guitar and then I'd turn around, shake my butt like George Michael did, and that would be the closing.

It was the best night of my life ever. Then I got off, and when Budd saw me he said, "Jimmy, well done. That was great."

I was like, "How cool is that? Budd Friedman said hi to me."

And then he said to my manager, "Let's have him back next week during the week."

"Wow," I said, "now I'm a working comic at the Improv."

For which I got paid $8.25. I still have the check that's unused because obviously there's nothing you can do for $8.25. But the best thing about the Improv is that they would feed you. My mom loved it when I played there because that meant I could eat. She knew I was eating. She was like, "God bless Budd Friedman. He's feeding you. Please tell him thank you from the Fallons." I didn't tell her I was eating chicken fingers, but it was still great because I was flat broke.

After about three months, Budd invited me to sit at his table, which was big because the unwritten rule was that you could say hello anytime you wanted to, but you didn't just sit down. Before I sat, he told me to get out of the aisles. Then he said, "I think you're ready for Saturday night." That actually was a paid gig and your name even went up on the marquee like a movie opening. It was exciting, and I was so happy that I went back to my apartment and began practicing that night, everything over and over.

So finally, Saturday night came and I showed up at the Improv with my doll and my guitar and everyone was congratulating me. And when I told them how excited I was, they said, "Yeah, it's a big night. Seinfeld's here." I looked over and, sure enough, Jerry Seinfeld was eating dinner with Budd. I was like, "My God," because this was at the height of *Seinfeld* and it couldn't be any bigger. I was like, "Oh my, gosh. I've got to call my mom and tell her Seinfeld's at the club." So I ran outside to the pay phone and I called her collect. I said, "Hey, it's Jimmy."

"How's everything?" my mom said.

"I'm at the Improv and Jerry Seinfeld's inside."

My mom went berserk. She was like, "What? My God, I've got to tell everybody."

I hung up and when I went back into the club, just as I was about to go on, somebody tapped me on the shoulder and said, "Seinfeld's getting ready to go up. He's going to go up and do ten minutes." So everyone, all the comedians, went back to watch and he came up and they announced him. No one else knew he'd been there in the audience.

He got a standing ovation just walking to the stage. And he killed, just a great stand-up. And I was standing over near the sound booth when the sound guy said, "Who's next?"

Whoever the other comedian was said, "I'm not following that." Then the next two guys after that said the same thing, so the sound guy said, "Who's Jimmy Fallon?"

"That's me," I said.

"Okay, you're up."

I thought to myself, "I'm following Jerry Seinfeld my first night. This is like the worst ever." And I was freaking out, but my manager tried to reassure me.

"Okay, okay," she said. "You can do this, you can do this."

So they announced my name, and I went up with my troll doll and my best ten-minute act—in fact, it was my only ten minutes, but I switched the order of my impressions and started with Seinfeld. I said, "Welcome to the auditions for the new spokesperson of Troll Doll, Inc. First up, Mr. Jerry Seinfeld." And I did my impression of Seinfeld and it worked. I'll never forget that night. Electric.

THIRTY-SEVEN

Passing the Baton and Looking Ahead: The Early 2000s to the Present

L ike everyone else, the extended Improv family awaited the dawn of the new millennium with anticipation and hope, and with a bevy of both established and new acts coming to our stage in Los Angeles and other clubs around the country each year—a small handful of which currently includes: Jeff Ross, D. F. Sweedler, Rich Vos, Jim Norton, Zach Galifianakis, Demetri Martin, Chelsea Handler, Louis C.K., Andy Dick, Ricky Gervais, Seth MacFarlane, Patton Oswalt, Steve Carell, Dean Edwards, Dane Cook, Jeff Dunham, Mitch Hedberg, Aziz Ansari, David Cross, Dov Davidoff, Kevin Brennan, Lynne Koplitz, and Rachel Feinstein—the twenty-first century has proven to be all of that and more.

Ever since I started out in New York in 1963, the thrill for me then, as it is now, has been watching our performers emerge and then forever continue to evolve. A lot has changed even since 1963, and practically everything has changed on the comedy scene, most significantly the exponential number of opportunities for performers.

However, the basic fundamentals of stand-up haven't changed, and I am confident about the future because I have no doubt that the value of what it offers will only continue to increase. On a more personal note, following the sale of the Improv to Levity Entertainment Group in 2012, I am no longer as actively involved as I once was, even though I still own the rights to the Improv name.

As for the current keepers of the Improv flame—Robert Hartmann of Levity Entertainment Group; our franchisees; and last, but certainly not least, the comedians—my wish for each of them is that they will always have the good fortune that I've had as I settle into that distinguished status called "elder statesman" without, I think, cause for too many regrets.

I know you can't get where I've gotten without putting some of what makes Seinfeld Seinfeld, Leno Leno, Fallon Fallon, and the thousands of other performers who've spent time on our stages over the years into the equation. I'm also acutely aware that the concept worked and continues to flourish here and at countless other comedy clubs across the globe because the constellations aligned to bestow upon me the funniest men and women on the planet, and I happened to be in the right place at the right time. How lucky I was. How lucky I am. How lucky I will always be.

DAVID STEINBERG, comedian, director, actor, writer, and talk-show host:

They always say a comedian needs a place to fail. I've never quite understood that logic, but Budd gave them a place to fail and he would guide them. He loved them and they love him for it.

NORMAN LEAR, television producer and writer:

It had to take a great deal of astuteness and love for comedy to do what Budd did, and that's his legacy. You can't spend the kind of time he had to with stand-up comics, both good and bad, without understanding the foolishness of the human condition and what makes a good laugh. Budd Friedman will be remembered for both things because he understood both.

JAY LENO:

You know what it is? When people make it comfortable for you, it becomes like an old sweater. That's how I've always felt about the Improv, and to this day it's a place where I know I can get onstage, try out material, and work. And it's the same kind of thing with Budd in the sense that even if I haven't seen him for six months, we can still pick up the conversation exactly where we left off.

PAUL PROVENZA:

I really believe that Budd will be remembered as the George Washington of the comedy business because he single-handedly created a paradigm shift. That's why a lot of comics know Budd's name the way they do George Washington's even though they've never met him.

MIKE PREMINGER:

Budd's legacy should be what it is. You can't say he was the father of stand-up comedy because there was stand-up before, but just look at all the people who started at the Improv. Before Budd came along, there was no place to try out things. You weren't just getting up there and telling jokes. You were talking about yourself, observing, and commenting. From that vantage point, Budd really opened up things.

ED BLUESTONE:

How will Budd Friedman and the Improv be remembered? Together, they were the primary catalyst of America's comedy wave. Before the Improv came along, there was an era of small places like The Duplex, The Bitter End, and the Blue Angel where people like Shelley Berman, Nichols and May, and Mort Sahl got their starts, but after that there was a period when comedy was sort of flat and the Improv was the renaissance.

DAVID STEINBERG, film producer and talent manager:

In the comedy business, the Improv was and is the place to be, and Budd was always the comedian's friend. He is the consummate ringmaster. He's the guy who would always be at your housewarming party. Even though he can act like a braggart and is sometimes full of shit, he gets away with it because he's fun to be around and you know he's really going to be there for you if he likes you.

MICHELE LEE:

Budd is an icon. He brought comedy into our culture and it's never changed. There's no one like him. Obviously, there have been other clubs that have introduced comics, but the Improv and his concept of introducing people who would be and who were was all Budd's.

JIMMIE WALKER:

Love him or hate him, I think Budd will be remembered as the Mount Rushmore of comedy. He's the face of it.

RICK NEWMAN:

He will go down as a frontiersman and an original in the world of comedy for starting the Improv. He's an explorer who made it work.

JOE PISCOPO:

Budd is the man who institutionalized comedy. He took it from joints to an industry, and he's still relevant to this day.

JUDD APATOW:

Budd will be remembered as someone who helped invent the whole form of the comedy club. He was a champion of some of the greatest comedians of all time. We have a lot of their work today because of that early support.

BOB ZMUDA:

If you think about it, the Budd Friedman story is kind of like the Frank Capra film *It's a Wonderful Life*. I mean, if the Improv hadn't existed, there would have never been a *Sex and the City* or *The Sopranos*, because those are all shows that Chris Albrecht green-lit at HBO and it's a job that he never would have had if he and I hadn't walked into the Improv. It was the springboard for all of our careers.

The money we raised for Comic Relief never would have happened without Budd and the Improv either. The connections back to this guy are amazing. There's a saying about being in the right place at the right time, but there's also another saying about knowing where the right place is, and in comedy it was the Improv.

RICHARD LEWIS:

Without question, Budd is the father of modern-day stand-up. He made it possible for people to feel good about themselves with a real comedy audience. I say this because there were nightclubs where you could perform before the Improv, but they didn't represent stand-up. It was like you were going on after Richie Havens and you had three minutes. You were like a hanger-on. Budd Friedman was the first to give praise and recognition to great comedy and great comedians. He was the first guy to give real prestige to comedy. Budd turned us into stars.

Acknowledgments

To the lucky few who are given a second chance
and make it work, we love you all.
—ALIX AND BUDD

Budd Friedman

This book is dedicated to my beautiful wife Alix, who has been my rock of Gibraltar through good times and bad from the moment we unexpectedly met at the Hollywood Improv nearly forty years ago.

I would also like to thank our four wonderful children: my daughters Beth and Zoe, and Alix's sons Ross and Dax, whom I have loved as my own ever since they came into my life. I could not be prouder of who they have become. And their spouses Kim, Beth, Steve, and John, and the incredible grandchildren they have given Alix and me: Noah, Sophia, Jacob, Bronte, and Gibson. More than anything else I have ever accomplished in my life, it is they who fill me with the greatest sense of joy and accomplishment.

As for the other members of my immediate family who have known me the longest—my sisters Kala and Helene—I love you with all my heart. My two wonderful brothers-in-law, Eddie and Gene, who are no longer with us and I will always remember fondly.

My late mother Edith, who served as two parents after my father Benjamin died when I was five years old and always supported my dreams.

Also, Fran Cowan, who was my first cousin and secretary/assistant for more than three decades at the Hollywood Improv. She masterfully rose to the occasion whenever it came to being a buffer between me and the other comics.

I would like to make a special acknowledgement to my co-author and collaborator, Tripp Whetsell, for helping me sort through the memories and persevere to write this book.

When it comes to my extended Improv family who spent time on our stage, many of whom also generously contributed their stories, my gratitude is equally profound. To Jay Leno, Robert Klein, Richard Lewis, and Jimmy Fallon. Thank you. To Danny Aiello, Chris Albrecht, Judd Apatow, Lewis Black, Drew Carey, Dick Cavett, Billy Crystal, Larry David, Tom Dreesen, Jeff Foxworthy, Al Franken, Gilbert Gottfried, Larry the Cable Guy, Howie Mandel, Kevin Nealon, Joe Piscopo, Paula Poundstone, Paul Provenza, Carl Reiner, Paul Rodriguez, Bob Saget, Adam Sandler, Jerry Seinfeld, David Spade, David Steinberg, Fred Willard, and Alan Zweibel. Thank you.

Also, to Nichole Davis, Rita Piazza, Jack Knight, Howard and Patricia Storm, and Lou and Arlene Alexander. Thank you. To all of my other friends, business associates, and members of the Improv family too numerous to mention—some of whom were unable to be a part of this book because of other commitments, but were no less a crucial part of the story—thank you. To Robin Williams, Rodney Dangerfield, David Astor, Richard Pryor, Anne Meara, Milton Berle, Andy Kaufman, Freddie Prinze, Dennis Wolfberg, Max Alexander, and all the others who provided years of laughter and are no longer with us, I hope that each of you knows how much you meant to me wherever you are.

And last but not least, my endearing appreciation to our customers. Because of you, I unexpectedly found my life's calling—and, despite a few bumps in the road, it has been an incredible adventure.

Tripp Whetsell

Although I was only the messenger, I also have many people to thank for their support and encouragement as I helped Budd write this book. As someone who has always wanted to be a comedian ever since I first discovered *An Evening at the Improv* as a teenager back in the mid-eighties, it has been a dream come true in every way. So has getting to know Budd, who not only welcomed me into his world with open arms, he never once failed to do whatever was necessary to help me get key interviews that would otherwise have been impossible.

I am grateful as well to Budd's wife Alix, his sister Kala, his daughter Zoe, and his son Ross. I would also like to thank Budd's assistant Nichole Davis and all the dedicated staff at the Hollywood Improv, including longtime manager Rita Piazza, bartender Eddie Berke, and photographer Mike Carano. At Levity Entertainment, which now owns the Improv, the support I received from Robert Hartmann and the rest of his team was no less amazing.

This book would also never have happened without my friend and super-agent extraordinaire Peter Rubie. Peter has loyally represented me for the past seventeen years and never once strayed. True to form, he was passionate about this project's commercial merits from day one—first in guiding me as I put together a proposal and then getting it into the enthusiastic hands of Glenn Yeffeth, publisher of BenBella Books, who was always generous with his time and availability whenever I needed him.

So was our editor Vy Tran, whom I would like to thank for her keen editorial eye and unfailing patience, both when it came to suggestions for improving the manuscript and giving us multiple extensions needed to complete it. Additional salutes to Adrienne Lang, Jessika Rieck, Lindsay Marshall, Sarah Dombrosky, and Scott Calamar, whose individual and collective contributions enhanced the final product immeasurably.

I am appreciative beyond words to Alan Zweibel, Rick Newman, David Steinberg, and George Shapiro, as well as David and George's assistants Tanner Gibson and Tammi Armitage. Their generosity in reaching out to many key Improv alumni whose fame is such that it required an extra nudge beyond Budd's was truly amazing.

I am also indebted to Jeff Abraham, Rory Rosegarten, Michael O'Brien, and Sheri Rosenberg Kelton for their help. Because I was too young to go to the original New York Improv during its heyday, I must especially salute three individuals—Shelley Ackerman, Judy Orbach, and Pat Buckles—for their invaluable guidance in giving me the lay of the land, as well as sharing their memories and pictures.

When it came to other books that were invaluable for helping to fill in critical reporting gaps, three in particular were especially useful: *I'm Dying Up Here: Heartbreak and High-Times in Stand-Up Comedy's Golden Era* by Bill Knoedelseder; *Comedy at the Edge: How Stand-Up in the 1970s Changed America* by Richard Zoglin; and *Stand-Up Guys: A Generation of Laughs* by John DeBellis.

Shani Friedman was an absolute godsend. For many months—and often on a moment's notice—she meticulously transferred hundreds upon thousands of words from audio recorder to computer screen at mind-boggling speed with many invaluable suggestions to boot. A major hats-off also to Carol Kraemer whose invaluable help in copy-editing early versions of the manuscript made it far more readable than it would have been otherwise.

On a more personal note, I am grateful beyond words I can ever properly express to my family for all of their unwavering support while I was writing this book: my mother and father, Anne and Bill Whetsell; my sister and brother-in-law, Holly and Gabe Coltea and their three daughters; my aunt and uncle, Porter and Carol Rodgers; my cousins John and Melinda Couzens and Susan Drumm; and especially Brent and Melissa Padgett for lending a helping hand when I needed it the most.

I am also forever grateful for the love and support of my treasure trove of friends, teachers, and professional colleagues. To Linda Evans, Ann Anello, Candyce Francis, Carol Scibelli, George James, Jesse Nash, Rob Bates, Susan Shapiro, Marsha Della-Giustina, Sharon Klein, Steve Zisk, Linda Alexander, Jon Satriale, Neil Vineberg, Wayne Jacques, Mike Kornfeld, Michael Caputo, David Kougot, Bruce Fretts, Richard Rubenstein, Adam Weiss, Angela Trostle, and Bob Greenberg. Thank you all from the bottom of my heart.

Index

Sinatra, Frank, 12
singers, 73–74, 127
sitcoms, 314, 323
Small, Charlie, 34
Smilers Delicatessen, 22
Smirnoff, Bruce, 212–213, 221–222, 280–281, 289–290, 307–308, 309–310
Smith, Sammy, 9
Smothers Brothers, xxii
Snyder, Marvin "Dusty," 245
softball league, 135–136
Sogoloff, Lennie, 161
Spade, David, xviii–xix, 285, 302, 306–307, 317–318
sports, 5
St. Louis, Louis, 84, 85
Stand Up NY, 177
Steinberg, David, 65, 105–106, 107, 111, 193, 196, 236, 241, 329, 330
Stiles, Norman, 190
Stiller, Amy, 78, 79, 202–203
Stiller, Ben, 78, 79
Stiller, Jerry, 66, 77–81, 88, 90, 110, 142, 202
Stiller and Meara, xii, 77–81
Stone, Stewie, 74
Storm, Howard, 54
Strauss, Arlene, 8
strike, 269–273, 281, 282
strippers, 26–27
substance abuse, 237, 278
suicide
    Lubetkin's, 272–273, 281
    Prinze's, 244, 245
    Williams's, 237
Sullivan, Ed, 145
syndication, 297

T

tabloids, 313
taping, of acts, 108–109, 115
Tartikoff, Brandon, 288
Tennis, Craig, 50, 130, 144–145, 146–147, 152, 243
Texaco Star Theater, 8
theft, of jokes, 240
Thomas, Betty, 275
Thomerson, Tim, 255
Times Square, 175
Tomlin, Lily, xii, xvi, 84–86, 220, 318
Tonight Show, The, 49–51, 59, 61, 72, 114, 130, 143–147, 171, 172, 173, 174, 183, 191, 192, 238, 242, 243–244, 285, 314–315, 318, 324
Torres, Liz, 68–69, 111, 118, 190, 195, 240, 251–252
Trillin, Calvin, 128

20 Years of Laughter at the Improv, 304
Tyson, Mike, 312

U

Untouchables, The (musical group), 47, 104, 137

V

Vallee, Rudy, 22, 23, 27
Van Dyke, Dick, 260
Variety, 13, 313
Verbit, Helen, 44, 45
Vernon, Jackie, 57–58, 107
Vietnam War, 35
vulgarity, 124

W

waitresses, singing, 36–39
Walker, Jimmie, 37–38, 94, 112, 119, 126, 127, 149, 151, 184, 190, 243, 249, 258, 261–262, 331
Wallace, George, 98, 286
Warfield, Marsha, 269
Wayans, Keenen Ivory, 319
Weber, Gene, 154
Weeden, Bill, 72
Weintraub, Fred, 62
Welch, Raquel, 144
Weld, Tuesday, 30
Werner, Tom, 314
West, Mae, 45–46, 52
Wexler, Norman, 211–212
What's a Nice Country Like You Doing in a State Like This? 176, 177–180
Willard, Fred, 56, 93–94, 111, 204
Williams, Paul, 252
Williams, Robin, 111, 157, 169, 231–237, 253, 263, 270, 271, 278–279, 280, 281, 293–294, 298, 305, 314, 316, 318
Willis, Bruce, 312, 313, 318
Wilson, Earl, 26, 151
Wilson, Flip, 304
Wilson, Tom, 267
Winger, Debra, 197
Winters, Jonathan, 316
Wisdom, Norman, 28
Wuhl, Robert, 98–99, 236

Z

Zmuda, Bob, 168, 183–187, 204–205, 211–212, 222, 305, 331
Zweibel, Alan, xvii, 91, 109, 126–127, 168, 202, 219, 229, 240–241

About the Authors

BUDD FRIEDMAN is the original owner, founder, and emcee of the legendary comedy club The Improvisation (better known as The Improv). Opening in 1963, The Improv was the first of its kind to present comedians in a continuous format and the first one to give unknown performers the opportunity to try out new material in front of a live audience—with the chance to be discovered by talent agents and late-night TV bookers.

TRIPP WHETSELL is a New York–based author, entertainment journalist, and critic specializing in comedy, television, film, music, and pop-culture history. His work has appeared both in print and online for such publications as VanityFair.com, *Variety*, *TV Guide*, the *Wall Street Journal*, the *New York Post*, the *New York Times*, *New York* magazine, the *New York Daily News*, *Closer Weekly*, the *Los Angeles Times*, and the *Hollywood Reporter*. This is his third book.

© David Kogut